Real Estate Sales Handbook

NATIONAL ASSOCIATION OF REALTORS®
developed in cooperation with its affiliate,
REALTORS NATIONAL MARKETING INSTITUTE®
of the NATIONAL ASSOCIATION OF REALTORS®
Chicago, Illinois

NATIONAL ASSOCIATION OF REALTORS®
developed in cooperation with its affiliate,
REALTORS NATIONAL MARKETING INSTITUTE®
of the NATIONAL ASSOCIATION OF REALTORS®
Chicago, Illinois

CHARLES SCRIBNER'S SONS/NEW YORK

1 3 5 7 9 11 13 15 17 19 B/P 20 18 16 14 12 10 8 6 4 2

Printed in the United States of America

Library of Congress Catalog Card Number: 80-81153
ISBN: 0-684-16507-4

Foreword

A Real Estate Sales Handbook has been part of the educational publishing program of the REALTORS NATIONAL MARKETING INSTITUTE® for the last third of a century. Distribution of almost 900,000 copies has been made through its seven editions and the Handbook has become an essential tool for both new and experienced real estate salespeople.

This reference book will not solve salespeople's problems but can help them when they have problems to solve. Any mention of local and state laws and methods of operation mentioned in this Handbook refers only to specific instances and/or sources cited and does not apply generally. Readers are advised to check policy and procedures, forms and contracts against whatever regulations apply in their company, municipality and state and to keep informed of changes in the laws at all levels.

Among the changes in society in the United States in the last quarter of the twentieth century two notable ones are the professionalism in the real estate industry and the sophistication of the consumer and business public. Both demand of real estate salespeople the fullest knowledge obtainable and a real dedication to serving the public. Continuing education in their chosen profession is available through print and audio-visual materials and attendance at courses offered by local, state and national real estate organizations. Real estate salespeople who avail themselves of these educational opportunities will be better equipped to render the kinds and quality of service both buyers and sellers have come to expect.

The Institute wishes to acknowledge with gratitude the contribution made to this eighth edition by Marketing Institute members Dorothy M. Yates, CRB, Tampa, Florida, and Charles A. Trowbridge, CCIM, Denver, Colorado. Thanks is also extended to Glenn Crellin, Research Economist with the NATIONAL ASSOCIATION OF REALTORS® in Washington, D.C., who helped with the tables. Statistical contributions were made by the U.S. League of Savings Association, the Mortgage Bankers Association of America, the Federal Home Loan Mortgage Corporation, the National Association of Savings and Loan, and the Chicago Title Insurance Company. This book was edited by Laura H. Wall and produced under the supervision of Meg Givhan.

Table of Contents

1 Getting Started

The real estate business offers rewards commensurate with the enthusiasm, skills, creativity, dedication, self-discipline and determination you bring to it. Each day presents new opportunities to meet interesting people and help them realize their goals at the same time you are working to reach yours. It is a business where a salesperson can make a lot of money and still be independent.

Real estate is a business of unusual working hours and frequently working weekends. It's a business where it's important to know how to organize time and understand the relative monetary value of the various steps involved in listing and selling real estate. When a salesperson makes productive use of his working hours he can still find time to spend with his family or in whatever recreation or hobbies he enjoys.

The arrangement of working hours in real estate usually differs from selling in other fields. Although unusual hours and weekend work may be necessary, well-managed schedules can provide freedom at other times. And as a real estate salesperson learns how to make maximum use of each working hour the same time use habits will spill over to help him enjoy every free hour to its fullest.

A people business

Successful real estate salespeople like to work with people. They meet a host of interesting buyers and sellers; they are called on to work with bankers, lawyers, leaders in business and government, architects, planners and others who influence the sale or development of land and buildings. They need to know and be known by the civic, education and other leaders of the area they are working to "sell" to the property-buying public. They have to learn to deal with some people they may not enjoy being with and have to accept their idiosyncrasies as part of a day's work. That situation is encountered in any business. The advantage in real estate selling is that the people "mix" changes with every listing and sale.

Subject knowledge needed

Real estate salespeople need to be skills-oriented. They should understand the following areas.

market analysis: understand market conditions in order to advise both buyers and sellers of the proper time to act

appraising: be aware of the approaches to value of property which include being versed on neighborhood trends, the climate of opinion and municipal ordinances that might affect values

finance: be able to guide buyers and sellers on how purchases can be financed and help to arrange it

law. advise potential parties to a contract of the need for expert legal counsel

interior decorating: be able to present a word picture of how a different color scheme could change the appearance of a room or how rearrangement of furnishings could alter the illusion of space

landscape architecture: know what changes in planting can do to improve the appearance of a property

construction and architectural details: be capable of advising sellers on the value of home improvements or point out to a buyer how major or minor changes could enhance the value of a property they are considering

community information: introduce new buyers to neighbors, showing them nearby schools, churches and recreational facilities

psychology: know just the right word to say and the time to say it and have insights into touchy domestic situations that could make or break a sale

Some problems in selling

Like every other business, real estate has problems. Sometimes they approach crisis proportions, either for the salesperson or his family. The most common ones are listed here, with a reminder of the ancient Chinese whose calligraphy for "crisis" combines the forms for both danger and opportunity.

Real estate salespeople learn to deal with "down" periods common to every selling field. They are almost predictable both in character and timing. The first critical period is likely to come after you get your first contracts and have conquered a natural fear of failing. You may be discouraged by more experienced salespeople who tell you the good habits you've just begun to establish aren't necessary. That is the time to forget how other people work. Do things the way you've been taught: use a daily work plan; follow up every lead and every sale; maintain a prospect list and work it regularly for development and follow-up; and work a full day, free of excess socializing and paper shuffling.

The next critical period usually comes during the second year. Maybe you've become a little cocky or a little sloppy and thus less efficient and effective. You may have begun to think you don't really need your broker and you can make it on your own; you may have become lazy and let good habits slide; you may have turned away from working to get listings, taking the easier route of walk-in buyers and ad calls; and you may have got so enthusiastic about your own real estate investment program you are looking at every property for your own potential use and not that of your clients. Now's the time for some retraining and self-analysis.

The third critical period is largely ego-centered. You may become bored with residential sales or you may begin to think about opening your own office or going into some other phase of real estate. It's great to grow. New fields bring new challenges. But remember, you can grow right where you are. Before making any major change, analyze carefully just what it is you think you can do and analyze that market just as carefully. Find out what special real estate knowledge and administrative know-how you'll need in the new field. How much lead time will you need before a new venture is profitable? The industry has many case histories of people who plunged into new ventures without enough preparation and capital and ended in failure.

Smart salespeople recognize any of these periods for what they are—temporary slumps. The smartest ones take effective action to work out of their slump.

What the business is like for families

There are family-related dilemmas for anyone who sells real estate. Some of the most common problems include the complaint that the business does not allow enough time at home. Real estate has been likened to the medical profession in that family matters always seem to take second place. The spouse has to know what to expect and what's involved in succeeding in real estate. One answer to this is to make whatever time is available quality time. Good time management practices can be carried over to personal time with the family. Rearrangement of children's schedules can give more time with parents. Vacations can be difficult to schedule. Even when the real estate salesperson is an independent contractor whose vacation schedule is not controlled by a broker, the timing of a transaction can cause delayed departures or cancelled trips. This is just as common in many other businesses.

Income can be a matter of feast or famine. Lean months may be caused by a bad drop in business or a personal slump. Either way, it's no fun. Some families can budget; some can't. Some find it best to pay bills in advance when big commission checks come in. Others are able to save enough from big checks to carry them over lean months. Some take out a short-term loan at the bank.

A spouse can be an extra set of eyes and ears without being aggressive about it. He or she may hear things around town that a salesperson doesn't. Sometimes it's ordinary gossip; many times it's real news that can result in a listing or a sale.

Specialties in real estate

Real estate offers a wide range of sales careers, from residential to commercial-industrial to investment. Residential selling is a challenging, rewarding career. Success demands the discipline of good work habits and mastery of selling skills. The other fields require special knowledge and training; each offers unique opportunities. The specialty may be defined by a type of real property, i.e. residential, commercial, office, industrial, etc.; or the specialty may relate to serving users or investors, buyers or sellers. In any specialty field, services your firm may offer include exchanging, trade-ins, leasing, appraisals, syndication, renovation and redevelopment, counseling, selling for builders, referral services, property management, insurance and financing. Whatever the specialty and its required body of technical knowledge, selling skills remain at the heart of success. The purpose of specialization is to provide the best possible service to your client.

Your license

Licensing laws give both the public and real estate brokers protection against unethical and irresponsible operators. Fifty states, the District of Columbia and several provinces of Canada regulate real estate brokerage through a system of licensing brokers and salespeople. Most licensing laws have been drafted and sponsored with the assistance and cooperation of REALTORS® to strengthen the professional standing of people legitimately engaged in the real estate business. Your license is your "right to work." Your obligation as a licensee is to work professionally, legitimately and ethically.

For detailed, up-to-date information, contact the Real Estate Licensing Commission in the state(s) where you'd like to practice.

Professional associations

Firms that encourage professional attitudes among their salespeople usually belong to the local Board of REALTORS®, where people associated in the same field work to maintain both the spirit and letter of professionalism. When you become an active member of your local board you will benefit from the exchange of ideas and experiences of fellow professionals. Make every effort to carry out the special assignments given you and to participate in all the programs and discussions at board meetings.

Commissions

In real estate brokerage today, money is made from commissions earned. Most salespeople work on a commission basis, operating as independent contractors. But some firms now employ salespeople and offer them a salary in lieu of commissions. Since compensation arrangements vary from company to company and even from salesperson to salesperson within a company, the arrangements are whatever the broker and the salesperson mutually agree on, within the acceptable legal limits for independent contractors and employed salespeople.

Working with other salespeople

Cooperation with other salespeople and coordination of effort is important to the success of a sales staff. It is not unusual, for example, for two salespeople to team up on certain transactions, dividing the commission on a predetermined equitable basis. Joint efforts of this kind often lead to a sale that might otherwise be lost. But occasional efforts of this sort should not be confused with the need for a continuing willingness of salespeople to help one another without expecting to be paid for it. A true spirit of cooperation exists in an office where everyone both gives and accepts help, knowing that such coordinated efforts result in greater volume for all. Conflicts of interest will occur from time to time but can be worked out in an office where a spirit of fairness prevails and judgments are made on what is right rather than who is right.

Listings are the property of the company. Your broker will tell you what the firm's procedure is for obtaining and filing listings. The sooner a new listing is filed and every salesperson is informed of it, the more active a sales staff can be. A salesperson who holds a "hot" listing for himself is unfair to his associates and can give the broker cause to terminate their relationship. When firms have a good stock of listings they help build the firm's reputation with both customers and clients because they know their needs can be met.

The company you work with

It pays to work for a reputable firm. Whether you work as an independent contractor or an employee, it's important to spend your working hours among people you respect and who respect you. You need your company's prestige and you have an obligation to maintain its good reputation, being careful to do nothing that will lessen the public's regard for it.

Large firm, small firm

Whether a small owner-operated business or a massive, multi-office operation, each size has advantages and attracts good salespeople. Small offices give salespeople an opportunity to work closely with the broker himself, learning and being guided on a one-to-one basis. This same advantage can be found in some large companies with a strong training program. Many large firms offer salespeople a chance to train for and move into a specialty without changing companies.

5

Most good real estate firms share the following attributes.

sufficient experience to understand the fundamentals of real estate practice

a staff of efficient, effective people

enough capital to conduct the business without limitations

principals who are service-minded and civic-spirited

sensitivity to changing conditions

strictly professional attitude toward the public

memberships in good standing in local, state and national real estate organizations and specialized institutes as well as active participation in their programs

considerate treatment of salespeople and employees

training and educational programs for personal and professional development

Services supplied by the company

In addition to office facilities, REALTORS® provide their salespeople with the name and image they have built in the community. This is complemented by the advertising program and public relations and publicity efforts.

One important service the company may provide is a referral program or network of offices with which it is affiliated, a service valuable to salespeople because such a high percentage of real estate listings and sales originate in referrals. As you become well-known and fully productive you will build your own referral business. Until then, you will depend heavily on business that comes to you through the firm.

Another service most companies provide is a set of forms used to collect data on your listing and sales production and guidance in using these data profitably.

Training programs

Your broker may have a system for training new salespeople. Many brokers also have a continuing training program which keeps the whole staff up-to-date on real estate practices in general and the company's response to changing conditions in the market, whether local, regional or national. In addition to the firm's training program, there may be an occasional training session organized by a cooperating group of brokers.

The REALTORS® NATIONAL MARKETING INSTITUTE offers training courses for members to help them develop professionally and learn to serve buyers and sellers more effectively. These courses cover professional sales techniques, human behavior, self-awareness and the awareness of others; setting personal and professional goals and the concepts and techniques that build professional stature. They challenge the individual to increased personal development and growth as well as provide guidelines to successful client counseling.

Training at some firms may be less formal and structured than others but all training is important. Independent contractor salespeople should avail themselves of every learning opportunity presented (on their own time, at their own expense) even though attendance is optional. Employee-salespeople can be required to attend whatever training the firm offers.

Certain kinds of on-the-job training are used in some firms. A veteran salesperson may take a newcomer under his wing, going along on the first calls or perhaps working with him until several sales have been made.

Whatever the training method used, ask your broker to explain it to you and how you can benefit from attending training sessions.

Sales meetings

You will have an opportunity to attend sales meetings. They can be excellent training grounds. Here, with fellow salespeople, sales managers and management you will discuss company policy and procedures, hear sales ideas being developed and exchange information. Sales meetings can be used to help improve selling skills through role playing or audio-visual instruction materials or to hear guest speakers discuss real estate related topics.

REALTOR® policy and procedures

A policy and procedure manual helps an organization run smoothly and effectively. When important guidelines are put in writing they save the salesperson's time in asking direction and help prevent misunderstandings. Knowing exactly what the company policy is on listings procedures, commissions and the differences between what is mandatory for employees and optional for independent contractor salespeople can prevent abrasive situations from developing. Checklists of the steps followed in taking and servicing listings, qualifying and servicing buyers and handling closings go beyond being guidelines and become salespeople's tools.

The nature and content of a policy and procedures manual

varies widely from company to company. Here are items common to most.

Advertising
  Program
  How classified ads submitted
  Brochures
  Buyer source records
Commissions
Disputes
  How to settle
Financing
Interdepartmental cooperation
  Appraisal
  Escrow
  Insurance
  Loan
  Maps, plat book, forms
Job description
  Checking in with office
  Dress
  Floor time
  Personal conduct
  Training
Legal counsel
  When necessary
  Where available
  When in doubt, where to ask
Securing listings
  Details of property
  Motive for selling
  Check neighbors
  Check list as guide
  Definition of salable listing
  Protection to listing
    salesperson—when it
    begins and terminates
  No "pocket" listings
  When listing fee is earned
  Survey selected properties
  Pricing the listing
Servicing listings
  Get listing into system
  Prepare property to show
  Caravan
  Open house
  Tell 20
  Advertise
  Keep in touch
  Counsel on possible price
    change
  Never remove a listing
  Canceling listing
  Changes
Office policy and Code of
  Ethics
Office procedures
  Clerical assistance
  Conduct with public
  Cooperation and
    coordination with other
    brokers
  Floor call
  Floor time
  Giving information
  Holidays
  Insurance: car, health, life

Office supplies
Petty cash
Telephone
  Answering techniques
  Long distance calls
  Personal calls
  Trunk lines
Vacation
Sales kit
  Reason to have
  Contents
  Rules and regulations
  Plan your work—work your
    plan
  Leaving business card
  "Sign Out" routine
Sales meetings
  Day and time
  Local real estate board
Selling
  Open houses—schedule and
    attendance
  Qualifying buyer
  Presenting offer
  Negotiating price
  Earnest money
  Mortgage information
Time management
  Records
    Agenda for the day
    Daily time report
    Monthly progress report

The Company Dollar

After a broker pays sales commissions, fees and splits to the staff and cooperating brokers, the remaining money is known as the "Company Dollar." From this must be paid the bills that provide a place to work and the services and supplies needed to do business. This may include such expenses as office furnishings, a pro rata share of office space and related maintenance costs, telephone, stationery and printed forms, clerical and secretarial services, advertising, promotion and publicity programs, salaries of supervisory and management personnel and any other items necessary to the operation of the business.

Every salesperson has a responsibility to produce income to keep the company going and assure its profitability. "Desk cost" is the term used to describe the average expense per salesperson, his assigned share of the broker's operating overhead. Desk cost is the broker's yardstick of dollar sales each salesperson needs to produce so the business is profitable. It becomes the yardstick for measuring your goals against what it costs the company to have you associated with or employed by them. It is important to plan your time so you achieve your goal and cover your cost to the company as well.

REALTOR®-salesperson relationship

The relationship between a REALTOR® and the salesperson affiliated with him is either that of "employer-employee" or one in which the salesperson is affiliated with the REALTOR® as an "independent contractor." It is of critical importance that every salesperson clearly understand the respective rights and responsibilities of each. To assure this understanding, it is highly desirable that a written agreement exist between the REALTOR® and at least those salespeople who desire to function as "independent contractors." The terms of such an agreement should be carefully reviewed and strictly adhered to. The agreement has effect only to the extent the parties to it observe its requirements in fact.

Employees

A salesperson employed by a broker is under his direct supervision and control. The broker may determine not only the objectives to be attained by the employee salesperson but also the manner and means of accomplishing them. The broker may pay expenses, license fees and board dues, compel attendance at training sessions, require floor time and assign administrative duties and organization titles. The salesperson-employee is subject to federal withholding tax on the compensation received from the broker-employer, who is required to pay FICA taxes and any other applicable workmen's compensation, unemployment compensation or other federal, state or local employment taxes. Moreover, the salesperson-employee is entitled to participate in the broker's pension and profit sharing plans, if any, on a non-discriminating basis with all other employees.

Independent contractors

If a salesperson is affiliated in an "independent contractor" status, the broker may still determine the objectives to be attained by the salesperson but he may not control the manner and means whereby those objectives are attained. He may not reimburse or pay selling expenses, license fees and board dues, compel attendance at meetings or adherence to a specific schedule, require attainment of sales quotas or control vacation times and may not include the salesperson in employee benefit programs. The salesperson-independent contractor is obliged to pay his own income and FICA taxes and may, if he desires, establish his own H.R.-10 Plan if he is unincorporated.

Comparison of relationships

The relationship which exists between a REALTOR® and his salesperson must be mutually satisfactory. There is no one ideal relationship and in fact the relationship may change from time to time. For example, a newly-licensed salesperson may find the employee relationship most satisfactory since it furnishes him a higher degree of security. The REALTOR® may find the employee relationship desirable because it permits him closer supervision and training of inexperienced salespeople.

On the other hand, an experienced salesperson may find the freedom and independence offered by the independent contractor relationship most desirable and profitable. At the same time, the REALTOR® may find this relationship entirely consistent with his operational and administrative objectives and capacities.

The important point to be observed is that the REALTOR® and the salesperson select the relationship they want and adhere to its requirements. Any attempt to create an "independent contractor employee" status defeats the objectives of REALTOR® and salesperson alike and results in confusion and misunderstanding which can lead to disputes and possible litigation.

Regardless of the relationship established, the REALTOR® provides an office for the salesperson and pays the overhead expenses of maintaining it. He contributes a stock of goods to sell (listings) and is available as a counselor and negotiator, especially in complex transactions.

2   Professionalism

Brokers and salespeople have certain legal performance responsibilities as well as ethical standards to maintain if they are to enjoy professional standing. Fifty states, the District of Columbia and several provinces of Canada regulate real estate brokerage through licensing. Most real estate licensing laws have been drafted and sponsored with the assistance of REALTORS® to strengthen the professional standing of people legitimately engaged in the real estate business. Licensing laws protect both the public and real estate brokers against unethical and irresponsible operators.

Professionalism is strengthened by continuing education. Information covered in state licensing exams should not be forgotten once the exam is passed; it should remain part of the salesperson's store of knowledge and added to by reading and keeping abreast of trends in the real estate business. In this context, professionalism requires that although you will not always have the answer, you must know where to look for it and be willing to find answers that satisfy the needs of buyer and seller.

One of the basics of professionalism is a clear understanding of the roles people play in real estate and the organizations through which they operate, whether as a principal, a sales associate or an employee.

A principal, in the law of agency, is the one giving authority to another to act for him. This person can be one who employs a real estate broker, the broker's client or it can be the one responsible for paying his commission. An agency is an agreement between an agent and his principal wherein the agent represents him in dealing with a third party.

A REALTOR® is a professional in real estate who subscribes to a strict Code of Ethics as a member of the local board and state association and of the NATIONAL ASSOCIATION OF REALTORS®. The term REALTOR® is a trademark owned by the National Association. It was adopted officially in 1916 and since then has been used continuously. Similarly, the term REALTOR-ASSOCIATE® is a registered trademark. The designation refers to a membership classification adopted in January 1974, which permits a salesperson employed by or affiliated with a REALTOR® to join the local board, state association or National Association.

A Board of REALTORS® is the REALTOR® organization at the local level that exemplifies the REALTOR® concept and organizational intent. It is the REALTOR® organization that is most visible and best known to the general public.

Membership of local boards consists of REALTORS® and REALTOR-ASSOCIATE® s who are members of the National Association through their local board or state association. Local boards provide many services to members including but not limited to a library on real estate; training films for REALTORS® and REALTOR-ASSOCIATE® s; training cassettes; standard business forms; decals, engravings, mats, pins, emblems, maps and other supplies related to the business; advertising, publicity and public relations on behalf of the board and its membership; and opportunities for civic participation and educational meetings and seminars on real estate. The possibilities of service to its members are limited only by the imagination and determination of the board's leaders.

The thrust to professionalism

Professionalism has been the concern of real estate leaders since the beginning of the movement for a national organization in the 1890s. The National Real Estate Association, formed at meetings in Birmingham in 1891 and Nashville in 1893, was the forerunner of the present organization. The panic of 1893 and ensuing depression killed the infant organization; but its aims of making real estate rules and regulations uniform from state to state, making title to real estate more secure and having real estate recognized as a profession remained uppermost in the minds of early leaders. Several meetings were held between 1894 and 1908, when the National Association was officially founded. The name was later changed to the National Association of Real Estate Boards. In 1973 the NATIONAL ASSOCIATION OF REALTORS® came into being.

National Association services and facilities

The NATIONAL ASSOCIATION OF REALTORS® has more than 1,770 member boards of REALTORS®. There are nearly 243,000 REALTORS® and approximately 462,000 REALTOR-ASSOCIATE® s. It is the largest business trade association in the world. Through its annual convention and the work of committees and departments, education, research and exchange of information about real estate takes place in order to raise the standards of real estate practice and preserve property rights.

Communications

real estate today®, the official publication of the NATIONAL ASSOCIATION OF REALTORS®, is published monthly by the NATIONAL ASSOCIATION OF REALTORS® and the REALTORS NATIONAL MARKETING INSTITUTE® of the NATIONAL ASSOCIATION OF REALTORS®. *real estate today*® is sent to every member of the Association. Other services include a quarterly clip art service, national Yellow Pages advertising and audio-visual presentations.

The NATIONAL ASSOCIATION OF REALTORS® also sponsors a national advertising campaign to promote the images of the Association and the REALTORS® and REALTOR-ASSOCIATE® s. This campaign uses national publications and electronic media to tell the REALTOR® story and increase public awareness of REALTORS® and the valuable services they perform in the community.

An annual ongoing program that is created and coordinated from the communications division is Private Property Week.

The aim of Private Property Week is to demonstrate that REALTORS® are citizens who are committed and concerned about private property rights and the community in which they work and live.

Education

The Graduate REALTORS® Institute (GRI) designation is awarded by all 50 state associations. The associations are authorized by the National Association to present the courses and award the designation after they have met the curricular standards set by the Board of Directors of the National Association in 1974. The National Association also offers the Residential Sales (RS) courses, which are developed by the REALTORS NATIONAL MARKETING INSTITUTE® and taught by instructors supplied by the Institute. The courses (described on page 18) are part of the Institute's requirements for candidates of the CRS designation. The Institutes, Societies and Councils which make up the National Association also offer instruction in their fields.

Legal Affairs

The Legal Affairs Division is charged with the responsibility of assisting in identifying and resolving legal problems that affect the National Association and its membership.

The Division consists of two departments, the Legal Affairs Department and the State and Municipal Legislation Department. The Legal Affairs Department provides legal advice to Member Boards and State Associations concerning current legal developments and their effect on the Association's policies, programs and activities. The staff also assists local counsel for Member Boards and State Associations in responding to myriad legal challenges and issues and coordinates the Association's Legal Action Program. The State and Municipal Legislation Department monitors important legislation at the state and municipal level in all states and advises the leadership and membership as to the manner in which these state laws and local ordinances may affect them. Additionally, this department monitors relevant uniform legislation, coordinates member legislative activities at the state and local levels, and publishes the "REPORTER," the "State and Local Legislative Update" and the "Barometer of Accomplishments."

Political Affairs

The Political Affairs Division strives to increase the Association's awareness of how the political system functions and how REALTORS® as individuals and as a group can have a substantial impact on that system, at the local, state and national levels.

The Division is organized into two separate departments: the REALTORS® Political Action Committee (RPAC) Department and the Political Education Department. RPAC's goal is to establish the real estate industry as a concerned and involved political constituency which will give active support to those political candidates who recognize the needs of REALTORS®, REALTOR-ASSOCIATE®s and property owners. The Education Department assists state associations and local boards in developing and implementing programs that encourage immediate individual involvement in grassroots political activities and the development of long-range grassroots programs.

Economics and Research

The Economics and Research Division conducts research on all aspects of the real estate industry and the national economy. In the process it produces a steady flow of reports which contain information extremely beneficial to members of the Association.

Each month the Division distributes its "Real Estate Status Report" to all state associations and local boards. This report contains up-to-the-minute data on trends in the real estate market and two or three times a year provides a forecast of future real estate activity. Every issue of the report also covers some particular area of interest to National Association members. The topics include franchising, housing affordability, turnover in sales associates, etc. Local boards may use the information contained in "Status" in their local publications.

The Division also performs special studies which are useful in daily business. The studies include: *Existing Home Sales Annual Report; The Income and Expenses of a Brokerage Firm* and *Profile of a Single-Family Homebuyer.*

Member and Board Services

Services to members is the mission of the Member and Board Services Division. Its purpose is to provide tangible benefits to members through policy programs and activities approved by the Board of Directors. Direct service to members has now been combined into a unified staff structure. This structure will provide service and assistance to Committees through the resources of Division staff experience and expertise.

The Member and Board Services Division has responsibility for direct service to members through the Library and the Convention Department and for service to Member Board and State Association Executive Officers through the Executive Officers Liaison Department. Member and Board Services is also responsible for the Education, Equal Opportunity, Home Protection, Make America Better, Membership Development and Community Revitalization committees and programs, as well as the REALTOR® Institute and the Total Energy Program of the NATIONAL ASSOCIATION OF REALTORS®.

Government Affairs

The Government Affairs office of the NATIONAL ASSOCIATION OF REALTORS®, headquartered in Washington, D.C., maintains continuous liaison with all branches of the federal government, federal agencies and related trade groups. The Department communicates complex legislative and administrative issues to the National Association. The Government Affairs Department is also responsible for informing the REALTORS® Legislative Committee (RLC) of all current issues before the Congress or under consideration in other parts of the federal government so the Committee's expertise and analysis can assist in formulation of REALTOR® policy. A timely legislative Bulletin keeps members informed of the office's activities.

Library

The National Association facilities in the Chicago headquarters house the Herbert U. Nelson Memorial Library, which contains more than 14,000 titles on all facets of real estate. An extensive mail circulation program is available and is used by members throughout the country.

Specialized divisions

In 1923 the National Association began to develop specialized divisions to aid members in perfecting their skills. REALTORS® and REALTOR-ASSOCIATE®s who avail themselves of these organizations of specialists are offered professional publications, technical journals, educational programs and research facilities as well as the business contacts essential to progress.

Education and certification in each of these specialties enable Association members to receive professional designations which mark them as qualified specialists to their business associates and the public.

REALTORS NATIONAL MARKETING INSTITUTE®

REALTORS NATIONAL MARKETING INSTITUTE® awards three designations: Certified Residential Specialist (CRS); Certified Real Estate Brokerage Manager (CRB); and Certified Commercial-Investment Member (CCIM). The Institute's members either hold one or more of these designations or are candidates for them.

It is the purpose of the Institute to enhance the professional competence of its designees, candidates and other REALTORS® and REALTOR-ASSOCIATE®s in the marketing of real estate and to provide special recognition and service for its members. One of the goals of the Institute is to continuously expand the quality and quantity of education, training programs and services to better serve its members and all REALTORS® and REALTOR-ASSOCIATES®s.

The Institute's publications are aimed at developing expertise and competence in all aspects of real estate; residential marketing, management, and commercial marketing and investment. The books dealing with the residential aspect of real estate can increase the reader's competence in the areas of listing, farming, house construction knowledge and interaction with buyers and sellers. Books with material helpful to managers offer information on defining and understanding management functions, applying management principles to operating a real estate office, and communicating effectively with salespeople. Information on commercial-investment includes market and feasibility studies and new techniques of discounting cash flows to calculate Internal Rates of Return.

Books that offer specific help to salespeople involved in residential real estate include this, the eighth edition of *Real Estate Sales Handbook; HOUSES: The Illustrated Guide to Construction, Design & Systems; Real Estate Advertising Ideas; The Art of Persuasion in Selling Real Estate;* and *The Competitive Edge in Selling.*

Titles aimed specifically at those involved in management are the classic *Real Estate Office Management: People—Functions—Systems; Real Estate Sales Meetings: Techniques and Topics;* and *Readings in Management.*

Commercial-investment titles include *Marketing Investment Real Estate: Finance—Taxation—Techniques* and *Analyzing Real Estate Opportunities: Market & Feasibility Studies.*

One book that encompasses all aspects of real estate brokerage is *real estate today®: Ten Years of the Best,* an anthology of articles from *real estate today®.*

The book list is being expanded constantly, each title chosen to fulfill a present need or anticipate future needs of people in the real estate industry. All the material published by the Institute is written by REALTORS® or experts on the topic.

real estate today®, the official publication of the NATIONAL ASSOCIATION OF REALTORS®, is published monthly by the NATIONAL ASSOCIATION OF REALTORS® and the REALTORS NATIONAL MARKETING INSTITUTE® of the NATIONAL ASSOCIATION OF REALTORS®. This award-winning magazine is a professional periodical devoted to the many aspects of real estate practice. Typical subjects include sales techniques and aids; financing; Association-related, economic, and legislative news; and new developments in residential, commercial and investment properties.

Real Estate Perspectives® are three publications of the Marketing Institute designed specifically for candidates and designees in residential sales, marketing management, and commercial-investment. Initiated in 1979, *Real Estate Perspectives®* are published bi-monthly and contain in-depth sophisticated articles and columns geared to each specialization.

Marketing aids are colorful pamphlets distributed by the Institute to use in direct mail promotions, as a handout to prospective clients and for office displays. They facilitate communication between salespeople and customers. These pamphlets can be imprinted with individual company names and logos. The professional business forms provide a framework for collecting and disseminating information, primarily in the field of commercial-investment.

The Institute also offers a large and constantly growing multi-media program. Some of the available training films for salespeople are *Prospecting for Listings,* which details ideas and techniques for acquiring listings; *A New Way of Living,* demonstrating closing techniques and approaches to selling the condominium way of life; and *What the Seller Doesn't Know Can Hurt You,* stressing the importance of educating the seller about financing. Also available are training programs consisting of tapes and slides. These can be used either by a manager to train salespeople or as a self-training device by individual salespeople. Two examples of this aspect of the multi-media program are *How to List Real Estate* and *How to Sell Real Estate.* These programs are designed to increase the sales skill of the user. Another multi-media aid to individual training is the cassette tape program.

All of the Institute's training aids—books, marketing aids, multi-media—are available for rent or purchase. A growing number of Boards of REALTORS® operate their own Marketing Institute lending library. The Institute puts out a catalog of all its educational and training tools, with instructions on how to order them.

Chapter Activities

The REALTORS NATIONAL MARKETING INSTITUTE® has established local chapters for each of its designations—CCIM, CRB and CRS—in order to provide a variety of opportunities for participation by members of the Institute in on-going specialized programs.

The Institute chapter programs provide support services for the local chapters which include: assisting in developing the professional abilities of its members; establishing local recognition and promotion of the image of the designations as an achievement earned through proven demonstration of professionalism; providing a forum for information exchange among Institute members.

Education

REALTORS® and REALTOR-ASSOCIATE® s who successfully complete REALTORS NATIONAL MARKETING INSTITUTE® courses earn credits toward an Institute designation in the area of their proficiency. While specific requirements may change, the qualifications for both residential and commercial-investment awards attest that those who earn them have a superior level of knowledge through the successful completion of prescribed courses, have proved their competence in the application of that knowledge through documented practical experience as approved by the Admissions Committee and have demonstrated and maintained a high standing of character, ethical practice and financial responsibility in their community and marketplace.

Current Institute designations

CRS, Certified Residential Specialist, is awarded to those individuals who have met certain education and experience requirements and who have demonstrated expertise in the field of residential marketing.

CRB, Certified Real Estate Brokerage Manager, is awarded to individuals who have proven competence in the management of a real estate brokerage operation.

CCIM, Certified Commercial-Investment Member, is for individuals primarily active in selling, exchanging, leasing, managing, developing and syndicating commercial and investment real estate.

The REALTORS NATIONAL MARKETING INSTITUTE® develops and provides the material presented in all the courses offered to the candidates for each designation. The Institute also furnishes the trained instructors for all the courses and offers the CRB and CCIM courses. The RS courses are offered by the NATIONAL ASSOCIATION OF REALTORS® through its state associations. New courses are continually being planned as subjects evolve and skilled instructors are found to teach them.

Residential Sales (CRS)

RS 101: *Advanced Listing Practices* defines the salesperson's job and teaches the everyday practices of the top producers in real estate listing and marketing.

RS 102: *Advanced Selling Practices* stresses those concepts and techniques that increase the salesperson's professional stature and increases professional gains in real estate marketing.

RS 103: *Successful Career Planning Through Organization and Time Management Practices* assists the salesperson in developing the potential to be productive, efficient and well-rewarded.

Marketing Management (CRB)

Marketing Management 201: *Introduction to Real Estate Office Management* is the new "overview" program to assist the manager in charting a course toward proficiency in every aspect of real estate sales and office management.

Marketing Management 202: *Communications and Leadership* is designed to give the manager an awareness of his position within the organization, provide him with several leadership styles he can apply and help him to understand where his organization is going.

Marketing Management 203: *Principles of Real Estate Marketing Management* introduces various marketing philosophies while looking at the real estate brokerage firm as an integrated marketing organization.

Marketing Management 204: *Recruiting, Selecting, Training and Retaining Sales Associates* takes a look at the manager, the firm and its goals, then helps to identify the characteristics needed in the sales associate.

Marketing Management 205: *"Broker": A Computer Simulation of Marketing Management Techniques* is an opportunity to test marketing judgment and learn and try new strategies through a computer-based simulation.

Guaranteed Sales Plan Clinic is a management study of sophisticated marketing methods for building company volume and thus greater income.

Commercial-Investment (CCIM)

Commercial-Investment Intro: *Introduction to Commercial & Investment Real Estate* serves as an introduction to the principles and concepts of commercial-investment brokerage and can lay the groundwork for the basic knowledge needed in the development of an investor clientele and acquisition of one's own real estate portfolio.

Commercial-Investment 101: *Fundamentals of Real Estate Investment and Taxation* prepares participants to aid clients in comparing after-tax profitability of alternative real estate investments as well as comparing real estate with other forms of investment.

Commercial-Investment 102: *Fundamentals of Creating a Real Estate Investment* teaches participants how to use comprehensive methodology to analyze a specific site and draw conclusions about its financial feasibility.

Commercial-Investment 103: *Advanced Real Estate Taxation and Marketing Tools for Investment Real Estate* acquaints participants with Federal tax laws as they affect real property transactions, including tax-deferred exchanges and the principles and techniques of tax planning.

Commercial-Investment 104: *Case Studies in Commercial and Investment Real Estate Brokerage* provides participants an opportunity to apply the principles, tools and techniques presented in C-I 101, 102 and 103, solving investment and user problems.

19

Commercial-Investment 105: *Skills and Techniques of Effective Communication for Commercial-Investment Selling* demonstrates the application of human behavioral theories to the day-to-day real and practical business relationships between salesperson and investor client.

Other Institutes, Societies and Councils

The SOCIETY OF INDUSTRIAL REALTORS® serves specialists in marketing industrial properties and meeting the real estate needs of industry. The SIR designation has been awarded to more than 1,350 members, including Active, Salesmen Affiliates, Associates, and International Associates. Active members have at least eight years' industrial real estate experience. Salesmen Affiliates have five years' experience. Both Active and Salesmen Affiliate members must pass a comprehensive written exam. Associate members include corporate real estate executives; industrial park developers; industrial development departments of major utility companies and railroads; insurance and investment companies with large industrial portfolios, and Canadian charter banks. Additionally, the Society has International Associate members in several foreign countries. Services include a bi-monthly market letter listing properties wanted for sale, a newsletter issued ten times a year featuring industry news and member activities and industrial mailing lists for members' use, as well as various educational and promotional materials, seminars and courses. In addition, special reports on industrial topics are issued periodically. The SIR Educational Fund published the third edition of Industrial Real Estate in 1979, available to NAR members at the SIR price of $20. The courses offered by SIR are *Industrial Real Estate I* and *Industrial Real Estate II.*

The INSTITUTE OF REAL ESTATE MANAGEMENT serves nearly 4,300 specialists who manage residential, commercial and office building properties. An individual receives the CPM®—CERTIFIED PROPERTY MANAGER®—designation upon successful completion of experience and educational requirements and compliance with the Code of Professional Ethics. Firms meeting standards of experience, education, integrity and fiscal stability earn the AMO®—ACCREDITED MANAGEMENT ORGANIZATION®—designation and offer management services to the investing public. In 1974 an accreditation and education program initiated the ARM®—ACCREDITED RESIDENT MANAGER®—recognition for on-site managers of apartment buildings or complexes. Regular services to IREM members include the bi-monthly *Journal of Property Management*, the bi-monthly *Operating Techniques and Products Bulletin* and the monthly newsletter, *CPM® Aspects*. Additionally, CPM®s receive the *Income/Expense Analysis—Apartments, Condominiums, and Cooperatives*, a unique research book. Other research services and educational materials are also available. Courses offered by IREM include: *Marketing and Management of Residential Property; Leasing and Management of Office Buildings; Leasing and Management of Commercial Buildings & Shopping Centers; Managing Real Estate as an Investment; Preparing the Long-Range Management Plan; Long-Range Management Plan for Residential Properties; The Long-Range Management Plan for Office Buildings; The Long-Range Plan for Commercial Stores and Shopping Centers; The Management of Condominiums; The Workout of Troubled Properties; Managing the Development Process* and *Managing the Management Office.*

The FARM AND LAND INSTITUTE serves more than 7,300 members and has the specific responsibility of developing educational courses, publications and programs for the benefit of REALTORS® specializing in land. Members who follow a prescribed course of study set forth by the Institute receive the designation of AFLM (Accredited Farm and Land Member). Member services include a monthly bulletin, *The Farm and Land REALTOR®*; a quarterly journal publication; an authoritative tax book, *Tax Planning for Real Estate Transactions*, written exclusively for the Institute by the accounting firm of Coopers & Lybrand; and the *Farm and Land Real Estate Manual*, a reference and guide for REALTORS® interested in the land segment of the real estate profession. Institute-sponsored courses include: *Introduction to Land Brokerage; Federal Taxes and Real Estate; Land Return Analysis; How to Establish the Market Value of Agricultural Land; Exchanging Farms, Ranches and Rural Properties; The Planning of Your Personal Estate; Subdivision Development; Listing, Packaging and Presenting Properties Effectively*. Also offered are one day tax seminars on: *Disposition of Real Estate Interests/Capital Gains and Losses; Basis of Real Property/Depreciation; Taxes Affecting Residential Property/Landlord and Tenant.*

The AMERICAN INSTITUTE OF REAL ESTATE APPRAISERS serves almost 5,000 REALTORS® who specialize in land economics and the complex field of real estate valuation. REALTOR® members who meet the educational and professional standards of the Institute receive the MAI (Member Appraisal Institute) designation or the RM (Residential Member) designation. Services include the quarterly *Appraisal Journal* and monthly *Appraiser*, as well as an educational program focusing on the case-study method. Courses offered by the Institute are: *Real Estate Appraisal Principles; Basic Valuation Procedures; Capitalization Theory & Techniques, Parts 1,2,3; Residential Valuation; Case Studies in Real Estate Valuation; Valuation Analysis and*

Report Writing; Standards of Professional Practice; Rural Valuation; Litigation Valuation; Introduction to Real Estate Investment Analysis; Industrial Valuation; Review and Evaluation of Appraisals.

The REAL ESTATE SECURITIES AND SYNDICATION INSTITUTE (RESSI®) serves 2,000 members who are specialists in the creation, issuance, analysis, promotion, marketing and management of real estate securities. Through RESSI®'s educational offerings and its national publication, *RESSI® Review,* members have the opportunity to learn the latest procedures and newest ideas in the fast-paced and highly competitive real estate securities field. The Institute's educational standards and professional guidelines, which it established for its members, are becoming increasingly important as this relatively new facet of the real estate industry begins a period of rapid growth. The Specialist in Real Estate Securities (SRS) designation is available to members meeting standards of excellence in education, experience and ethical conduct. Courses offered by RESSI® are *Course I—A Workshop in Syndication* and *Course II—Advanced Techniques in Real Estate Syndication.*

The AMERICAN SOCIETY OF REAL ESTATE COUNSELORS serves 471 members who specialize in giving competent advice and professional, unbiased counsel on real estate matters on a fee, per diem or retainer basis. Membership is by invitation only. Members who meet the Society's stringent qualifications, which include ten years' experience in real estate and three years' specialization in counseling, receive the CRE (Counselor of Real Estate) designation. Services include a professional journal, *Real Estate Issues,* published twice a year, also available by subscription to non-members; *The Counselor,* a quarterly newsletter, and other professional materials.

WOMEN'S COUNCIL OF REALTORS® is open to all women and men who are members of the National Association. It is dedicated to the advancement and recognition of women in real estate and supplies members with leadership training and educational aid, especially in residential sales. About 20,000 members receive the monthly publication, *WCR Communique,* which features educational articles on real estate and related business topics, plus news of council activities, and also the *WCR Referral Roster,* a business contact tool. Annual Regional Leadership Conferences, sales training seminars and special education sessions are among the benefits offered members.

The American Chapter of the International Real Estate Federation (FIABCI) serves REALTOR® members as an international exchange of ideas and techniques in the real estate business. Federation headquarters are located in Paris, France, with chapters in 37 countries. Each year a World Congress of real estate professionals is held in one of the member countries to consider the major issues and problems confronting the profession in various countries, with a view to finding broad solutions.

REALTOR® Code of Ethics

The NATIONAL ASSOCIATION OF REALTORS® has constantly worked to unify and standardize the practices of real estate professionals in this country and to establish and maintain a common feeling of professionalism among members. Part of such professionalism is adherence to the following Code of Ethics.

PREAMBLE

Under all is the land. Upon its wise utilization and widely allocated ownership depend the survival and growth of free institutions and of our civilization. The REALTOR® should recognize that the interests of the nation and its citizens require the highest and best use of the land and the widest distribution of land ownership. They require the creation of adequate housing, the building of functioning cities, the development of productive industries and farms and the preservation of a healthful environment.

Such interests impose obligations beyond those of ordinary commerce. They impose grave social responsibility and a patriotic duty to which the REALTOR® should dedicate himself, and for which he should be diligent in preparing himself. The REALTOR®, therefore, is zealous to maintain and improve the standards of his calling and shares with his fellow-REALTORS® a common responsibility for its integrity and honor. The term REALTOR® has come to connote competence, fairness and high integrity resulting from adherence to a lofty ideal of moral conduct in business relations. No inducement of profit and no instruction from clients ever can justify departure from this ideal.

In the interpretation of his obligation, a REALTOR® can take no safer guide than that which has been handed down through the centuries, embodied in the Golden Rule, "Whatsoever ye would that men should do to you, do ye even so to them."

Accepting this standard as his own, every REALTOR® pledges himself to observe its spirit in all of his activities and to conduct his business in accordance with the tenets set forth below.

ARTICLE 1

The REALTOR® should keep himself informed on matters affecting real estate in his community, the state, and nation so that he may be able to contribute responsibly to public thinking on such matters.

ARTICLE 2

In justice to those who place their interests in his care, the REALTOR® should endeavor always to be informed regarding laws, proposed legislation, governmental regulations, public policies, and current market conditions in order to be in a position to advise his clients properly.

ARTICLE 3

It is the duty of the REALTOR® to protect the public against fraud, misrepresentation, and unethical practices in real estate transactions. He should endeavor to eliminate in his community any practices which could be damaging to the public or bring discredit to the real estate profession. The REALTOR® should assist the governmental agency charged with regulating the practices of brokers and salesmen in his state.

ARTICLE 4

The REALTOR® should seek no unfair advantage over other REALTORS® and should conduct his business so as to avoid controversies with other REALTORS®.

ARTICLE 5

In the best interests of society, of his associates, and his own business, the REALTOR® should willingly share with other REALTORS® the lessons of his experience and study for the benefit of the public, and should be loyal to the Board of REALTORS® of his community and active in its work.

ARTICLE 6

To prevent dissension and misunderstanding and to assure better service to the owner, the REALTOR® should urge the exclusive listing of property unless contrary to the best interest of the owner.

ARTICLE 7

In accepting employment as an agent, the REALTOR® pledges himself to protect and promote the interests of the client. This obligation of absolute fidelity to the client's interests is primary, but it does not relieve the REALTOR® of the obligation to treat fairly all parties to the transaction.

ARTICLE 8

The REALTOR® shall not accept compensation from more than one party, even if permitted by law, without the full knowledge of all parties to the transaction.

ARTICLE 9

The REALTOR® shall avoid exaggeration, misrepresentation, or concealment of pertinent facts. He has an affirmative obligation to discover adverse factors that a reasonably competent and diligent investigation would disclose.

ARTICLE 10

The REALTOR® shall not deny equal professional services to any person for reasons of race, creed, sex, or country of national origin. The REALTOR® shall not be a party to any plan or agreement to disciminate against a person or persons on the basis of race, creed, sex, or country of national origin.

ARTICLE 11

A REALTOR® is expected to provide a level of competent service in keeping with the Standards of Practice in those fields in which the REALTOR® customarily engages.

The REALTOR® shall not undertake to provide specialized professional services concerning a type of property or service that is outside his field of competence unless he engages the assistance of one who is competent on such types of property or service, or unless the facts are fully disclosed to the client. Any person engaged to provide such assistance shall be so identified to the client and his contribution to the assignment should be set forth.

The REALTOR® shall refer to the Standards of Practice of the National Association as to the degree of competence that a client has a right to expect the REALTOR® to possess, taking into consideration the complexity of the problem, the availability of expert assistance, and the opportunities for experience available to the REALTOR®.

ARTICLE 12

The REALTOR® shall not undertake to provide professional services concerning a property or its value where he has a present or contemplated interest unless such interest is specifically disclosed to all affected parties.

ARTICLE 13

The REALTOR® shall not acquire an interest in or buy for himself, any member of his immediate family, his firm or any member thereof, or an entity in which he has a substantial ownership interest, property listed with him, without making the true position known to the listing owner. In selling property owned by himself, or in which he has any interest, the REALTOR® shall reveal the facts of his ownership or interest to the purchaser.

ARTICLE 14	In the event of a controversy between REALTORS® associated with different firms, arising out of their relationship as REALTORS®, the REALTORS® shall submit the dispute to arbitration in accordance with the regulations of their board or boards rather than litigate the matter.
ARTICLE 15	If a REALTOR® is charged with unethical practice or is asked to present evidence in any disciplinary proceedings or investigation, he shall place all pertinent facts before the proper tribunal of the member board or affiliated institute, society, or council of which he is a member.
ARTICLE 16	When acting as agent, the REALTOR® shall not accept any commission, rebate, or profit on expenditures made for his principal-owner, without the principal's knowledge and consent.
ARTICLE 17	The REALTOR® shall not engage in activities that constitute the unauthorized practice of law and shall recommend that legal counsel be obtained when the interest of any party to the transaction requires it.
ARTICLE 18	The REALTOR® shall keep in a special account in an appropriate financial institution, separated from his own funds, monies coming into his possession in trust for other persons, such as escrows, trust funds, clients' monies, and other like items.
ARTICLE 19	The REALTOR® shall be careful at all times to present a true picture in his advertising and representations to the public. He shall neither advertise without disclosing his name nor permit any person associated with him to use individual names or telephone numbers, unless such person's connection with the REALTOR® is obvious in the advertisement.
ARTICLE 20	The REALTOR®, for the protection of all parties, shall see that financial obligations and commitments regarding real estate transactions are in writing, expressing the exact agreement of the parties. A copy of each agreement shall be furnished to each party upon his signing such agreement.
ARTICLE 21	The REALTOR® shall not engage in any practice or take any action inconsistent with the agency of another REALTOR®.
ARTICLE 22	In the sale of property which is exclusively listed with a REALTOR®, the REALTOR® shall utilize the services of other brokers upon mutually agreed upon terms when it is in the best interests of the client.
	Negotiations concerning property which is listed exclusively shall be carried on with the listing broker, not with the owner, except with the consent of the listing broker.
ARTICLE 23	The REALTOR® shall not publicly disparage the business practice of a competitor nor volunteer an opinion of a competitor's transaction. If his opinion is sought and if the REALTOR® deems it appropriate to respond, such opinion shall be rendered with strict professional integrity and courtesy.
ARTICLE 24	Where the word REALTOR® is used in this Code and Preamble, it shall be deemed to include REALTOR-ASSOCIATE®. Pronouns shall be considered to include REALTORS® and REALTOR-ASSOCIATE®s of both genders.

The Code of Ethics was adopted in 1913 and amended at National Conventions in 1924, 1928, 1950, 1951, 1952, 1955, 1956, 1962 and 1974.

Competition, antitrust and the real estate salesperson

Real estate salespersons are expected to compete for business actively and efficiently. They are expected to seek and find new ways of obtaining listings of properties for sale and rent.

A thorough understanding of the nature and form of competition which exists in the real estate industry is important, not merely to success but also to legality.

Laws, sometimes known as antitrust laws, have been enacted by Congress and the legislatures of the several states which are designed to protect competition. They do so by a wide variety of prohibitions of which two are of particular relevance and importance to real estate salespersons.

25

The first prohibition is that against any form of price fixing. Price fixing is the formation or an agreement or understanding, express or implied, direct or indirect, between a brokerage firm and one or more of its competitors to fix, control, or maintain the price of real estate services to the members of the public. A price-fixing agreement is, in legal terminology, illegal *per se.* That means there is and can be no excuse, defense, or justification for a price-fixing agreement which the law will recognize.

But real estate salespersons should recognize that similarity or even uniformity in the commission rates of different and competing brokers does not signal the existence of an illegal agreement to fix prices. Price uniformity is a fundamental characteristic of a highly competitive market wherein competitors cannot charge more for their services without losing business to others and cannot reduce the charge for services without impairing their profitability.

Few, if any, real estate salespersons are in a position to fix, control, or maintain the prices at which listings are taken since this is a decision of the broker by whom they are employed or with whom they are affiliated. However, every salesperson must know who his competitors are. He must also understand that real estate commissions, like the price of all other goods and services not monopolized or regulated by government, must be established independently by the broker and never by agreement with a competitor.

Real estate salespeople within the same office are not competitors for purposes of the antitrust laws. Likewise, the salesperson's sponsoring broker is not his competitor. Thus, it is not contrary to the antitrust laws for a broker to establish independently the real estate commission to be charged for the services of his office.

Real estate commissions must always be negotiable; that is, the commission established with respect to any transaction will always reflect the "most" that the property seller is willing to pay for the services he requires and the "least" the broker is willing to accept for the services he is required to render.

If any real estate salesperson believes that the commission required by his broker for his services is unreasonable, he should either affiliate himself with a broker charging a commission rate he deems reasonable or reduce his share of the commission to that which he can justify.

The real estate salesperson who seeks to ingratiate himself with a potential property seller by suggesting that he is "compelled" to value his services too highly because of some agreement among brokers in the marketplace not only devalues his services but exposes innocent brokers and salespersons to civil and criminal litigation and liability.

For any salesperson to suggest or even intimate that commissions are the product of agreement between competing brokers or that they are dictated by a real estate board or its multiple listing service is to accuse the brokers or the board of a serious crime; a felony punishable by heavy fines and long terms in jail. Moreover, for any salesperson to honor such agreement, whether or not he is the author of it, is to share the guilt and hence become subject to the punishment.

The second prohibition of the antitrust laws of particular relevance and importance to real estate salespersons is that against "boycotts and concerted refusals to deal." The antitrust laws prohibit a group of competitors from "ganging up" on a competitor in order to force him out of business or to force him to change the way he does business. Boycotts, like agreements to fix prices, are illegal *per se.*

Each real estate salesperson and his broker is required to respond to the challenges of his competition by individual, as opposed to collective, action. The proper response to competitive innovation, be it a different, better, or cheaper service, is to meet or beat such competition, one on one. The antitrust laws permit one competitor to extol the value of his services and even to question the value of the services of his competitor. They do *not* permit agreements in any form to harass or suppress the operations of a competitor. No salesperson should ever suggest or infer that any response he makes to a competitive challenge is the product of agreement by other brokers or the real estate board.

The ultimate success, prosperity and survival of a salesperson depends on his ability to provide the services the public requires at a price the public is willing to pay.

A client who thinks of a real estate salesperson as a mere MLS catalog clerk and real estate brokerage as nothing more than a guided tour of properties for sale or rent will consider himself "overcharged" regardless of the commission he pays. On the other hand, a client who recognizes the real estate salesperson as a professional qualified and dedicated to securing the highest price and the best terms for his property will also recognize that the "value added" by the services of that salesperson will substantially exceed the cost of those services. It is the responsibility of the real estate salesperson to demonstrate that his services "pay for themselves."

The antitrust laws are intended to establish an economic environment in which the operation of the marketplace determines what goods and services will be produced and the price at which they will be bought and sold. Efforts to collectively restrict supply or artificially control demand distort or destroy this marketplace and are illegal.

The mandate of the antitrust laws as applied to real estate salespersons is clear—compete one-on-one for every client, customer and listing.

The Civil Rights Act and the real estate salesperson

The Civil Rights Act of 1866 requires that "All citizens of the United States shall have the same right, in every State and Territory, as is enjoyed by the white citizens thereof to inherit, purchase, lease, sell, hold, and convey real and personal property." In the case of *Jones* v. *Mayer,* decided on June 17, 1968, the U.S. Supreme Court held that the 1866 law prohibits "all racial discrimination, private as well as public, in the sale or rental of property."

In Title VIII of the Civil Rights Act of 1968, which is known as the Federal Fair Housing Law, Congress declared a national policy of fair housing throughout the United States. The law makes illegal any discrimination or differentiation in treatment based on race, color, religion, sex or national origin in connection with the sale or rental of housing.

A salesperson who denies equal professional services to any person for reasons of race, creed, sex or country of national origin violates both the law and his responsibilities under Article 10 of the REALTOR® Code of Ethics. The consequences of such denial are serious and can involve loss of license, expulsion from the Board of REALTORS®, narrow solicitation restrictions or broad record keeping and advertising requirements, civil damages and penalties and in some cases criminal prosecution, fine and imprisonment.

No REALTOR® can afford to employ or have affiliated with him a salesperson who takes his obligation to comply with the Code of Ethics and civil rights laws lightly. The REALTOR® has been held responsible for the salesperson's civil rights transgressions and only rarely has been able to escape liability.

It is not enough that a salesperson be familiar with the civil rights laws and take no action contrary to them. He should follow daily procedures and safeguards which will permit him to affirmatively establish his compliance with the law and his innocence of discriminatory conduct. Thus, he should be able to demonstrate that a minority prospect was offered the same number and range of listings as any other prospect of comparable financial means; that a minority prospect received the same degree of "followup" and the same level and quality of sales effort. If anything, the minority prospect must be given more and better service if only to secure the benefit of any doubt which may be raised.

And doubts inevitably will be raised, not only because of the high degree of civil rights sensitivity which exists among minority groups, but also because of the broad range of groups and agencies, public and private, concerned with enforcement of the civil rights laws.

There are two basic theories under which the conduct of a real estate salesperson may be challenged as violating the civil rights laws.

The first theory involves the general allegation that he made housing unavailable on account of race, creed, sex or country of national origin. The specific complaints supporting this allegation usually takes two forms: The minority seller or purchaser received less favorable treatment than that given non-minority clients, or the salesperson foreclosed the minority customer from obtaining housing in the community of his choice.

Complaints of "less favorable" treatment normally find the salesperson being accused of failing to service the minority customer as fully as a non-minority customer with regard to any facet of the services rendered, or differentiation in the treatment of any minority customer to his detriment in any manner.

Complaints of "less favorable" treatment of minority clients and customers are easily made and can be difficult to disprove because of their inherently subjective and qualitative nature. In dealing with minority clients and customers, care and restraint must be exercised and performance on behalf of such persons carefully and accurately documented.

The complaint that the salesperson foreclosed the minority purchaser from obtaining housing in the community of his choice is commonly known as a charge of "steering."

The complaint of "steering" normally finds the salesperson accused of actions which have been characterized by the Civil Rights Division as "attraction" and "avoidance" or more precisely actions designed to "attract" minority buyers to minority or changing communities and to cause minority buyers to "avoid" non-integrated communities. Such actions include the broker misrepresenting the truth regarding the availability or desirability of property in any area, whereby minority persons are primarily directed in any manner to minority, integrated or transitional neighborhoods, or non-minority persons are primarily directed in any manner away from such neighborhoods.

Complaints of "steering" like complaints of "less favorable treatment" also assume a subjective quality which makes their refutation difficult in the absence of documentation. Such documentation should include, at a minimum, evidence that the minority purchaser was offered a range of listings available to the salesperson and that such listings encompassed all areas served by him.

While emphasis has been placed on the need for non-discriminatory treatment of minority clients and customers, the salesperson should be equally alert to the danger of being charged with discriminating against non-minority prospects. Such charges arise primarily from allegations of "steering" and involve a complaint that a non-minority prospect was not shown listings in minority or changing neighborhoods or was discouraged from purchasing in such neighborhoods by direct or implied derogatory references to its racial, creedal or ethnic character.

Documentation of non-discriminatory performance becomes particularly important because of the use of so-called "testers." These are persons utilized by civil rights enforcers, public and private, who pose as potential clients of customers for the purpose of verifying compliance with the civil rights laws. Such "testers" use a variety of techniques designed to induce salespeople into making illegal racial representations or otherwise engage in discriminatory conduct. They may carry concealed tape recorders to document the salesperson's performance.

"Testers" normally operate in pairs: a minority couple and a non-minority couple. They will represent themselves as being substantially the same in all respects other than their minority status. The test they pose is whether or not they are shown the same listings in the same areas on the same terms with the same interest.

The second theory under which the conduct of a real estate salesperson may be challenged is on the ground that he has used the presence or proximity of minorities as a means of inducing non-minority residents of a neighborhood to sell their property. Such conduct is known as "blockbusting." Charges of "blockbusting" normally stem from the following complaints:
a. that a salesperson has used the fact that minority group persons are moving into the neighborhood as a reason for a homeowner to list his property for sale
b. that a salesperson has engaged in an intensive telephone, mail or door-to-door convass for listings in a changing neighborhood or an area adjacent to minority or changing neighborhoods.

Here again, the concern is with the subjective interpretation which will be placed by minority and other clients and customers on his comments and conduct. It is not necessary, for example, that the salesperson expressly refer to the proximity of minority groups if his comments or conduct in soliciting a listing create the impression that he is "panic peddling." This is particularly true of minority salespeople who seek listings in a non-integrated community. They are well-advised to avoid intensive listing activity or high visibility in any neighborhood which is adjacent to an area of minority concentration.

Compliance with the civil rights laws as they relate to the sale of real property requires a thorough understanding of them. These laws look not merely to the intent of a salesperson's conduct but to its effect. For this reason, salespeople should keep abreast of the developments in the law and should study with care the REALTORS® Guide to Practice Equal Opportunity in Housing, which describes in detail greater than this brief summary the obligation and duties of the salesperson under the law.

Equal opportunity in housing is an ethical principal to which every REALTOR-ASSOCIATE® must subscribe. It is the law of the land and it is good business practice.

3   Successful Sales Qualities

Of all the personal qualities required for success in selling, emotional stamina is perhaps the most important. In short, this means the ability to handle the stress and emotional pressures that inevitably arise in the interpersonal relationships involved in selling.

Each individual has a different tolerance for pressure and stress. However, everyone can learn more about the causes of stress and how to cope with it more effectively. A person entering selling must recognize that emotional tension and pressure is unavoidable. This is called the "law of the situation." It means that it is the duty of the salesperson to understand the customer; it is not the customer's duty to understand the salesperson. Further translated, "the law of the situation" means that to be effective in selling, the salesperson must be well-fortified in dealing with the stress factors of interpersonal relations.

Meeting sales challenges

The guidelines that follow will help you handle the pressures of emotional stress.

In all interpersonal dealings, ask yourself, "Is the action I am taking directed to my real goal and purpose?" This will lead toward acting objectively and not according to whether you feel "justified." Acting as we feel justified usually means actions directed by emotions. Acting objectively means acting logically toward a specific purpose.

Be tolerant of others. Tolerance is the ability to accept other people's capabilities. Frequently we develop stress by trying to push other people to behave as we would like them to. We measure their abilities by our own and become frustrated when they do not make decisions or judgments as quickly as we might under the same circumstances. Whether with customers or your own children, you must adjust to what others are capable of doing or undue emotional pressures will arise.

Dismiss grudges, grievances and hard feelings. Strong emotions are barriers to good communications; therefore, it is essential that you take the initiative in creating a favorable climate for communicating with your customers.

Recognize that you may not get the praise you feel you deserve. The further up the ladder you climb, whatever ladder you might be climbing, the fewer people there will be around to tell you what a good job you are doing. The more successful you become, the greater the need to be able to recharge your own emotional battery without relying on other people to do it.

Developing positive attitudes

Selling is an attitude. It takes a good many aptitudes to be qualified in real estate sales work but the process of selling is basically an attitude. Your success as a salesperson will depend a great deal upon how well you can build a positive image of what you are trying to do. Build a positive image of what you want to earn. Beyond putting a dollar figure on paper as a goal, it means visualizing the kinds of activities you will have to accomplish in order to achieve that earning level.

The human mind is very much like a computer: it is programmed to go through thousands of actions skillfully because you have practiced them over and over again until they are performed subconsciously. To become expert at anything requires practice. Mental practice is just as important as physical practice. A positive mental attitude really means seeing things in your mind in a positive manner and seeing yourself succeed in what you are trying to do. These are steps in programming your computer toward success.

Financial goals should be realistic; at the same time, they should challenge you to think beyond routine, to try new ideas and to build selling skills that become uniquely yours.

Positive company attitude

Just as you build a positive attitude toward your own success and toward service to your customers, you must build a positive attitude toward your company. It is unlikely that you will succeed without your company being successful or that your company will be successful unless you and other salespeople succeed. This means teamwork and having and expressing a positive view of your company's reputation. It means loyalty to those with whom you work and an effort to further the objectives of the company and its people.

One of the major judgments made by customers is the source from which they buy. Everything you do to build the stature of your firm enhances your own image as a successful person.

There will be times when company decisions are made with which you do not agree. That's natural and your broker will welcome your viewpoint and suggestions as the occasion warrants. However, once a policy or decision is made by your firm, your positive attitude must take charge. Think of reasons the new situation will work; don't brood over things that cannot be changed.

A thing called rapport

The word rapport is not often used in daily conversation. We talk about things like "personal chemistry", "different wave lengths" and "getting off on the right foot" to describe how we interact with people. Favorable interaction depends a great deal upon your personal behavior and attitude. There are hundreds of traits that cause people to feel comfortable or uncomfortable with us. Studies indicate there are five traits that appear to be most important in professional selling.

Enthusiasm means belief in what you're doing and not noise or a cheerleader attitude. It is a spirit that permeates your approach to your customer. It is the most contagious of all human traits; if you wish to generate enthusiasm, show enthusiasm.

Aggressiveness, a quality of courage, is the ability to keep on trying and testing situations without giving up. It is the trait that causes the successful salesperson to start where other people quit.

Self-reliance sustains a person through difficult times. It is that part of emotional stamina that helps an individual rebuild confidence when defeat has entered the picture.

Tact lubricates abrasive situations that are encountered in selling. While you must always be honest, there is never a need to be brutally frank. Speaking softly and helping others feel comfortable is a more rewarding response.

Accuracy in technical details and information is a must for the successful salesperson. Accuracy is a form of dependability, a most important trait in the eyes of your clients.

Understanding human behavior

Some individuals go through life feeling that people are insoluble puzzles; some simply refuse to try to understand others. No two customers will be alike in their thinking, feelings, attitudes or behavior. Therefore, it becomes important to see each person as an individual and to recognize some fundamental aspects of human behavior that can guide you in getting along with people as they are and not as you might wish them to be.

You can't "love" people into buying. You must recognize that people buy to fulfill very fundamental needs. When you realize that every question a customer asks and every comment or attitude he expresses is related to one of four fundamental needs, then you can really counsel, guide and assist that customer toward a successful sales conclusion.

A salesperson who lacks a basic understanding of behavior is like a ship without a rudder. Steering people toward achieving needs is the key to personal service in selling.

The four basic needs all human beings seek to fulfill are the same needs every buyer or seller must fulfill in reaching selling or buying decisions.

Physical needs

These are the needs of a person to feel comfortable, to protect health and improve well-being, to save work, time and energy and to assure a sense of personal security and independence. They may not be expressed outwardly but are inherent in the way buyers evaluate features of a property or the services of your company. Physical needs are often expressed through concern about the safety of the neighborhood or the house itself.

Social needs

Every person seeks love and wants to express love; we all want to fulfill the desire to do for those we love, to make them comfortable, to improve our domestic lifestyle and to enhance the romantic values of living. These needs are strongly presented by customers who express interest in the spouse's satisfaction and the children's comfort, convenience and well-being. The salesperson must listen for these needs.

Ego needs

All people need a sense of identity, belonging, esteem and approval in the eyes of others. This need is frequently a dominant factor in decisions about real estate and can cause buyers to be unrealistic about what they can afford in a house. The successful salesperson realizes that to deflate a person's ego is tantamount to building an immovable roadblock to concluding the sale. One experienced instructor in selling reminds us that every customer should be seen wearing a sign: "Make me feel important." This is a reminder that we should not only see the best in others but express it to them.

33

Spiritual needs

These are more difficult to recognize. They become active after lower-level needs have been fulfilled. They have to do with achieving a lifetime ambition. The person begins to question if he has realized his full potential. It causes many people who have achieved material success to take on responsibilities as teachers or in social service work that pay little in money but much in satisfaction or self-fulfillment.

Managing yourself

One of the first things you will hear in real estate is that you are "on your own" and therefore should discipline your time and your effort. These are wise and worthy words but they really boil down to personal management. Applying management's fundamental aspects to selling real estate will enable you to organize your thinking and increase your effectiveness.

Plan your work for each day and week. Establish priorities to help you achieve objectives.

Organize the resources you need to accomplish your plans. Decide if you need help from others and how you will get it.

Serve your customers effectively and with genuine interest and the commissions will take care of themselves.

Evaluate by reviewing both successful and unsuccessful transactions to see what you could have done better. Ask your manager for criticism and accept it in a positive way.

Self-improvement

One of the most important qualities of a successful salesperson is to recognize that professional growth and development is a continuous process. There are many sources of information on self-improvement, development and the sales process in the programs presented by the REALTORS® NATIONAL MARKETING INSTITUTE, in university and adult education courses in your community and in published materials that are readily available for your study. Self-development should be viewed in three areas of potential growth.

Technical competence

Build your knowledge of real estate and periodically

evaluate those areas where you need further information, study and skill. Your customers will not have faith in your advice if your knowledge of your field is not sound and up-to-date. This can also apply to fields which are not exclusively real estate but are closely related, such as banking, construction or architecture, in which you may get questions from your customers. Develop your knowledge according to your interests and capabilities but know where to find answers in those areas beyond your technical competence.

Human relationships

There is no limit to building insight, understanding and depth in our dealings with people. Much of this comes from the everyday practice you will develop in selling but much also comes from willingness to assess your understanding realistically and take steps to improve through further education and learning.

Creativity

Many people let success become a rut. Truly successful people are open-minded to new approaches. Creativity does not mean some monumental invention; it can often be a small matter that you have learned to handle in a way that leaves a lasting, positive impression on your customer.

Good health

Personal health is a highly important part of self-improvement. Without good health there is little likelihood a person can achieve full potential in anything. If your body does not serve you well, neither will your mind. Never be too busy to have a regular medical check-up and to develop sound health habits.

Good health, vitality and energy are important first impressions to project. In this same light, first impressions are enhanced by good grooming and personal appearance that bespeak quality and concern for self-image.

Your success image

Many people think success is usually a matter of luck depending on whether one gets the breaks or is in the right place at the right time. Certainly these things can help but every study of success shows that the individual wanted to succeed and did something to make success happen. Unfortunately, some people have trouble visualizing themselves as a success. These people are found to have a failure image which was often developed early in their lives.

Building a success image is a matter of recognizing the great value of the service you are bringing to your customers, recognizing that you are truly helping the customer make one of the most important decisions of a lifetime and recognizing that you have a positive influence over the thinking, plans and decisions of many people. The professional in selling never underrates him- or herself. This does not mean developing a big "I Am" complex. To the contrary, it means never declaring that you are that which you do not wish to be! It has been said that the world largely accepts us at our own estimate of ourselves. If so, it is because we usually live up to our own self-estimate. People are successful because they really believe they can be successful. Much enjoyment from your career in selling will come from the satisfactions that develop as you see your service to other people produce happiness and value. Never was the old philosopher's statement more true than in selling: "... as you think—you are."

Time Management

Setting goals is the first step in effective time management. You need to decide first what you want, how you're going to get it and then plan your time accordingly and discipline yourself to follow the plan. Look at the desks of successful salespeople and executives and you'll likely find a written plan or schedule of work for the day and/or week. These people know that time is money and that any time they waste is wasting money.

Why set goals?

People are basically oriented in two ways: to goals and to tasks. Experienced salespeople in real estate have proved that goal orientation works best for them.

Goals provide the means whereby people make a commitment to themselves. Goals generate the internal motivation to get on with the day's work. Your desire to reach your goal will encourage self-discipline. People do not fail because of lack of skills but because they do not organize their time well and discipline themselves to follow their plan.

Elements of a goal

If your goals are to help you achieve success they must be attainable, flexible, cover a definite time period, be measureable and put in writing. They are performance objectives aimed at doing rather than at good intentions.

Attainable goals

Both salespeople and brokers should be realistic when setting goals. Goals should be neither too easy nor too difficult. For example, if you know you can make $15,000 in commissions in a year, a goal of $25,000 may be unrealistic. But a goal of $18,000 will challenge you to make an extra effort beyond what you know you can produce. In this case, an $18,000 goal is attainable.

Flexible goals

The real estate market and the general economy can change a lot in six months and flexible goals allow for changes. For example, a goal of two exclusive listings per month should permit a variance up or down as financing becomes more difficult or easier to get. Or suppose you get an exclusive on all the lots in a new subdivision. After a brief celebration, make sure your goals are flexible enough to allow for this change. Don't count on those subdivision lots to get you to your goal for the year. Your goal should still include getting two additional exclusive listings every month.

Time period for goals

Generally speaking, one-year goals are most important; but

progress should be checked weekly or monthly. Periodic reevaluations will help you measure your progress and make any changes needed; they will also help remind you what you're working toward and how much further you've got to go. (See Fig. 1.)

Monthly Goals

Goals for the year

Listings ___*120*___   Sales ___*12*___

Listings sold ___*12*___   Escrows closed _____

Month	Listings	Sales	Listings Sold	Total Transactions	Sales $ Volume	Commission $ Total	Escrows Closed
Jan.	*10*						
Feb.	*10*						
Mar.	*10*						
Apr.	*10*						
May	*10*						
June	*10*						
July	*10*						
Aug.	*10*						
Sept.	*10*						
Oct.	*10*						
Nov.	*10*						
Dec.	*10*						

Fig. 1 This record shows what you must produce each month to reach your yearly goals. Your monthly production can be checked against these figures to measure your progress toward yearly goals.

Many firms set longer goals of three, five and even ten years. The longer the term of a goal the less control you have over it because of the variables in the market and the general economy, the people you will be serving and your own performance capabilities.

The time element is also necessary to keep your enthusiasm high. If you set a goal of 24 listings but don't set a time period for getting them, you won't have a target date for getting the job done. Without a target date, goals tend to take second place to what appears to be more pressing matters.

Measurable goals

If your goal is "to list 24 exclusives between January 1 and December 31", your goal is measurable. But if you had written, "List as many properties as I can between the beginning and end of the year," that is not a measurable goal. Why? Because if you list 20 properties, maybe you could have listed 24 if you'd worked harder.

Written goals

Putting your goals in writing provides a silent reminder of the commitment you made to yourself as well as the means of measuring your progress. This is important to both you and your broker as well as anyone else involved in helping you achieve your personal, professional and income goals.

Who needs to know

Your spouse or whoever will be involved personally in helping you attain your goals and enjoy the results of your achievement will naturally need to know your plans. The other person who needs to know is your REALTOR® who will also help you. No one else in the organization need know what your goals are if you decide to keep them to yourself. Some people are reluctant to share this kind of information with their peers, fearing ridicule if they should fail. Others want to share, believing a team spirit will spur them on to do a better job.

Your REALTOR® has to know what your goals are because they are also a part of the organization's. He needs to know early enough to counsel you on their practicality and whether you can realistically expect to make your income dollar goal in the market area the firm serves. He may want to show you how your dollar goal fits into the overall company goal, too. He will likely know how to help you achieve your professional goals through instruction available from your local board and state and national association; and he can show you how to work out your time schedule to avail yourself of additional training.

How to set goals

Determine your goals by personal needs. For example, ask yourself how much over and above what is needed to feed and clothe the family will I need to get that new boat? Personal goals could be as basic as keeping ahead of the cost-of-living increase; to buy a second home or a different house or education or recreation for the family. Perhaps you want to start a personal investment program or establish your own retirement fund. The important element in personal goals is that nobody else can tell you what your goals ought to be and nobody can limit your long-term goals.

Writing down your personal goals and a few details about each one is just as important as recording your income goal. Writing them down will help you sort out your priorities. You might want to redecorate the house and buy a new car. Only you can decide which should come first.

Professional goals can include added training for the professional skills you want to achieve during the given time period. Your list of professional goals will show you what you want to do to advance in real estate and stay ahead of the competition.

Personal goals should also include the things you want to do as a private individual to participate in the community in which you live and/or work—the civic, religious, recreation and sports activities that are important to you. Many of these activities also contribute to your business success but they are chosen to fulfill purely personal needs.

A written list of goals might look something like the following.

Goals for 19 _81_

Earn $ _120,000_

Get _120_ listings

Close _12_ sales

Purchase a new house

Spend three Saturdays a month with the family

Complete three real estate courses

Reduce liabilities from $_____ to $_____

Join local board and attend meetings

Read six new books on real estate

Subscribe to the bank's newsletter on finance

Become an officer in the Chamber of Commerce

Converting goals to a work plan

You'll need records to convert your income goals to a daily work program. Most salespeople keep monthly or yearly data on the number of listings taken, the number of showings needed to make a sale, the number of sales completed and a record of both listing and selling commissions.

To relate your goal to the number of showings, for example, let's say you are now making $15,000 a year, that you average ten showings a week and want to increase your income by $3,000.

10 showings × 50 weeks = 500 per year
500 into $15,000 = $30 per showing

If everything else remained constant (average sales price and commission) you will need to increase showings to 12 per week.

2 showings × 50 weeks = 100 per year
At $30 per showing = $3,000 additional income

If you can improve the use of your time enough to enable you to show two more houses per week, you can increase your earnings as much as 35 percent. The following figures are based on an eight-year study of salespeople's activities in one real estate firm. These figures are presented here to furnish guidelines only; they are not factual data on a national scale.

	Former time plan	New time plan
Number of showings made	240	340
Number of offers received	30	40
Number of sales	20	28
Average value per sale	$20,000	$20,000
Average commission per sale	$ 480	$ 480
Listings taken	20	25
Average commission per listing	$ 240	$ 240
Sales commissions	$ 9,600	$13,440
Listing commissions	$ 4,800	$ 6,000
Total commissions	$14,400	$19,400

Increasing the efficient, effective use of your time need not mean working longer hours. It can mean working fewer hours if you learn to make each working hour bulge with productive action.

The trick is to control the 1,440 minutes you have every day and not let the minutes control you. Almost every successful person has some kind of written plan for each day and week. Such a plan is a strength, not a weakness. As these people write their working plan they also are establishing priorities for what they will do, assigning top place to their most productive activities.

**Analyzing time
values**

The first step toward controlling your time is to analyze exactly what you are now getting out of each hour of your working day. Start by writing down how much time you spend on listing, selling, renting and other activities.

Real estate salespeople's time can be broken into four classifications.

Class "A" time: spent face to face with someone who can make a listing or purchasing agreement

Class "B" time: spent in preparing for "A" time, lining up listings, making appointments, preparing listing presentations and sales negotiation papers

Class "C" time: spent on all other real estate activities such as putting up signs, keeping listing book up to date, writing letters, attending sales meetings and keeping records up to date.

Class "D" time: spent on non-real estate activities like coffee breaks, personal business, recreation and social life

It may shock you to look at the finished analysis and realize how much time you have spent on unproductive work.

With this time classification in hand, you can put priorities on what you plan to do each day. The plan will fall into three categories.

what you must do (keeping appointments to list and show
  property)
what you should do (canvassing for new listings)
what you could do (to give you broader exposure to the
  market)

Such a plan will provide incentive to eliminate the non-
essentials from your working hours. You'll soon find yourself
establishing a timetable for the day based on who you need
to see and when, what calls have to be made and what
paper work has to be done. Planning the work day in
increments of half hours has proved best for many
successful salespeople.

**Making every hour
productive**

Allocate the most productive selling hours to being out in   41
the field. You can do this if you get to the office early every
day and get paper work and other office chores out of the
way with dispatch. That leaves peak daytime hours for work
in the field. Lunch hours can be used productively with
buyers or sellers or seeing important business and
community contacts.

Learn how to cope with interruptions. When people come to
you with an unimportant interruption, ask tactfully if it can
wait until another time and if necessary make an
appointment to handle it later.

Plan your travel to use minimum time and gasoline. Avoid
doubling back by being fully prepared for the job at hand.
And while you're in a neighborhood, use being there as an
excuse to stop and say a brief hello to former clients. When
you're on the road alone, use driving time to listen to
cassettes on some phase of the business about which you
want to know more.

Closing out the working day can be part of your plan. If the
office closes at five o'clock, spend a little time planning the
next day, scan the evening paper and perhaps do a last
minute check of a listing presentation to be made the next
day. Whatever is left to be done, do it and get home to the
family!

Measuring your day

It's important to have a way to evaluate your activities at the
end of the day, the week or the month. Evaluation can show
whether you're being both efficient and effective.

Peter F. Drucker, writing in *Management*, says efficiency is
concerned with doing things right. Effectiveness is doing
the right things. This applies to real estate to the degree that
the most efficient time management system cannot succeed
unless that system is put to work effectively. You can make
your system work effectively by developing good work
habits and using tools that enable you to get the job done
every day and recording progress toward your goals and by
developing habits that use time and tools most effectively.

A checklist or comment sheet for noting what you
accomplished each day and what remains to be done is
one way to measure effectiveness. It is a reminder of the
progress you are making toward achieving your declared
goals. Fig. 2 "Plan for the day" and Fig. 3 "Action for the
day" show how one salesperson manages his time.
Fig. 4 shows how to record hours invested.

Plan for the Day

January ___, 19___

Phone calls	Number	Topic
Attorney White	779-0084	Status of title search - 12 Good St.
Competition Rlty.	778-0202	Is Grove St. still available?

42

Personal contacts	Number	Address	Result
Mr. Black	229-9006	Know anyone moving into area/town?	
Mr. Smith	779-7766	169 Pine St.	Listed
Mr. Wood	778-6677	199 Walnut St.	Not home

Appointments: name and place

9:00 **Phone calls**	12:30 **Lunch**	4:00			
9:30	1:00 **Lunch**	4:30			
10:00	1:30	5:00			
10:30 **Listing calls - visits**	2:00 **Mr. Bell at office**	5:30			
11:00	2:30 **see homes**	Evening **8:30 Present**			
11:30	3:00 "	**offer to Mr. Wilson**			
Noon **Lunch Mr. Green**	3:30 "				

Remarks

Fig. 2 Salesperson's appointment book provides space for planning a day tailored to real estate.

Action for the Day

Phone calls made | Number | Topic

	Number	Topic
Jones	776-4228	Appointment this weekend
Last Natl. Bank	776-4456	Going interest rates
Peterson	776-7849	Reaction to houses seen, monthly income of wife
Mr. Wilson	776-7992	Appointment to present offer

43

Appointments made | Day, hour and place

	Day, hour and place
Jones	Sat. 17th. 2:30 at office
Mr. Wilson	Tonite 8:30 at his house

Personal contacts made and results

Mr. West	Introduced by Joe Green at lunch

Listing contacts | Number | Address | Result

	Number	Address	Result
Mr. Blue	776-0092	128 Nice St.	Call Monday

Showings | Properties

	Properties
Mr. Young	See showing report #14

Listing obtained: name and address | Type

Mr. Smith 169 Pine St.

Property sold | Buyer | Seller

Mr. Bell 334 Perfect Lane

Remarks

Drop off Mr. Bell's contract on way home to co-broker.

Fig. 3 A valuable record to keep and to check against your Plan for the Day. Unfinished business from these two pages can then become part of next day's plan, or on some specific future day.

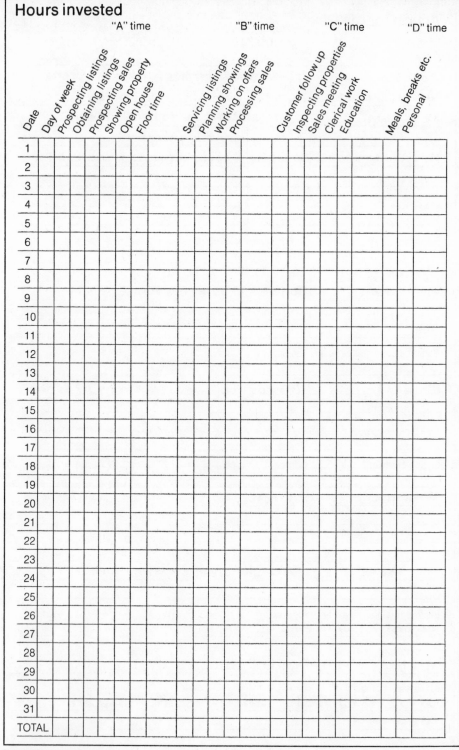

Fig. 4 This chart will give you a quick picture of how you use your time every day for a month. You can see at a glance how much time you spent with people whose decisions can affect your income.

| Time management tools | In addition to a desk calendar-appointment book, you'll need a pocket calendar and whatever forms the company provides to help you keep track of your progress toward your goals. What you add beyond that is up to you. |

A pocket calendar is your mobile adjunct to the desk appointment book. Form the habit of transferring dates, names and numbers from this book to your desk appointment book and vice versa. Writing phone numbers in the pocket calendar alongside daily appointments saves time when you have to make phone calls away from the office.

Many salespeople use a spiral bound stenographer's notebook in the car to record important action taken outside the office. When filled, it goes into office files as a permanent record. This same notebook also provides a place to jot down ideas and questions. This kind of information also needs to be transferred to office records regularly.

Don't form the habit of writing important things on tiny scraps of paper that can be dropped as you get out of the car or blown or brushed from the top of a desk.

Another way to record important parts of a business day is to use a battery-operated tape recorder. It requires the services of a secretary to transcribe the tapes, adding one more operation to the office routine, but many busy people regard it as invaluable.

Optional tools might include a tape deck for the car, a car telephone or a radio-operated beeper system.

Telephone calls

Because so much of your business is transacted by telephone, it's important to keep a daily log of your conversations. If your firm doesn't have forms for such a record, a spiral bound stenographer's notebook will do. The important thing is to list the person called or calling and a summary of what the call was about.

Staying in touch with the office is important. A growing number of real estate salespeople use car telephones or a radio-operated beeper from office to field. This service has some spectacular results in the quick sale of new listings when salespeople are notified of them while showing properties and the new listing falls within the price and style the customer wants. The important point is to keep in touch with the office whatever method you use.

Regular chores

No matter what form your daily schedule takes, certain things need to be done. This list of office and field chores is a memory jogger, a reference for the things you should be doing consistently to create listings and sales. How you do it will be up to you, assisted by your broker.

In the office:

Arrive on time

Review daily plan

Read newspaper ads

Check message box

Check new office and MLS sheets

Match buyers with property

Promote your listings with staff people

Review escrow sheets

Review listing check sheets

Call other brokers for their listings

List follow-up calls to make

Get comps for appraisal

Verify appointments

Call "For Sale by Owners"

Call potential buyers for appointments

Call criss-cross directory

Call expired listings

Call old clients for referrals

Call escrows for follow-up

Address direct mail

Make cold calls

Field work:

Check "For Sale by Owners" and expired listings

Preview new office and MLS listings

Show property

List property

Prospect

Lock boxes and signs

Get escrow instructions signed

Get loan documents signed

Identify yourself to people as a real estate salesperson

Using free time

Every working day has some unexpected free time, "found" time, when you are waiting for a customer who's late, waiting for a phone call or when you think there's nothing to do at the end of the day. Put this time to work and you'll soon accumulate hours of productive effort.

Following are things you can do to use unplanned free time productively.

Organize sales aids so they are ready for immediate use

Reconstruct the last listing interview or showing to determine what needs to be changed

Develop contacts with people responsible for relocating personnel

Read newspapers for transferees, promotions and new businesses moving into the area

Make appointments to inspect all listed properties not yet seen

Read articles, bulletins and books on real estate and selling

Get out and meet new people and hand out business cards

Check old listings that may have been taken off the market

Call exclusive sellers to report all activity

List competitors' expired exclusives and call these sellers

Do a little digging for undeveloped land

Make a list of the developers and builders doing business in the area and present the vacant property to them

Get organized for tomorrow's activities

Rewrite ads

Evaluate work habits

Mail a thank-you to a past client

Offer referral assistance to sellers leaving the area

Contact sellers who may be looking for another house in the area

Concentrate on how to render better service to buyers and sellers

Update listing book

Survey neighborhood of a new listing

Read the building permit section in the newspaper

Offer to help a friend with a tax problem by showing him income property

Promote new listings to another salesperson

Read engagement and wedding announcements in the newspaper and call to see what their housing needs will be

Read the "For Sale by Owner" ads

Call and see two "For Sale by Owners"

Maintain a book of owner ads and assist in listing these properties

The opposite of found time is "time out"—the moments we lose each day in idleness or unproductive business. Think of an eight-hour working day as a bank of 28,800 seconds, each worth one dollar, given you to invest. Time is a bank from which one can make withdrawals but never make deposits. The withdrawals can be converted into profitable investments or can be lost through wasteful habits.

In a survey of real estate salespeople earning about $15,000 a year, a list of time lost in an average day included the following.

Coffee breaks: 3 per day at 10 minutes each equals 1,800 seconds

Idle talk in the office: 15 minutes or 900 seconds

Driving the same route to and from the office each day, a non-creative practice that takes away from the opportunity to see new properties available for sale: 40 minutes per day or 2,400 seconds

Lost creative time from not having tape cassettes or other training devices in the car to listen to when driving: an average of 40 minutes per day or 2,400 seconds

Poor planning, causing a need to double back to pick up signs or secure loan commitments: approximately 30 minutes each day or 1,800 seconds

Having to do a job twice because it wasn't done right the first time: about 45 minutes or 2,700 seconds

Going to lunch with people who can't help you in business or the advancement of your career: about 60 minutes or 3,600 seconds

Daydreaming on non-productive subjects: approximately 20 minutes a day or 1,200 seconds

Remember, the eight-hour day has 28,800 seconds, each worth a dollar. From the $28,800 available to "invest," a total of 16,800 seconds ($16,800) was lost in time-stealing habits and practices, leaving only $9,600 invested wisely.

5 Selling with Psychology

There was a time when selling was viewed as a manipulative process in which the skillful salesperson could induce a customer to agree to buy. The salesperson was regarded as one who had a strong impact on personal relations, could motivate people toward buying and find psychological advantages with which to close.

Psychology basics

Perhaps there is some element of these factors in all buy-sell relationships. However, it is far more important in examining the modern science of selling and the professional concepts of buy-sell relationships to recognize some important fundamentals of sales psychology.

First, the salesperson does not motivate other people. Motivation is not something we do to others; it is something that happens when appropriate conditions are developed, both in personal relationships and in satisfaction of buyer needs, that cause other people to become motivated toward a particular goal.

Second, the psychology of buy-sell does not vary from one occasion to another. The fundamentals of buying and selling are immutable and unvarying. No matter what the product or service, a professional salesperson must understand clearly and specifically the three basic elements of buy-sell psychology.

what people buy
why people buy
how people buy

When these fundamentals are clearly understood, the skilled salesperson can guide, counsel and assist the customer in making favorable decisions, satisfying needs and reaching conclusions that are permanent and lasting buying decisions.

What

What do people buy? Certainly, they do not buy the tangible substance of an automobile, a dishwasher or a home. They are not purchasing the bricks, lumber, plaster and architecture in a home; neither are they buying the steel, rubber and porcelain in the dishwasher. People buy what a product or service will do for them. They buy advantages and benefits. Therefore, the successful salesperson learns how to translate all the features of what is being sold into advantages and benefits to the customer.

Why

To translate features into advantages and benefits, the

successful salesperson must understand the basic buying motives—the needs of human beings as discussed in Chapter 3.

How

While it is essential to understand what and why people buy, the real key to successful selling is both understanding and control of how people buy. Every sale of any product or service is based upon the positive conclusion of five decisions. Every lister or buyer must make these five decisions and when the salesperson understands how to assist these decisions, how to develop agreement and how to measure progress, control of selling is assured.

First, the customer must both understand and agree that there is a clearly defined need to buy. This need will be related to one of the motivations discussed earlier but it may not always be clearly recognized by the buyer. For example, a salesperson may not recognize at the start that an important reason for buying a particular property is ease of maintenance and commuting convenience (physical need). The salesperson may also not recognize that a real need is to make the spouse happier in a more spacious home, keeping friction in the family to a minimum (social need). Until the salesperson has clearly identified these needs and helped the customer evaluate them, an important buying decision cannot be made.

Second, the customer must decide this property or service is the one to fulfill the recognized need. A particular home may or may not fulfill the need as recognized by the customer. Accordingly, the salesperson must make sure that time, attention and effort are given to alternatives and questions are answered to give the customer information to decide if the property will fulfill the need.

Third, the customer must decide that he is buying from the right source. You and your firm are the source. You are assisting the source decision when you answer the telephone, making your first impression on the customer and when you carry out your sales work. Many times you have decided to purchase something but somehow the source of supply did not satisfy you, so you went somewhere else to seek the same product or service. So it is with your customers. They must decide you are the right source. Much of what this handbook is about is how you can become the most reliable and professional source available.

Fourth, the customer must decide the price is right. Sometimes this seems the impossible hurdle in selling but it doesn't have to be. When price is clearly related to the recognized need of the buyer, it becomes meaningful, realistic and understandable. When the buyer's need is not clearly defined, price represents a real problem. You can agree that the greatest bargain ever offered does not attract you if you don't need the thing being offered. (A free appendectomy would hardly be to your liking if you didn't need one.) The successful salesperson learns how to express price in terms of fulfilling needs.

Fifth, the customer must decide the time to buy is now. This decision is really what a closing is about. The theory that there is a psychological moment to close a sale often creates considerable pressure in the salesperson. Closing is a continuous process, starting with the first decision about source, continuing through your advice and assistance with determining need and developing into a final conclusion when you request a time decision. If the time decision is not favorable, it is evident that one of the other four decisions has not been successfully completed. At that point, the salesperson can confidently go back and review the other four decisions with the customer and make sure which one needs further information or guidance for agreement or conclusion.

Listening

As mentioned, your personal attitude toward a lister or buyer influences the source decision. Your ability to "tune in" to the individual, to put yourself in that person's place and try to understand what he is trying to accomplish are tools in making buy-sell psychology work. These can best be summarized by stressing the importance of listening. When you speak, you talk about what you already know; when you listen, you learn some things you very likely do not know.

A listening attitude

Make sure that you have chosen a physical set-up that encourages expression from the other person. Beware of distractions and any intimation that you are in a hurry or preoccupied. Overestimate the other person's point of view. Be careful not to answer questions too quickly. Agree that it is a good question and ask for some more information before answering.

Listen with a purpose

Listen for feelings as well as to what a person is saying. Listen for clues about the needs of the individual. Feelings are essential to understanding the real meaning behind communications. When communications are expressed at an emotional level or come from a highly assertive, evaluative attitude (indicated by words like should, ought, mustn't, ridiculous, foolish, etc.), you can be sure that communications will not be productive. Ask questions that give your customer a chance to come back with facts, logic and reasoning, rather than emotions.

Test your understanding

It is easy to jump to conclusions about what people say. Avoid this by trying to restate in your own words either the feeling or the content that has been expressed. A customer may state: "I'm very disappointed with the way you have handled this situation; you haven't done any of the things you said you would do. . ." It will be futile to come back and argue that you have done what you said you would do or point out how mistaken the customer is. To test understanding, you might say: "I'm sorry you are upset but let me make sure I understand; I gather you feel that you have not received all the information you need to go ahead with your personal plans. Is that correct?"

If the customer comes back and says: "That's what I'm telling you; I haven't got anywhere near the information I expected. . .", you are in a position to ask: "What kind of information would be most helpful to you?"

This approach enables the salesperson to keep communications at the level of logic and reasoning. When they deteriorate into emotional levels, it becomes very difficult to apply psychological concepts to selling.

A-I-D-A

According to the A-I-D-A method, every sale carries the prospect through four psychological steps: attention, interest, desire and action. These must be taken in sequence by the salesperson; it is seldom that any one of the steps can be omitted.

How A-I-D-A works

Getting the prospect's attention is the first step in this process. You cannot get anybody to buy anything or even to look at it unless you are first able to get his attention. This is the first psychological reaction that must occur in the prospect's mind. You make him want to listen to what you are saying.

Attention is a mild form of interest. The difference between the two is only in degree. But attention is casual and temporary. It may be objective and it may be broken off at any moment. Hence, you must work to develop a real and sustained interest as quickly as possible.

In bridging the gap between attention and interest you will find maps, pictures, blueprints and layouts highly effective. When a prospect holds in his own hands any object you have given him, he is hardly able to resist some interest in it. This is especially true when it explains something about which he is already interested or presents some constructive new idea which can be of benefit or profit to him.

Arousing the prospect's interest can also be achieved by simply explaining more details about the property and by showing him how he will personally gain from ownership.

When the salesperson has been able to develop a reasonable amount of interest, desire follows. In this stage of the psychological process the prospect is no longer on the defensive. He and the salesperson are meeting on a common ground. He is willing to listen while the benefits which he might enjoy are explained. If the salesperson does a good job and paints his word picture vividly, the prospect's interest grows until the desire for possession is created. This third step, desire, is very crucial. You can see that the salesperson has not made any real progress until this stage has been reached.

The last step in the A-I-D-A process is the one in which the prospect says, "All right, I'll take it." From attention to interest to desire to action: is the course every sale must take, according to this method. The same sequence of mental reactions takes place when you buy a new automobile or a new suit. These steps have occurred in your mind thousands of times. They are logical steps in selling real estate or any other commodity.

Take it step by step

When you understand the A-I-D-A formula, you realize the folly of trying to close a sale before desire has been built in the prospect's mind. Desire is an emotional reaction and it can only spring from interest. And interest starts with attention. Each step is the result of the previous one; it is impossible to take them in reverse order.

Sometimes you hear a salesperson begin his conversation with, ''Would you like to buy a nice new bungalow?'' Perhaps he should not properly be called a salesperson, yet that is the technique of many who try to sell. They jump to the action step and skip the other three. This frightens the prospect who jumps to the defensive and promptly answers no. There is no reason why he should say yes because interest and desire have not yet been aroused.

Advantages of home ownership

In creating desire, you must interject into the conversation facts which are convincing. If you were trying to sell a home, the following list of arguments for home ownership would be extremely useful. You would not use all of the items for every prospect but could select those which seem most applicable to each prospective buyer.

53

Financial independence: more people have started on the road to financial independence through home ownership than in any other way

Security: in times of stress the home is always something to fall back on

Cash equity: a well-bought home is in this respect like a savings account

Credit: home ownership gives financial and credit rating in the business world because it is recognized as a fundamental principle of stability

Place for your children to play without criticism

Interest in civic and municipal affairs

Chance for individual expression: exterior and interior of home can be decorated to express the personality of owner

Permanent environment: finding neighbors and friends whose friendships last over the years

Healthful exercise: pride of possession inspires work in home and garden

Character development: responsibilities of ownership develop business acumen and responsibility

Savings: the undertaking encourages systematic savings. Over a period of years the buyer is money ahead by buying and occupying a home.

Beautiful furnishings: high quality carpeting and draperies can be purchased because they fit into a decorative scheme that will last for years.

A place for a family's lifestyle

Pets: as many as desired both indoors and outdoors

Appreciation of value

Peace of mind: provision has been made for family

Interest and property tax deductions

Commercial-investment advantages

Many of these points are true for commercial and investment real estate as well. The commercial-investment salesperson must be knowledgeable in and stress the tax advantages of depreciation, interest, property tax deductions and investment credit (for both real and personal property), which may create a tax shelter. It is also essential to understand the principles of leverage and estate building. To the user or investor of a piece of commercial or investment property, the best arguments to convince the prospect how a building or site will fulfill his distinctive needs are enhanced by using demographics in addition to stressing the physical characteristics of the property.

Empathize

Regardless of which approach to selling you use, the ability to place yourself in your prospect's shoes is very important. In this position, you can begin to see yourself as a salesperson; you can determine how and why the client reacts in a certain way to the sales presentation and to you. Do you really act and seem sincere? Is the sales presentation one that you (the salesperson) would believe from someone else if you were the buyer? With empathy, the salesperson can answer these and many other questions and adjust his selling according to the kind of answers he gives himself.

54

Ask the prospect to buy

After spending much time and effort getting to know the prospective buyer, determining needs, talking persuasively and generally bringing the prospect right up to the point of purchase, many real estate salespeople neglect a very important item: knowing the right time to ask the prospect to buy. Such salespeople often lack the courage to ask for action. They get the prospect in the mood to buy but do not strike when the iron is hot.

In every sale there comes a climactic moment when the buyer is most likely to react favorably to the suggestion to buy. Knowing exactly when that moment arrives is partly a matter of experience and partly intuition but it is of the utmost importance.

It often helps to ask questions which, if answered affirmatively, indicate that the time has arrived: "When will you want to take possession of the home?" or "Shall we see if the owner will sell that vacant lot next to the property?" Either of these questions, or a thousand others like them, may tell you that it is time for the contract to come out of your briefcase. If the questions do not produce a favorable response, you must continue to sell until you feel the time for action has arrived.

Sometimes the salesperson does not realize the state of mind of the prospect when he has to make the final decision. Often a real estate salesperson, in the middle of a busy period or thinking about his own affairs, forgets his prospect's frustration and fear at the moment he is asked to sign a contract. Regardless of the amount of money involved in the transaction, it may loom as large as a mountain to the prospect. It is, after all, his money. Again, the salesperson must put himself in his prospect's shoes; he must empathize. The element of fear must be overcome if the sale is to be made. You can do much to alleviate the fears of the prospect simply by imagining yourself in his position and assuming an attitude of helpfulness from there.

The atmosphere for a closing

It is very important that the closing take place under conditions with minimal interference and interruption. This is an important moment for your prospect because he should be able to participate in the closing in a strictly businesslike manner. The closing should take place wherever there will be few interruptions—in the prospect's office if there will be no interference or at his home if children will not be a distraction.

As you guide the buyers through the closing, you should remain as calm and as confident as you have been throughout the selling process. You should continue to take into consideration the feelings and thoughts of the buyer. By consulting with him about each item of the contract as it is written, by answering questions patiently—even those asked a hundred times before—by having the contract legally amended where needed and by insisting that the client read the contract carefully before signing, you can be confident you have sold property that will stay sold. You should work with, and not as, legal counsel in the closing process.

Sometimes the most assured, practiced salesperson will reach closing time with a prospect who wants time "to think it over." At that point, you should tell him that you would like to have him think it over to be absolutely certain everything is in order and no mistake is made. Then you should keep right on selling as long as there is any hope for an immediate decision. However, you should be careful not to make an issue of anything that will make the resumption of your sales program impossible if an immediate decision cannot be obtained.

Throughout the selling process, it pays to be aware of the psychological processes going on and, moreover, the psychological needs of the people you are working with. His own needs are important but when it comes to working daily with people, the successful salesperson is one who likes people and is genuinely concerned about them.

6 Listing and Servicing the Seller

Listings are the key to success in real estate. They are the inventory of the business—the products brokers must have to attract buyers. A real estate sales cycle starts with a good listing that is priced right. The more complete a broker's inventory of well-priced listings, the more buyers he can serve and the more money he and his sales associates will earn.

Two sales equal one

To sell one property a broker has to, in effect, bring two sales to a successful conclusion. He must first sell himself and his firm to the property owner; then he must sell the listing.

Success in the first sale, the listing, depends on you and your firm having a good reputation in the community and on your skill in persuading owners that you will do a good job of finding people interested in buying their property and then selling it to them.

Success in the second sale depends on the skills you and the firm have for servicing the listing by advertising it, finding people interested in and qualified to buy it and negotiating the sale.

Obtaining listings

Your first objective is to obtain listings, the first sale mentioned above. What are your best sources? How can you cultivate them? There is no single "best" source. Good sources are everywhere, everyday. You cultivate them in ways that fit your personal style, are acceptable in your market and conform to your firm's policy. Your success in obtaining listings will grow as you expand your sphere of influence.

Systems and techniques

Experienced brokers and salespeople know that certain systems and techniques work successfully to bring listings. Proven methods are highlighted here but there are always refinements and innovations waiting to be developed as both people and markets change. Your future is as unlimited as your creativity.

A listing "bank"

Build a "bank" of listings. Your deposits consist of all the people who could list their properties with you; withdrawals are the properties sold. If you know 400 or 500 owners in your market area better than any other salesperson, chances are you're the person they'll turn to when the time comes to sell.

Your listing bank can be opened when you have made a definite plan and set a goal for a specific number of listings in a certain time period. You can start by getting acquainted with 25 owners each month. It will give you a great feeling of accomplishment as you build your personal inventory of prospects and realize how many people may come to rely on you as their real estate professional; another sense of accomplishment will come when you know that if you contact a certain number of people every month your efforts will produce the listings and sales needed to reach your goals.

Farm systems

In a farm system, each salesperson is responsible for a specific part of the area the firm serves. A farm system may be structured by the broker, who assigns the territory according to company policy, or it can be an area chosen by the salesperson or it may be optional. The basic concept of the system is that it is best to specialize in one area rather than running all over the marketplace. Most people prefer to work the area where they live, where they already know some people and where it is easier to become better known to many more. Get to know as many people as you can and become expert on property values and sales activities in your farm area. Develop your own plan to call on owners regularly by phone or in person, sending notes or a newsletter or items of special interest to the people you know and want to get acquainted with. A well-organized plan that is followed carefully will pay handsome returns.

Canvassing

Every owner thinks about selling his property before he actually puts it on the market. A successful lister finds a lot of these properties before anybody else knows about them. He does it by cold canvassing. Two methods are used widely: telephoning from criss-cross directories and door-to-door contacts.

If you use the telephone method, introduce yourself slowly and give the name of your firm. Explain that you are looking for a specific type property for which you (or someone else in the firm) have a legitimate buyer. Describe briefly what the requirements are. Inquire whether the person you are talking with knows of a similar property in the neighborhood whose owner may be thinking of selling. (Never ask if his property is for sale. The answer will inevitably be No.) This canvassing technique has proved successful over many years. A typical average is to get one good lead out of every 25 cold canvass calls. There is at least one person in every neighborhood who will confide in you. Make copious, careful notes. Then follow through.

Call the specified owner, using the same opening. Many will say they are thinking of selling and will invite you to inspect the property.

Face-to-face visiting is the second successful cold canvassing method. If you do it at a specific time every day when you don't have a conflicting appointment with a buyer or seller you'll soon establish a work routine that gets you out where the prospects are. This method requires persistence and regularity. You'll need to devote many hours to getting acquainted and becoming recognized in the neighborhood. After your first sign goes up (and, it is hoped, a Sold sign soon follows) you'll have begun to gain a foothold in the neighborhood. An average area with 400 to 500 homes will take anywhere from six months to a year to pay off. But once this happens, you should have a permanent and continuing source of listings. Your listing bank is full.

Some salespeople say canvassing is best done on an informal basis on Saturday in residential areas, when you can meet people as they work in the yard, wash their cars or play outside with the children. The mood and tone of Saturdays is more relaxed and you are likely to make many good personal contacts this way. Others believe cold, dreary days are best because owners are more likely to invite you indoors.

If cold canvassing is prohibited or frowned on in the area you serve, you may need to approach it in a different way. Make a list of 25 homeowners and you can send them a letter of self-introduction. It might read like this:

_____

Date

Dear Mr. and Mrs. Smith,
May I take this opportunity to introduce myself to you. I am Jim Searcy, associated with ABC Realty. I will be representing homeowners in your neighborhood and will stop by in a day or two to meet you.

Sincerely,
(s) Jim Searcy

Use your personal envelopes when you mail these letters.

Then you can go and call on them. Ring the bell, step back a pace or two and face away from the door. When the door opens, start the conversation something like this (You'll say it in your own words, but be sure to have it memorized!):

"Good morning, Mrs. Smith. I am Jim Searcy of ABC Realty. Did you receive my note of introduction? It should have arrived today. (They'll usually say yes.) I just stopped by to make your acquaintance. I will be representing ABC Realty in this area and hope you will help me. And for your help, may I please give you this small token of my appreciation?" (Hand her some small, useful premium along with your business card.) Usually the owner will accept the gift because she has already received the letter and you've not asked her for anything. You are there only to serve.

Be prepared with a series of pertinent questions:

Have you enjoyed living in this area?
How long have you been here?
Do you feel the neighborhood is improving?
How many children do you have?
What are their names and ages?
Do you have any pets?
What do you like most about living here?

Having got this information, thank the owner for the opportunity of discussing the area with her and go to the next door without mentioning anything about wanting to list her house. Twenty-five calls, data on 25 families, and you have started your listing bank. You have your name and association in 25 homes and they now know you.

Keep going on that 25-a-day routine. Soon you will discover people are eager to discuss the neighborhood and to ask your views on the real estate market. They may even comment that you are the only real estate person who has not asked them to list their property.

Know your community

Most successful real estate people become involved in civic groups and community projects. When they do, they are not only building their own reputation and making social contacts, they are also representing their firm. Community activities often provide a way of finding out what local leaders have in mind for the future of the area. If you are known to these planners and doers they may turn to you when they need real estate services.

Clients

Satisfied clients are a prime source of future referrals. Keep in touch with the sellers and buyers you've served, reminding them occasionally that you'll appreciate their referring friends and associates to you when they need the services of a REALTOR®. Clients themselves are potential customers for more business when the time comes to buy another house or when they are looking for income investment or business properties.

In addition to using direct mail and telephone to keep in touch with clients, a quick, friendly visit when you happen to be driving through the neighborhood can be profitable. Such a visit shouldn't be a hard sell situation; keep it brief, unless you are pressed to stay to tell them more about something they're interested in.

Advertising

Advertising, both institutional and classified, is used in varying degrees to obtain listings. Follow-up is important and is largely the responsibility of salespeople. Most firms have established methods for recording telephone response to ads. Other follow-up channels include keeping your ears and eyes open for every response or clue that comes your way.

Newspapers

Local newspapers can be a good source of listing prospects. Their news columns carry information of great value to you as they tell of transfers, promotions, births, marriages, deaths, civic plans and projects, all of which can involve the transfer of real estate. Following up on these leads is profitable.

REALTOR® referrals

Your association with other REALTORS® in your community, county, and state is an excellent source of both listings and sales. A REALTOR® in another city or state who knows you through the NATIONAL ASSOCIATION OF REALTORS® or REALTORS NATIONAL MARKETING INSTITUTE® will feel confident in referring someone from his area to you. Such referrals include not only people being transferred but also investors looking for commercial or investment property in your marketplace.

Other sources

Homes surrounding a new listing are often a good source for soliciting business. Many firms inform the sellers' neighbors of a new listing. This may bring you more new listings and may provide you with a buyer for the listing you are now promoting. (See "Tell 20" on page 77.)

Expired listings can also create new business. Old listings may seem overpriced or shopworn, when the real reason for failure to sell may have been bad timing (putting a house with a swimming pool and gardens on the market in winter) or financial (a tight mortgage market). Getting a listing of this nature back on the market calls for creative thinking and selling on your part to induce the owner that listing it with you is more likely to consummate the sale.

Vacant homes

As you drive through your market area and note a vacant home, find out who owns it. Then contact the owner and let him know you list properties in the area and may be able to sell his. If it's an empty rental property in need of repair, the owner may want to realize his equity without spending money to recondition it. This might lead to a second sale or even a referral to another broker if you induce the owner to reinvest the money realized from the sale of the vacant house.

Business cards

Business cards can be your silent sales tool. Put them to work for you every day. Give them to friends and business acquaintances as you stop for a brief hello or as you're leaving at the end of a business session. The law of averages will work for you in producing results that reflect the number you pass out.

See the people

Busy real estate salespeople spend every possible moment away from their desks, getting out to see people. STP has become a popular slogan that has nothing to do with gasoline additives. It means see the people and it works. As you get out among people and they ask, how's business?, reply that it's great but that you need more good listings and do they happen to know of any. Some of the most creative transactions in the business have begun in a casual street corner conversation between an alert broker and another person who had a bit of knowledge the REALTOR® hadn't yet heard.

When you think you've exhausted all the possible sources of listing referrals, check through the more than six dozen sources that follow.

Financial leaders:
bankers
insurance agents and adjusters
savings and loan officers
trust department officers

Business and labor:
personnel directors
planning departments
finance officers
labor leaders
union officials

Tourists:
motel and hotel clerks
airline clerks
car rental agencies
travel agencies
restaurants and coffee shops

Service people and vendors:
gas, electric and water meter readers
garage sales, house sales

mail carriers
Fuller Brush salespeople
Welcome Wagon hostesses
ice cream vendors
Tupperware salespeople
hairdressers and barbers
Avon ladies
waiters, waitresses

Institutions:
school directors, principals and teachers
colleges and universities
Army and Navy post officers
PTAs
librarians

Media sources:
for rent ads
newspaper, radio and TV people
printers
for-sale-by-owner ads

Merchants and salespeople:
moving companies
retailers
druggists
Chamber of Commerce
car dealers, gas station owners and garage owners
heating oil dealers
dry cleaners and laundries

Professionals:
doctors
management people
lawyers
CPAs
judges
dentists
employment agencies

Civic and municipal:
homeowner associations
municipal officials
county assessors
probate clerks

Social, church and charitable:
bridge clubs
country clubs
service clubs
garden clubs
block parties
open house hospitality parties
fund raising committees and canvassers
church groups
lodge groups
veterans' groups
bath and tennis clubs
fraternal organizations
recreation, sports, hobby groups
newcomer clubs

Building:
builders' agents
apartment and rental agents'
architects
landscape architects
nurserymen
decorators, interior designers
contractors
plumbers
electricians

Miscellaneous:
public bulletin boards
community centers
supermarkets
laundromats
barber and beauty shops

Good records

All your efforts need to be supported by useful, accurate records regardless of the sources and techniques you employ to generate listings.

If you work on a farm system, a tickler file of 3x5 cards is an effective way to keep track of your prospects (Fig. 1). The same card system can serve a broader territory but will require some method of segmenting by neighborhoods or areas. More elaborate prospect records can be kept (Fig. 2) using a three-ring binder. Whatever system you use, keep records and keep them up to date. If you note the husband's and wife's businesses and their companies bring in new people, they can be a source of referrals for you. If you call and there's no one home, note the date and put the name back on your daily calendar for another try soon. Use your records to refresh your memory prior to calling on them. They'll be impressed if you remember their names.

4903 S. 73rd. E. Ave.   663-8566
Block 17, Lot 3, Quail Creek Addition
Larry James - Cheryl
Salesman/IBM - Housewife
Saw 9-17-74 left brochure, saw 11-21-74 left pen.
Listed w/BOH-MONT for $38,500, 11-23-74
Sold 12-10-74 for $38,500 by BOH-MONT 80% loan
Sold to: Bill Green - Lynn

Fig. 1 No matter what system your firm employs to develop listings these cards can be central to a salesperson's organizing his work.

Listing Activity Report

Name _____   Spouse _____

Address _____   City _____   Zip _____

Children	Age	Thank you notes and follow up calls	
1 _____	_____	A _____	F _____
2 _____	_____	B _____	G _____
3 _____	_____	C _____	H _____
4 _____	_____	D _____	I _____
5 _____	_____	E _____	J _____

Dog _____   Cat _____   Phone _____

Referrals:

Name _____   Address _____

_____   _____

_____   _____

_____   _____

Hobbies _____   Sports _____

Calls:

_____   _____
_____   _____
_____   _____
_____   _____
_____   _____
_____   _____
_____   _____
_____   _____
_____   _____
_____   _____
_____   _____
_____   _____
_____   _____
_____   _____
_____   _____
_____   _____
_____   _____
_____   _____
_____   _____
_____   _____
_____   _____
_____   _____

63

Fig. 2 By using a separate sheet for each family, the salesperson can make sure he is servicing his listing area and retaining his contacts.

Every time a house in your area is listed, whether it's your listing or not, mark down the date and asking price. When it sells make a note of that along with the price, type of financing and the new owner's name. If a property sells "by owner," don't be afraid to ask who bought it and at what price. If you have kept in touch with him he'll regard your interest in that area as a natural one. Sales price information is necessary in building your comparable files for listing and appraising.

A complete file of comparables for your area will enable you to tell listing prospects the asking and selling price of places that have sold and those that did not. Sharing this information with people in your firm who might be thinking of selling can strengthen your position with them.

Make a checklist

Here is a list of things to do to expand your sphere of influence. Add to it as you think of new ways to make people aware of your real estate expertise.

Develop your own centers of influence
Contact owners of neglected property regularly
Contact owners of expired listings the day you receive
    notice of them, unless your local board disapproves
Contact owners of foreclosures
Check local tax records twice a year
Write absentee owners every three months
Give your business card to every new contact you make
Talk and listen real estate wherever you go
Ask people to tell you about people who plan to move
Keep in touch with every listing you've sold either by phone
    or mail
When a seller signs your listing agreement, ask him if he
    knows of anyone else who is contemplating selling
Drive to and from work a different route every day, looking
    for listing possibilities

Obtaining a listing

However your firm operates, certain elements are essential to successful listing practices. They are presented here with the suggestion that you may want to change the sequence to suit your needs.

Preparing for a listing appointment

Successful listers spend time getting ready for this important appointment. Preparation includes researching recent sales in the neighborhood, investigating available financing and knowing as much as possible about comparable properties for sale in the area. Use this data to prepare a competitive market analysis.

Listing kit

You'll make points with sellers if you have everything you need with you when you make your first call. Keep a kit of listing materials in your car and check its contents regularly. It's a time-saving arrangement and can save you the embarrassment of having to double back to drop off things you might otherwise forget. Keeping the kit in the car also makes it possible to handle an unexpected listing opportunity.

Listing kit tools
50-foot measuring tape
listing forms
amortization schedules

information on guaranteed sales, if applicable
referral forms for out-of-town transfers
Marketing Institute pamphlets for sellers: "You Can Help"
company brochures
copies of direct mailings you make on your listing
information on how MLS works
notebook for recording data you'll need
ballpoint pen
listing agreement

Listing presentation book

A listing presentation book needn't be elaborate. Its value lies in the content and the skill with which it is used. Arrangement of the content is important. The material can be assembled by the salesperson and put in a three-ring binder. Plastic page covers will keep the material clean and make the book more durable. Whole sections or individual pages can be changed as needed. A combination of print and illustrated material is more effective than straight typewritten text. You may decide to use colored mounting paper.

65

Material for a listing presentation book should include information about the company, about you, why listing with a REALTOR® is wise, and how your company markets properties.

Company qualifications include text, news clippings or brochures that tell how long the company has been in business, its growth pattern, the market area served, the number of offices and size of the sales staff and its qualifications and achievements. Be sure to include pertinent information about yourself, awards you have won news clipping of your professional achievements and complimentary letters from satisfied clients.

Reasons for listing with a REALTOR® emphasize the advantages to the sellers.

better control over inspection of the property by potential buyers
no showing without a salesperson
a schedule of reasonable hours for showing the property
sellers not tied down during the listing period
sellers kept fully informed on any offer obtained
in a Sale by Owner, the REALTOR®'S commission is always deducted by the buyer and the seller is left to do all the work for nothing

The marketing program is discussed as you show forms used to determine how houses are priced to sell (competitive market analysis), sample ads (both classified and institutional), MLS forms, any brochures the company produces on certain types of properties and the company For Sale sign design.

All this material is organized to give you an unwritten script to follow. Then all that remains to be done before a listing appointment is to complete the competitive market analysis on the specific property. Much of this data could be got in advance at the local court house: legal description, lot size, previous owner's name, tax assessment and tax rate, proposed tax changes, easements of record, recorded mortgages and liens. Some brokers feel the time spent assembling this data, especially when your office is near the county seat, is nominal compared to the information got. It may include some data you won't need, but if you have it and show the sellers you have it, your qualifications are not likely to be questioned. A contrary and valid attitude toward this work is that the time required could be better spent to get more listings and that these details can be got later.

A special folder carrying the sellers' names on the cover with your business card on the inside can be an impressive, functional supplement to your presentation manual. The folder holds a market analysis form, some Institute leaflets, a listing agreement and an offer-to-buy form. This folder can be studied by the sellers at their leisure, acquainting them with how you prepare a listing and the forms they'll be asked to sign for both the listing and the sale.

The listing presentation book and seller's folder cause the sellers to look at the marketability of their property in an informed rather than an emotional way. When the material is accurate and presented in a professional way it leaves little to chance.

What do sellers want? A buyer, of course. Beyond that, they want someone to take charge and handle details, someone to help them make decisions, someone to lean on and worry with, and top dollar for their property. The urgency of the sale may affect the price they will accept.

Your first visit is the time to establish in the seller's mind the fact that you are the real estate expert. Now is the time to take charge and get them in the habit of asking you what to do rather than telling you.

Your first appointment It is important to arrive on time. Get the conversation started by discussing the real estate business, not the property the prospect has to sell. This helps establish you as the professional the sellers want and need and opens the way to discuss what your firm can do that the buyer cannot do on his own. For example, you know the comparables, you market properties in the area, you screen all prospects, you find prospects the seller could not possibly reach, you handle negotiations on price and details of settlement. In a strong opening, you're selling your knowledge and skills as a real estate professional and persuading the sellers that you are the person to handle this important transaction. Inspection of the property may precede or follow this discussion. The sequence depends on how you want the interview to proceed.

When you look at the property, remain calm no matter how exciting the prospect may seem. Watch the effect your compliments have on the sellers, to be sure they do not affect the asking price. Make notes about what the property lacks, but don't discuss it at this time.

Discussing details After the property inspection, it's time to sit down and discuss details. Try to direct this session to a quiet place where you can sit facing the owners. It's important to be able to make your presentation without having to glance from one to the other. As you talk, make notes that will help you answer questions.

Learn why they're selling. Listen as they talk about themselves. Interrupt only as you need to further qualify what they're saying about jobs, children, where they plan to move and when and what housing they'll need. You should be building a family profile and know a lot about the personalities of the owners by the time this interview ends.

Show your listing presentation book

Now it is time to acquaint the sellers with your company and the service it offers. As you go through your listing presentation encourage the sellers to stop you when they have questions. It is said that we retain 10 percent of what we hear, 50 percent of what we see and hear and 90 percent of what we hear, see and tell. When you engage the sellers in conversation about the listing presentation you can get them to repeat back to you some of the things you've just told them about yourself and your firm.

67

Your listing presentation will show that your firm has well-trained salespeople, a reputation for reliability, will generate inquiries, qualify good prospects and eliminate the poor ones.

Explain how your firm qualifies buyers and where buyers come from. Research has proved that 65 percent of buyers are market-oriented, i.e., they are referrals to a salesperson or a brokerage firm or are contacted by real estate salespeople.

Stress the safety and convenience of having professionals bring prospective buyers to them, then act as an intermediary in negotiations and financing details and final settlement details.

Countering objections

Objections are the biggest hurdles to getting a listing. An objection is nothing more than a question that should be answered. One good way to answer an objection is to restate it in question form, agree with the sellers that their question is valid and go on and make a statement that answers the question. If they are still not convinced, offer proof. The proof will allow you to expand into more benefits.

When objections are the "I'll do it myself" sort, use your "For-Sale-by-Owner" techniques to persuade the sellers they need your services. A discussion of objections often enables a salesperson to lead into the close.

The real estate broker knows how to advertise properties to the best advantage, qualify prospects, show the property, secure financing and is experienced in closing details. Few owners have such expertise.

Real estate salespeople know the market and where the best buyers may be found. Few sellers do.

There are myriad psychological nuances to selling property; all are facilitated by using a third party as a sales intermediary. The owner may be willing to take a lower price but without the third party he dare not appear to consider the prospect's suggestion of a lower price, certain that if he makes one concession he will be asked to make two or three. Therefore, he must brush aside, without encouragement, any suggestion of a change in price or lessening of terms unless he is prepared for a substantially larger concession.

The same reasoning applies to the buyer's situation. With a REALTOR®, however, the principals can reach a satisfactory agreement with far greater ease. The REALTOR® negotiates between prospective buyer and seller an offer which can be considered by the seller with all available facts at hand. The seller has the assurance that if he accepts, the sale is consummated; or if he has another possibility in mind, the prospective buyer will be able to consider the counteroffer intelligently and make a prompt, wise decision.

A buyer may be timid and reluctant to talk frankly with the seller. He may shrink from bringing up criticisms that must be answered before a sale can be made. He may be too proud to discuss his financial resources or ask for the terms he needs. The owner cannot overcome this timidity but a good real estate salesperson can.

On the other side of the coin, the owner of the property is inclined to be sensitive. He resents criticism and his talks with the prospective buyer may end in argument. The salesperson, however, can present the buyer's point of view to the seller objectively so problems and stumbling blocks to the sale can be reasoned sensibly.

In relation to the advantages of having the sale handled by an expert, the commission charged by the broker is reasonable. In the long run, it usually costs more for the owner to act as his own agent than to use the services of a REALTOR®.

For sale by owner

Records show that thousands more people thought they could sell their property themselves than ever were able to bring it off. Here's where your real skill in selling your services is put to the test. It's also one of the most promising sources of listings. Train yourself well to meet this challenge, memorizing the objections commonly voiced by owners. You'll soon be able to persuade many of them of the value of a REALTOR®'S services. Here are some questions to pose as you talk to people who believe they can sell their own homes.

Do you really know what your property is worth in today's market? Will you price it too high and discourage potential buyers or too low and lose part of your equity?

Do you know what A-I-D-A means? Can you write the type of ads that will attract a qualified buyer?

Do you have a list of prospects and access to numerous buyers? Can you eliminate the lookers from the buyers?

Can you show other houses as comparables?

Are you familiar with the techniques of selling real estate? Have you the ability and skill necessary to make a sale?

Can you show your property as effectively as a broker? Are you prepared to expose your family to any stranger that knocks at the door to see your house?

Are you available to prospects on a full time basis until the house is sold?

Can you answer objections and criticism without losing your temper?

Do you have the time to call back on prospects without placing yourself in a poor bargaining position to negotiate an offer?

Can you draw a legally correct contract and include all the changes and conditions customary in this area?

Are you familiar with today's financing? Do you have several sources of financing?

Do you have the time to handle all these details?

Not one of these questions suggests that you already have a buyer for the property. You haven't even seen it, so how could you know who might be interested in buying it? And until you've seen it, you don't know whether it is a listing your firm will want. Sell real estate services first; then it's time to ask for an appointment to see the property. In asking for an appointment you can legitimately claim that from time to time you have buyers for homes in the area. All you've done is ask for a chance to see the home. The owner may agree to the appointment simply to be able to pick your brains so he will be able to deal with an eventual buyer himself! That's a risk you take; but it's also your chance to persuade him to list the property with a professional.

These same arguments can apply to commercial-investment selling. Because of the complexities involved in the commercial real estate field, it is very likely the services of a well-informed salesperson can be of even greater benefit to an owner or prospective buyer.

Selling the seller

You have to persuade the seller to list the property with you and your firm instead of trying to sell it on his own or listing it with another REALTOR®.

Talk about your firm's size. There are advantages to listing with small firms as well as large ones. Discuss the points that favor yours.

A good presentation also stresses what your company has that the competition doesn't—things like a national referral system, guaranteed sales program, good office location and a strong image in the marketplace. If the property is located in your farm area, remind the sellers that this is "your" neighborhood too. Speak emphatically but don't brag.

Promise only what you can deliver

Explain your firm's advertising program. Many people don't understand the difference between classified and institutional advertising, the value of the latter in selling real estate and the limited effectiveness of advertising a single property. Tell how institutional ads strengthen the base of a REALTOR® 'S daily efforts and how they attract buyers to the office. This is a good time to mention the convenience of having your firm answer all phone inquiries and how you qualify buyers. If your firm has an established policy on advertising individual listings, explain it fully so the sellers know what to expect. Don't promise more than you can deliver.

Touring the property

Three things are accomplished by a tour of the house:

Rooms are measured and other pertinent data collected

Condition is examined, permitting you to suggest tactfully what may need to be repaired; also to give guidance on what should not be done

Conversation will help you determine why the property is being sold, when it will be available and who makes decisions in the household

Some salespeople like to have the owners help take room measurements. Others leave the measuring to be done by the sales caravan of the listing firm. Suggestions for minor repairs are easy to make. Dripping faucets or loose doorknobs are easy to see. They may lead prospects to wonder what unseen defects exist. Overcrowded closet and other storage space may hold unessential clutter; it could suggest to potential buyers a lack of sufficient storage. A few hours' clean-up and reorganization effort might result in some empty storage space, giving the effect of a plentiful supply. A stained ceiling suggests a leaking roof. Even if the roof repair job is evident, urge the seller to redecorate that ceiling so buyers won't suspect a still-leaking roof. Cockroaches, moths and rodents are anathema. Call in the exterminators!

On the other hand, major renovations done to the seller's taste might spoil the sale for new owners whose tastes differ. Don't recommend spending sums the seller cannot hope to realize in the sale price.

Another reason for getting the reason for selling is that most buyers want to know. It's not important to them but if a reason is not given, it can trigger suspicion.

Do you want the listing?

At some point in examining the property and getting acquainted with the owners you will have to decide whether the listing is a viable one for you and your firm.

The real reason for selling is rarely given in response to the first inquiry unless it involves a business transfer or settlement of an estate. It's important to get the real reason so you know if you are dealing with a qualified listing Be sure to get the answer to this question in the presence of both owners. Until they agree, you are wasting your time. Find out when the owners plan to move, where to and what their future housing needs may be.

Why does the owner want to sell? Is it imperative that he sell? If the reason for selling is not strong, approaching compulsion, your chances of procuring an acceptable offer are lessened. Since many owners are evasive, getting an honest answer to this question may take more time than some salespeople are willing to give.

Is the property comparable in value to others in the area? An exclusive listing for a home that is not comparable in value to others in the area always presents a selling problem.

Do the owners give the impression of being cooperative? An exclusive agreement is similar to a partnership in which the seller and REALTOR® work together to accomplish the best results. If one of the owners is opposed to selling, you may encounter difficulties in arranging showings and getting

70

acceptance of a reasonable offer. If you sense you are not developing rapport and gaining the confidence of the sellers and that these are people with whom you simply cannot do business, it is futile to try.

Is the market favorable for a mortgage on this property? Availability and cost of mortgage money influence a sale. In an unfavorable market, you should explore availability of secondary financing either from the seller or some other source.

Will the exclusive run long enough to cover the peak period of the seller's motivation? Does he need to sell in 30 days or can he take six months? Market conditions can determine the time needed to get the job done. The weaker the market, the more time required.

Is the property the kind you believe you can merchandise under the customary exclusive agreement? Limiting characteristics in residential properties include such things as two bedrooms, large, cavernous rooms in older properties or deluxe houses located too close to properties of much lower value. Such listings normally take longer to sell.

Are you genuinely enthused about the property, believing you have a reasonably good chance to sell it during the term of listing? Will your enthusiasm and confidence survive the critical commentaries of lookers and bargain hunters?

Are you willing to be personally responsible to the owners during the term of the listing, to keep them advised of all activity and buyer reactions and to counsel them about price and terms? An informed seller is a receptive seller. He will be much more responsible to proposals when he knows and understands the basis for them and is aware of the effort it has taken to produce them.

Have you made a complete analysis of the property? Many salespeople do not and are unprepared to give professional guidance when the inevitable question is asked, What is the property worth? Since most owners have an inflated idea of the market value of their place, you must be ready with facts to justify your suggested price range. Your market analysis is invaluable in this regard.

Pricing the listing

Working with a seller to determine the price of his property requires both knowledge and tact. Often the price you believe the property is worth is not acceptable to the owner. He has heard about property values in his neighborhood or what several have sold for. Whether these prices are rumor or fact does not enter the owner's thinking.

At this point, you may wish to suggest an appraisal be made by impartial, expert authorities on real estate value. The owner pays the appraisal fee. He usually will not object if it can be demonstrated that an appraisal is to his advantage.

An appraisal may not be necessary if the seller understands how you arrived at your suggested price. You can do this in several ways. You can get files of comparable sales in the neighborhood with actual prices (which may not agree with the ones people have heard).

Some salespeople like to have the listing contract out where it can be seen all through the listing interview but steer conversation away from any talk of price until after they've seen the place and finished their presentation.

Every seller will want your opinion on the market value of the property. The first step in turning the discussion to price is to present your research. Show the sellers your competitive market analysis, explaining how reliable these studies have been over many years. Using the market analysis, discuss the comparables sold recently, those now for sale, their pricing and the financing available.

Ask some preliminary finance questions. You'll need to know how the property is presently financed. Learn whether or not the owners will carry a purchase money mortgage, either first or second. You should already know local sources of mortgage, funds such as banks, savings and loans, mortgage companies, insurance companies, fraternal orders and private investors. You should know the best financial resources. This information is vital in selling and closing stages and will also increase the seller's confidence in you. Lack of financing know-how has resulted in many a down payment and signed contract having to be returned because not enough work was done to satisfy the financial requirements of the transaction.

After you have explained what the price range of comparable properties has been for the past 60 days and discussed financing in a general way, stress the importance of pricing properly. Explain the difficulties in selling over-priced properties.

Homes offered for too long become shopworn and are often difficult to sell
Salespeople lose interest after a number of unfavorable reactions
Overpricing reduces the response from advertising
The property fails to compete with other offerings
Buyers expect more at high prices; failing to find it, they seldom become interested again even at a reduced price
When a property does not sell after proper exposure for a reasonable period of time, price is the problem

Be realistic. Don't allow your enthusiasm for a property to warp your judgment and lead to overpricing. Stress the importance of the time factor and the wisdom of pricing a property realistically at the beginning to avoid the danger of having to take a loss when a listing becomes shopworn. Attracting buyers is the name of the game.

One very successful REALTOR® suggests an asking price range by saying, "Here, for all these reasons, is the price range within which we believe the average buyer for your house will be. Does that seem logical to you?" The suggested price covers a three percent high-low range based on a careful market analysis. This manner of suggesting a price range tells the sellers you are not appraising their property but want to help them market it. The second part of the statement asks the sellers to accept (or reject) the logic of the REALTOR®'S calculations. It makes the decision theirs and it helps them make a decision.

Some owners will insist on asking an unrealistic price. If your company policy permits and if the listing contract covers the urgent time period, if the property is in good condition and is located in an area that is in demand, the listing may work out. But make sure the sellers understand you feel it will not sell at their price. Ask them to keep a record of the number of times it is shown at their price the first week of the listing period. From then on it is your job to keep in touch with them to try to persuade them to reduce the price.

Important data for sellers

Your pricing figures ought to show exactly how much the owner will realize on the sale and the optional ways of selling. Don't draw up figures hastily or make any estimates. Wrong calculations lead to great problems.

73

The owners may already be familiar with the listing agreement if you showed it to them in your listing book or left one with them during your first visit. As you explain it to them in detail, you are beginning your close. Be sure those who will sign it understand every part of it.

Guarantee and trade-in plans

If your company has a program to encourage equity purchase, enabling homeowners to continue with their plans to purchase another, explain it to your prospective listing clients. Such a program may give you the edge on your competition. As their real estate expert, you may become involved in both the sale of the home they are living in and the purchase of the new place. Be sure you understand your company's program thoroughly before you promote it.

Types of listings

You will want to get an exclusive right to sell. It is important to understand the basic types of listings.

An exclusive right to sell is a listing contract between owner and broker in which the agent is given the sole and exclusive right to sell the property. Under this form of contract, the REALTOR® earns the commission even if the property is sold by the named broker, the owner or by anyone else. The commission rate is negotiable.

Under the exclusive agency contract the owner reserves the right to sell the property himself and not pay a commission to the REALTOR®. If the owner sells the property through his own efforts, the exclusive agency ends without any liability for a commission and regardless of the employment period specified in the contract.

The exclusive contract should be for a definite period of time. This period will vary according to the kind of property, the activity of the market and the arrangement the salesperson makes with the seller when the contract is executed. In every case, the time period should be sufficient to enable the real estate office to conduct an effective marketing campaign and should cover the period of maximum motivation.

For the broker, an exclusive right to sell listing has many advantages. He is justified in spending time and money to locate qualified buyers and to negotiate a good sale. He can offer the property through other REALTORS®, thereby giving the owner a special service that includes both individual preferred attention and attention in a wide market. An exclusive listing gives the broker assurance that the property he is selling can be delivered at a definite price and on pre-established terms.

The seller also has advantages in listing exclusively. When he gives one broker an exclusive he has a right to expect a vigorous sales effort. He can confidently expect results, for no broker should accept an exclusive unless he honestly believes he can sell the property.

Closing

Ask a question which assumes the listing: "Mr. Smith, you've said you need professional service and, as you agreed earlier, if you could net $40,000 on the sale of your home, you would be glad to list. The terms of our listings are normally 90 to 120 days. Would you prefer that we started with 120 days or would 180 days be even better?" Here you have made it easy for the owner to answer. You haven't asked him to make a big decision, only to choose between the two options. This is known as "minor point" or "alternate close" and is a classic approach.

Another approach to closing is the stair-step arrangement where each objection (question) is met (answered), leading the owner a step closer to the close. Basically, a close is the combination of asking questions, meeting objections and summarizing benefits that are important to the seller.

As soon as the seller has committed himself to a preferred time period, begin to write up the listing contract. Discuss personal property that is to be included in the asking price. Be sure every item is listed fully in the agreement so there can be no question between you and the seller or between seller and buyer and so your office forms and MLS sheets are accurate.

Put it in writing

A written contract should always be used. The price of the property and the commission rate, which is negotiable, are clearly spelled out in a contract. The seller must understand clearly what commission rate is involved and that the commission is included in the sale price of the property. Be certain he understands, for example, that the commission must be paid out of the selling price of the property. This should be stated in writing as part of the contract, along with a specific statement of any other charges or costs to be paid by the seller. Either the salesperson, at the time of the listing, or the broker, when the listing is accepted by the office, should make and deliver to the owner an exact copy of his listing contract so that all conditions will be thoroughly understood. In many states this is law. Brokers, of course, have different forms for this purpose but all compile information pertinent to a listing.

Get all the facts

Every brokerage firm has its own way of keeping all the information on a listing together. It's important to get every detail needed for your own office and the MLS sheet. The more you know about a property the better job of marketing you can do. Prospective buyers are likely to ask about these things.

location of transportation, schools, churches, business and

shopping centers, recreation and amusement facilities

price asked, mortgage, who holds mortgage, interest rate, amortization rates, down payment expected and availability of other mortgages

year house was built, type construction, plumbing, wiring and roofing material

number and size of rooms on each floor, type basement, garage size and type

size of lot

heating system, air conditioning system, utility services, water and sewage systems

charges against property: annual taxes, assessments, special tax districts and other liens

date of possession

attractive special features (lake or river rights, stables, swimming pool, gardens, landscaping, separate living quarters for in-laws)

why selling (not because it matters but because buyers are curious)

zoning history and present zoning, including non-conforming uses

easements granted and deed restrictions

insurance information

exchange possibilities and kind or value of property considered for trade

Commercial-investment listings

It is of paramount importance that the most thorough and reliable listing information available on commercial-investment properties be obtained. In listing and selling residential property, a market data approach is most often the basis for determining value and/or price. Income producing properties are purchased primarily for their ability to produce an income stream after considering all tax aspects and also as a hedge against inflation. The amenities and physical characteristics of the property, which are of first importance to a single-family residential property, are important to an income producing property only to the extent that they influence the quality, quantity and durability of the income stream. It is, therefore, imperative that all of the financial information concerning a property be obtained before marketing it. The process of collection, analysis, reconstruction and finally the presentation of this information is thoroughly developed in *Marketing Investment Real Estate—Finance, Taxation, Techniques,* published by the REALTORS NATIONAL MARKETING INSTITUTE®.

Creative selling

A good commercial-investment salesperson looks at every parcel of real estate, improved or otherwise, with a critical and creative eye. He asks himself the following questions.

Is the property being used to its highest potential?
What other or better use might it have?
What transaction could bring this about?
Who are good prospects to participate in such a transaction?

A good commercial-investment salesperson listens all day every day for news and rumors involving the market he serves. He learns to filter fact from rumor and know the value of each. He's attuned to business, professional and personal news about people and things, aware that any change might involve possible use of his services. This is creative selling.

You may have heard that your community is thinking of adding a new swimming pool, branch library or neighborhood playground. Then you think of the old house or vacant building in a good location that could be renovated to fill the need or possibly be razed to provide a suitable site. If you have a list of such properties and brainstorm ideas for their private or public use, you may have the beginning of a creative transaction. Unused industrial buildings offer the same creative possibilities. As rail stations, warehouses and other single- or multi-story business buildings fall into disuse, new shopping and recreation complexes are being designed to continue their useful lifetime. Adaptive uses of historic buildings are a new and growing challenge in creative selling.

Factual information on every listing should be a permanent record in the REALTOR®'S office. Besides helping service the seller, it becomes a valuable record of real estate history in your area, valuable when the property is resold, reassessed or appraised.

Prepare the seller

Before you begin to show the property, you and the seller must cooperate to prepare for it. Tell the owner or tenant when you will be bringing people to see the property. Make them aware of the possibility of an unavoidable sudden showing.

Be sure the seller understands the pre-showing and MLS procedures to avoid misunderstandings and embarrassing situations. This may include asking for a key, taking a picture of the property, putting up a sign and having a caravan. The seller will not mind such procedures if he understands why they can help sell a property; they will, in fact, confirm his belief that your firm does its utmost to market the property.

How the seller can help

Homeowners can help sell their properties by getting the place in shape to show. REALTORS NATIONAL MARKETING INSTITUTE® publishes a "You Can Help" leaflet you can distribute to owners. It tells how important first impressions are, how a little decorating can improve the appearance and appeal of a house, what small repairs should be made before the first showing, how important it is to keep clutter at minimum from cellar to attic as well as outdoors, the importance of both daylight and artificial light in making visitors welcome, the reason to keep pets out of the way and music, radio and television turned off. It stresses the importance of the seller remaining in the background, letting you take charge of the showing and discuss price, terms, possession and other factors important to the sale.

The same principle of getting property ready to show applies in the sale of commercial property, where repairs and a general sprucing up help toward a successful showing.

Discussing these things with the sellers provides an opportunity to explain to them how you prefer to handle showings. Explain that advance appointments are set up (the first one can be the time you bring your firm's sales caravan to see the place), how open houses work (if your firm uses them), how to handle For Sale sign responses if they come to the door (refer them to your office for appointment), why whatever repairs, clean-up and decorating planned should be done at once (certainly before holding an open house) so the place makes a good impression on all the salespeople who'll be showing it and your firm will not need to apologize for or defend any bad points.

You may suggest leaving a fact sheet (whatever is given buyers in your market) near the main entrance so other salespeople can check it as they enter. Ask the seller to add a few notes about what they most enjoyed about the property and the neighborhood and what they'll miss most on leaving.

Getting the listing into the system

The selling process starts as soon as you get the listing into the system. Both speed and accuracy are important to getting the proper forms filled out and telling other REALTORS® and all your prospective buyers about it.

Multiple Listing Service
A Multiple Listing Service is the means of disseminating and correlating listing information to its members so REALTORS® can serve the buying and selling public better. Under the MLS, an owner lists his property with a participating broker who then submits the listing information to the service, making the information available to all participating officers in the market area. Cooperating REALTORS® then assist the listing firm find a buyer. When a sale results the commission is shared at the rate established by the listing office.

Getting your listings into the MLS promptly is important to starting the whole selling cycle.

This checklist will remind you of the things you'll need to do to get the listing into the system promptly and efficiently.

Put up the For Sale sign
Make sure the description for the fact sheet is clear, concise and complete
Include pertinent data on schools, churches, recreation and shopping facilities and special features and give directions for reaching hard-to-locate properties
Arrange for caravan to inspect the property
Get name and phone number of the person to be contacted for showing appointments
Decide whether to have an open house
Are you and owner in agreement on asking price? If not, have you gone on record to register your feelings and have you a plan for follow-through?
Decide where and how property will be advertised

Tell 20

Using your local cross-index street address directory, list the names, addresses and telephone numbers of 20 neighbors near your listing.

Find the street number of your listing. As a rule, the ten addresses and names up the list and ten down the list are the immediate neighbors to the right, to the left and across the street from your listing. These are considered the ideal minimum range or influence.

You can bracket the 20 names in the directory and work from it. A better plan is to transfer names, addresses and phone numbers to a form similar to Fig. 3. (These can be bought from cross-index publishers or you can make them up yourself.)

If a telephone cross-index directory is not available, you can get the full benefits of a Tell 20 system by calling on the neighbors in person.

What do you say?
Have your comments memorized or written on cards you can keep in front of you. Say "Hello, Mrs. Smith, please." When she responds, open the conversation by giving your name and the name of your firm slowly. Continue, "We have just listed the _____(name)_____ home at ____(address)____. I'm calling to let you know it is for sale and to tell you we will be very pleased if we can locate new owners. Would you mind if I ask you a few questions that will help us do that?" The usual response is affirmative.

Then be ready to ask specific questions that will help you locate prospects while you also impress the listener with your professional approach to selling real estate.

How long have you lived here?
Have any of your friends or relatives ever mentioned they would like to live here?
Do you know anyone who has outgrown his apartment or home?
Do you know anyone who is renting but would like to own his own home?
Have you considered buying a property here as an investment?
Can you think of anyone who might consider buying a home as an investment? I have some other homes for sale.
What do you like about this neighborhood? (A negative answer is a listing prospect).
Do you have children? How many? What ages?

When you've finished, 20 property owners will know that a neighbor's place is for sale and that you're interested in helping find neighbors for them.

Know other listings

You should be completely familiar with every listing your firm has and with all the listings in your farm area. Many brokers believe all the firm's salespeople should personally inspect every exclusive listing. Not only does this show the owner the firm's determination to be fully informed about the property, it helps individual salespeople do the best job of selling their listings.

Servicing seller

The first service performed for the seller after the listing is given is to get a copy of the listing sheet into his hands. It can either be hand delivered or sent in the mail with a covering letter. This serves three purposes. It provides an

TELL 20 FORM

Name	Address	Phone	Date Mailed	Date Phoned	Date Personal	Remarks
HUGH E. HARDAWAY	557 Markham	342-8299				
James L. HANSEN	558 Markham	344-9903				
Frank Kerns	559 Markham	344-3709				
T.H. BOLTON Jr.	561 Markham	344-3637				
William Allen Godwin	563 Markham	342-7936				
J.L. Champaign	564 Markham	344-4666				
KENDALL TOW	566 Markham	344-5346				
James L. Brantley	568 Markham	342-4627				
Dean A. Berry	569 Markham	344-2609				
Luther N. Davis III	570 Markham	342-3851				
Thomas G. Hart	571 Markham	344-1707				
Major P.R. Hare	572 Markham	342-1935				
H. Burgoyne TAYLOR	573 Markham	344-3636				
CHARLES Devan Dicks	574 Markham	342-9454				
BOBBY F. Rush	575 Markham	342-6561				
J.H. Freeman	576 Markham	344-9472				
Donald L. Williams	579 Markham	344-1745				
E.R. Williams	600 Markham	342-6176				
G. Murphy Small	602 Markham	344-0715				
D.G. Parmer	605 Markham	344-2099				
William J. Stewart	606 Markham	344-1587				

Fig. 3 Insert name and address of your listing between heavy lines in middle of page. Then use your local cross-index directory to obtain names, address and phone numbers of neighbors to left and right and across the street.

opportunity to thank him for listing with you, shows the sellers exactly how his property is described on the listing sheet and enables you to ask him to check it for accuracy. Sending it by mail with a covering letter can be important protection to both the seller and the REALTOR® if any question arises about details of construction, room measurements and personal property inclusions. Some REALTORS® ask sellers to initial an extra copy and return it for their files.

Throughout the listing period it is up to you to keep the owner informed of the progress of the sale. Data collected on your firm's efforts (Fig. 4) should be conveyed to the seller regularly. If the owner knows you are doing your utmost to sell the property he is most likely to be patient if the process takes longer than anticipated. You cannot expect this if you don't keep the owner aware of what you are doing beyond showing the house—how you're promoting it by direct mail or classified ads or telephone solicitation of potential buyers.

If the property doesn't elicit an offer from those who see it in the first few weeks and the price was higher than you advised at the time of listing, now is the time to sit down with the sellers and counsel them on the advisability of lowering the asking price. Your counsel is one of the services they have a right to expect for the commission they agreed to pay you.

One good way to remind yourself to keep in touch with the sellers is to put the listing on your calendar the day you get it. Then move ahead on the calendar, flagging dates for action at regular intervals. Be sure to note a date at least two weeks in advance of the listing expiration as a time to check out your own office and cooperating MLS firms for a full report on prospects' reactions to the property.

Some of the interim things you can do to build rapport with the sellers is to send copies of ads you run on the property and any institutional ads that help build traffic in your office and prestige for your firm. Sellers ought to be kept informed of the response to the property. If you keep them apprised in a continuing way, they may be the ones who first suggest a change in the asking price.

The way you service every listing you take will have a direct bearing on your ability to develop future business and your credibility in the marketplace. How do you keep in touch with owners? Successful salespeople use a variety of techniques. Sometimes they telephone, occasionally they drop the sellers a note or stop for a brief chat when they're in the neighborhood. It's important to call the owners after a caravan of salespeople have been through the place and give them feedback on the reactions of other knowledgeable salespeople. It's possible to give them tactful reminders about trimming the lawn or shoveling the sidewalk when you call to set up an appointment for an important showing. Once a week contacts with the sellers should suffice.

Be sure to keep the MLS up to date on price changes or personal property the owners may decide to include with

Marketing Activity Record

Property _____

Advertising

Classified   Publication(s) _____

                Date(s) _____

Open house   Date _____ Hours _____ Number prospects _____

Brochure   Date mailed _____ Responses _____

Solicitation

Tell 20   Calls made _____ Responses _____

                _____

MLS listing   Date _____ Number brokers _____

Other promotion _____

                _____

                _____

                _____

Number showings Our office _____ Others _____

Prospect comments _____

                _____

                _____

                _____

Offers   _____

                _____

                _____

                _____

Fig. 4 Record of marketing effort on each listing serves as factual basis for making regular reports to the sellers.

the asking price, a change in date of possession or any new information relative to financing the sale.

Every well-serviced listing may result in added business from the immediate neighborhood or from friends and acquaintances of the sellers who hear what a creditable job you are doing.

Perhaps the best way to do a topnotch job of servicing any listing is to put yourself in the seller's place and think of all the things you'd expect from another sales agent who listed a property you own. Then do them for this one.

Caveat

It is essential that you keep firmly in mind that every person, regardless of race, creed, color, sex or national origin is entitled to equal opportunity in housing. This subject is covered in detail in Chapter 2.

7 Advertising and Public Relations

Advertising objectives

While the quantity and kind of advertising differs from firm to firm, the reasons for real estate advertising are universal. Good advertising gets the name of the firm into the public eye and mind, helps create goodwill and prestige, leads to listings, attracts prospects, helps market specific properties and informs the public about real estate.

Although any and all of these objectives could be accomplished through personal contact, advertising is the most efficient and effective way to get the job done.

Scope of an advertising program

In most residential real estate firms the largest percentage of the company dollar is spent on advertising. In a small office advertising may be limited to For Sale signs, classified ads and occasional direct mailings prepared by salespeople or the broker. A large, departmentalized firm is likely to employ a wide range of media and may either have its own advertising department or retain an advertising agency to handle the work. No matter what size the firm or how much money is spent, it is important that all salespeople know about the campaign so they can tell clients what is being done on their behalf.

Two kinds of advertising

Real estate advertising can be divided into two categories: marketing and institutional.

Marketing advertising, aimed at obtaining listings and finding buyers, consists of classified and display ads in print media, use of radio and television commercials to promote specific properties, direct mail and outdoor advertising.

Institutional ads put the firm name before the public, explaining the services it offers or its philosophy of the real estate business.

While marketing ads seem likelier to produce profits for a firm, institutional ads are often more effective. A total advertising program should include both.

Consistency in advertising

Logos, slogans and company colors convey your company's image whether they appear on For Sale signs, stationery, direct mail pieces, premium giveaways or in classified and institutional ads. Changes should be made with great care and should not be made too frequently else they interrupt the continuity of the message. People inside a company tire of a theme or program long before it has made its maximum impact in the marketplace.

Evaluating effectiveness of advertising

Most firms follow regular routines to measure response to their classified and display ads and then use these data to determine the program's effectiveness. Each time someone calls or comes into the office, the salesperson or office staff member asks how he came to contact the firm. If it is in response to an ad, the client is asked the name of the paper or station and the date of the ad. By keeping this and other written records a REALTOR® knows which media generate action and which days of the week his ads pull best response.

It is more difficult to measure the effectiveness of institutional campaigns. The REALTOR®, his salespeople and office staff have to keep attuned to public reaction to advertising that does not draw measurable response.

The marketing campaign

Newspaper ads

Classified newspaper ads are the REALTOR®'S most common advertising tool. A good classified ad serves a variety of purposes.

brings buyers to a REALTOR® who has properties to sell
helps REALTOR® obtain more listings
builds familiarity with a real estate firm
brings traffic to a REALTOR®'S office
keeps firm name in the public eye
stimulates word of mouth advertising
promotes individuals when their name appears in ads
increases staff loyalty and pride in the firm
helps persuade people with down payment money to
    spend it on real estate
can tell the public the range of services a firm has
    to offer
helps persuade sellers your firm can market property
    better than he can

Writing classified ads

Since the listing salesperson is most familiar with the property to be advertised, it is up to him to describe the property whether he writes the ad or someone else takes the information from him. Whoever writes ads, it is important that the style conforms to the firm's ongoing program.

The classified ad should not tell the whole story but should leave some question or curiosity in the reader's mind so he will want to inquire further. If the ad tells a reader everything he wants to know about a property, chances are he may not call. When you omit certain essential information intentionally or use a technical term to describe a property's unique feature it usually generates inquiries.

When you write ad copy, the major objective is to create a visually appealing ad with good descriptive copy that embodies the points you'd make if you were selling the prospect in person.

Some do's

Collect all the facts. You're selling a way of life and not just a place to live. Once you're well acquainted with the property, think about what it has to offer the different members of a family, a person living alone or someone who wants to use it as a business investment. Then write the ad. Get the main benefits in the first five to eight words.

Start with the headline. It should dominate the ad and highlight the single most salable feature—location, view, price, emotional appeal, architecture, condition or size. Your ad caption can be bold, dramatic and original. The 12 most persuasive words in the English language, as determined by a group of researchers at Yale, are: save, need, easy, discovery, money, results, safety, proven, you, health, love and guarantee.

Make the body copy easy to read. Don't keep a buyer guessing. Give specific details about the number and kind of rooms, age of house, extras, esthetic features, neighborhood, schools, transportation, outdoor and recreation areas and terms. Appealing adjectives and colorful word pictures provide sizzle. A Newspaper Advertising Bureau survey of people planning to move indicates that each home buyer has one lifestyle element as his primary deciding factor. The most popular ones are spaciousness, a showplace, good place for children, solid comfort, easy maintenance, safe neighborhood, ease of commuting, privacy, place to swim, keep fit, lots of conveniences nearby, push button living (inside is most important) and natural surroundings (outside is most important).

Ask for action. Make it easy for the prospect to respond. Create a clincher that stimulates the reader to do something positive like call your office or attend an open house.

Give your firm prominent identification. Provide readers with an easy-to-spot phone number, address, office hours or even directions to your office (or the property advertised if it's an open house).

Plan a good layout. Let the headline stand apart from the rest of the copy. If you list more than one property, leave a little open space between each one.

Be truthful.

Some don'ts

Don't use vague generalities, worn out phrases and too many superlatives.

Don't use too many abbreviations. They make an ad look more like a puzzle than an invitation to buy.

Don't use headlines that tease or bully. It could turn readers away.

Don't paint an untrue word picture. It will destroy your credibility with a prospect who comes to look at the property.

There are, of course, many more techniques to good classified advertising. Study all the real estate classifieds in your papers and decide what makes a good ad and why.

If you write ads, one of your most important business contacts will be the classified reps of the papers your firm uses. In many cases these people are excellent sources of tips on wording, type size, style and other ad techniques. They can be a great help to salespeople who never thought they would be writing ad copy.

Display advertising

The big plus in display advertising is the use of pictures, showing what a REALTOR®'S best properties look like. Word descriptions under the pictures may not be complete; but since most people are basically interested in looking at the property pictured, a brief description sometimes helps. If it leaves several questions unanswered in the reader's mind, it can generate a call for more information.

Display ads can be used to describe several properties even when only one is illustrated.

Institutional classified

Classified ads can carry a firm's institutional message by brief mention of special services the firm has available, worded to generate phone inquiries for details.

An editorial column advertisement is effective when done well. Written by a REALTOR® or a member of his staff or agency, it looks like a regular news feature or other editorial column except that it must be marked "Advertisement" or "Paid Advertisement." Such a column can feature tips on investment real estate, the climate of the local real estate market, suggestions on buying and selling homes and other real estate topics. Regardless of the content, the fact that the column appears regularly with the firm's name on it (and perhaps a picture of the person who signs it) adds to the REALTOR®'S advertising impact. But it must be produced by someone who writes well and can meet a regular deadline. The cost of such a lengthy, regular feature may be high but in many instances the returns in sales and goodwill more than compensate for the dollar spent.

Radio and television

Though the initial cost is high, electronic media ads often bring results equal to newspaper classified at the same time they serve a strong institutional purpose. Effective radio and television advertising requires special competence in both choosing outlets and preparation of text and visuals. Firms using these media should get the best professional counsel available.

Direct mail

Small firms find direct mail campaigns particularly effective in telling their market audience about properties they have for sale, whether residential or commercial-investment. When possible, the mailing piece should provide a place for a salesperson's signature or a pocket for a business card enclosure to lend a personal touch. The best direct mail pieces include a return coupon or card by which the recipient can indicate further interest in the promotion and a record of responses provide the firm a measure of the effectiveness of the program.

Direct mailing brochures are usually effective in selling commercial-investment property. The brochure describes only one property; but if that property is worth a half-million dollars and the brochure helps sell it, the money has been well invested. Such a mailing would be directed to a carefully developed list of private investors, syndicates, corporate investors and others chosen for their natural interest in a specific property.

Signs and billboards

Your firm's For Sale and Sold signs are strong institutional advertisements, telling the local public how active you are in the marketplace. Colors, typeface and design are important. The signs should carry a minimum of text. Their visual strength is in a good logo, the identifying mark of your company.

Billboards also keep the firm name in the public eye. Giant versions of small property signs, they literally shout the firm's name and logo to people as they drive by. There is a rule of thumb that billboard text should be limited to not more than five words which can be read in four seconds. A costly form of advertising, billboards require the services of an ad agency for both design and placement. They are used most frequently to advertise a residential development or commercial-industrial complex. Some large firms now use them in an institutional way in large cities, keeping their name in the public eye.

Smaller versions of outdoor ads are used in public transportation spaces—airport corridors, buses and trains. Some taxi companies sell display ad space inside their cabs. These display ads not only catch the eye of local people but get a firm's name before newcomers quickly.

Truth in lending

The provisions of the Truth in Lending Act of 1969 are important in all kinds of advertising. Anyone in a real estate firm directly or indirectly responsible for advertising should be completely familiar with the act. Basically, the law restricts the language that can be used in advertising relating to terms of purchase or financing. A REALTOR® can advertise the annual percentage rate but not the pure interest rate or he can avoid mentioning any financing terms in his advertisement. Your broker will advise you how his advertising program conforms to the act.

Public relations, promotion and publicity

Public respect, goodwill and faith in your firm must be earned. Everything every member of the firm does becomes part of its public relations, creating an image that cannot be bought. Good public relations are "deeds first, words last." Implied in this is the public's trust in the firm, its people and its ethics and concern for the well-being of its clients.

How can a salesperson engender the respect, goodwill and faith of the public he serves? He can carry out the firm's policy by both actions and words. Actions include everything from a positive attitude to the job, the firm and the community he is selling. Enthusiasm for the job includes being on time and doing what you promised when you said you'd do it. Positive thinking about the firm can be conveyed all through the working day as you let people know you believe you're working with the best company in the business. Belief in the community begins with the job and carries through to devoting some free time to taking part in business, civic, service or other organizations that need help and support.

Promotion and publicity are the "words last" of public relations. The firm promotes its public image when it publicizes the addition of new salespeople to the staff, the achievement of individual or company goals or the opening of a new office. Promotion includes helping a worthy cause or project succeed by taking an ad in a benefit program, lending window space to publicize a project, donating premiums or prizes for benefits, sponsoring sports teams, having a float in the town parade or perhaps providing balloons for everybody who attends.

Promotion and publicity are bound only by what the company can do in good taste within the limits of its budget.

There are other things real estate firms can do that are a combination of promotion, public relations and what amounts to institutional advertising.

Working with news media people is one. Most newspapers, radio and television stations have a reporter assigned to cover real estate happenings in the local market. While you as a salesperson may not be assigned to work with these reporters, you can help your broker identify possible news stories to suggest to them. Some REALTORS® encourage their staff people to get acquainted with reporters and editors, knowing that it pays to be a reliable source of real estate news and facts. Media news people and REALTORS® share a common interest in promoting the attractiveness of a town or market area as a good place to live and/or work.

Radio talk shows offer another unique opportunity to cooperate. These shows, where a panelist discusses his area of expertise with the host, accept telephone queries from the listening audience. Such exposure is a fine way to widen the public's acquaintance with your name and your firm. Listen to these shows and become familiar with their format. Then list several suggestions for real estate topics you believe would interest their audience. Call the show's producer for an appointment and tell him briefly why you think real estate would be a good topic for his show. The producer may not accept any of your good ideas but may ask you to develop one you hadn't thought of. Cooperate. It could be the beginning of a profitable relationship.

8 Finding and Working with the Buyer

Once you have listed a property you are well on the way to successful completion of that first sale mentioned in Chapter 6. Your next challenge is to find a buyer, consummate the second sale and earn your commission on both.

Prospect sources

It's just as important in selling as it is in listing to let as many people as possible know you're in the real estate business. You should also be thoroughly familiar with every listing in your firm, well-acquainted with other listings in your farm area and study the classified and display ads so you'll be prepared to talk intelligently to whoever calls in response to them.

Your inquiries will come from a variety of sources. Ads locate some buyers and make the phone ring. The Tell 20 system mentioned in Chapter 6 is a good source to cultivate either in person or by phone. The wideness and depth of your acquaintance in your market can be a rich source of prospects. The long list of contacts in Chapter 6 will be just as valuable in cultivating buyer prospects. Open houses attract prospects, especially in areas that do not have multiple listing services. There'll be some casual walk-ins at the office, inspired by properties displayed in your windows or a spontaneous decision to start looking for another place to live. An especially promising source is referrals who call or come into the office because you or your firm was recommended.

All these sources are reasons to take floor time because it keeps you on the scene where important activity is taking place and gives you your turn at telephone inquiries.

Other sources will depend on your generating interest in specific listings. If you've kept a good file of potential buyers who have not found the place they want and go through these names regularly to try to match their needs to your listings it can generate new activity. Keeping in touch with these people will help you think of them when new listings are put into the system. You'll build their confidence in you by letting them know you remember them.

Getting ready for telephone calls

Ads make the phone ring. So do referrals. That's why it's so important to handle telephone inquiries with skill.

Early every day clip the classified ads for your market in your daily newspaper. Paste each on a separate 3x5" card, leaving room to list similar properties you know. With these cards, you are ready to talk about any advertised property being called on as well as suggesting similar listings the caller ought to see.

The caller has usually collected or marked a series of ads that interest or intrigue him. He doesn't want to see them all. He really wants to eliminate as many as possible in the first phone calls. You can help him do it by volunteering your knowledge of the properties he's calling about, whether they're your firm's listings or someone else's. As you do this, you are persuading him that he'd be smart to let you help solve his problem rather than running around to a half dozen brokers inquiring about the other ads he's collected.

Using the telephone skillfully

People skilled in telephone communications say that if you smile as you pick up the phone to answer it you convey a feeling of goodwill to the caller.

Successful salespeople also say they think "sell" as they pick up the phone. Whether you're smiling, thinking "sell" or doing both, answer the phone on the first ring if possible!

The salesperson's objective when answering a telephone inquiry is to get an appointment. During the first call you need to determine whether the person calling is an interested buyer or just a curious neighbor. Don't waste time on the nosy, "just checking" calls. (You'll learn to recognize them quickly.)

You want to establish rapport with the caller-prospect and get to know something about him. Do not try to sell the property. Instead, get an appointment for a qualifying interview.

The caller's emotions are at a high level. If he is a serious prospect, he is thinking about a very important purchase. It is your task to keep the caller's enthusiasm high and satisfy his curiosity about the property while you establish rapport and persuade him to make an appointment to see you in person. Learn how to give some information in response to each of the caller's questions, ending your statement with a return question to him, thus forcing him to respond with information you need.

Open the conversation by giving your name slowly and asking for the caller's name. Use the caller's name several times during this initial conversation. It will help to fix it in your mind and will flatter him. Get the caller's address and telephone number as quickly as possible, so you'll have complete information for follow-up.

Most companies have a prospect profile form to remind salespeople of every point to cover in qualifying. You begin to qualify during the initial contact. For example, if someone calls your office about an ad or in response to a For Sale sign, ask a few basic questions to establish rapport, then offer to set up an appointment to discuss his needs further.

Ask questions that elicit a response that is more than a yes or no. Stimulate conversational replies, then listen carefully. Arrange the appointment as soon as possible.

Phone problems

The following are a few problem situations you may encounter in your first telephone call from a prospect and suggestions for handling them successfully.

The caller won't give a name. It may be a nosy neighbor, in which case there's no way you can get the name. On the other hand, if the caller is sincere (and you develop an "ear" that can distinguish between the two) offer to send them something—a map, a packet about the area, or listing sheets. To do this you'll need the name and address, which you can usually get. It's good to get the phone number, too.

The caller is "just checking" or "calling for a friend." Continue the conversation until you know if it's authentic interest worth pursuing.

The caller has another salesperson. If you know that other person and he's good, assure the caller he's in good hands. You might suggest he make sure the other salesperson show him the property he inquired about, in case it's a firm that concentrates on its own listings. It's nice to call the other salesperson, telling him his client called about a certain listing and that you urged him to see it. The other salesperson may sound embarrassed but he's likely to be pleased.

The caller says he's not ready to look just yet. Probe a little to try and learn the reason. If he says he simply doesn't want to be bothered with calls, assure him you'll leave him alone and that your main interest is in trying to help. If he seems to be just procrastinating, you may persuade him to see you by offering alternate hours for a house call: "I could come out at either two or four o'clock on Tuesday. Which would you prefer?" That way you both sound like busy people trying to find a little time to discuss an important matter.

The caller wants to drive by the property. If you don't want to give out the address, one valid reason could be the owner's instructions not to give the address to anyone not accompanied by a salesperson. It might also be against company policy. Both reasons can be presented as a means of protecting owners.

Qualifying

Qualifying is the who, what, when, where, why and how of the customer's needs. You have to know the questions to ask and then listen carefully to the answers. Full communication is necessary if you are to select the right properties to show.

Why qualify? It is your obligation to yourself to determine whether or not your prospect is a qualified buyer. If he will not buy or cannot buy, you have not only lost time, you have also lost money. If you do not take time to qualify carefully, you could find yourself in an embarrassing position at or near the time of closing with a seller who is frustrated and angered by your carelessness.

Where does qualifying begin?
It should start with the initial contact and should never cease until a contract is negotiated and signed. If the buyer is under pressure to find a property quickly (as in the case of sudden transfers) you'll have to work more quickly and spend more time in an intensified qualifying check. Accuracy and thoroughness are essential no matter what the circumstances.

The qualifying interview is preferable in a quiet place where you can visit openly and frankly, as free of interruption as possible. Some salespeople prefer to arrange the initial meeting on their own ground, the office, feeling it puts them in the most favorable position to create confidence and because all the tools of the trade are available there to assist in the presentation. Others prefer to meet prospects in their home so they can see the prospects' living style and gauge more accurately the type of people they are dealing with.

What qualifying determines

Who the buyers are; who their friends are or will be; whom they work for or will be working for; whom they want to impress or are impressed by; and who referred them to you.

What type, style and size home they need; what is their income; what are their ages; what are their hobbies; what is their motivating factor; what grades are their children in; and what do they not like about their present home?

When will they have to move; when did they start looking for a home; when can you meet with them?

Where are they now living; where are they employed; where do they worship; and where will they go from here?

Why are they making this move (transfer, desire to move up or down, financial reasons, divorce, change of location)?

How do they plan to purchase (FHA, VA, conventional or cash?); how much do they plan to invest; how long do they expect to be in this location?

Qualifying interview
Begin the interview with a request for the prospect's permission to ask personal questions, so that midway through your interview the climate is not destroyed by his objecting to a question you pose. (One way to get this permission is to suggest that your desire to help solve his housing needs is similar to a doctor's need to know his patient's symptoms before he can prescribe treatment.)

Clues
You have a beginning clue to the prospect's needs in the ad to which he responded. You have even stronger clues if he called in response to a For Sale sign. (You know a house size and style that appealed to him, a neighborhood that interests him and a suggestion of the price range he's thinking about).

Ask pertinent questions about the size of the family and the number of people who will be living in the new home. Encourage the prospect to talk about his social and business expectations and ambitions and the importance to him of community and civic life. In answering these questions, buyers reveal a lot about themselves; but you'll still have to do some reading between the lines.

Urgency
Urgency can be an important qualifying point. Are the buyer's needs urgent enough for you to clear your schedule and give him your full attention? If he is living in a motel, has sold his former home and needs to locate the new property and get possession in a matter of weeks, you may

want to explain that you will give him 100 percent of your time for the next several days to solve his urgent housing problem in exchange for 100 percent of his time! This shows the prospect that you value your time, understand the urgency of his needs and will accommodate your busy schedule to his needs in a very professional way.

The "4-7-3" formula

The "4-7-3" formula is a series of qualifying questions. The sequence in which they are used is flexible. Many variations will produce the results you want. The strength of the formula is that your qualifying questions are structured. You should know in advance what you're going to ask prospects. The reason for using this structured approach is that the kinds of questions asked will produce useful information rather than just conversation; and you won't fumble and stumble through qualifying interviews.

Four questions

Four preliminary questions should be asked during your first contact which will most likely be by telephone. They help you determine if the prospect is a looker, a professional shopper or a real buyer. Failure to establish the degree of the caller's serious intent puts no money in your bank account. These are the questions to ask.

Do you own your own home now? (If the answer is yes, proceed to the next question.)
Are you planning to sell it before you buy another?
Is your property already listed with another broker? (If the answer is no, proceed to the next question.)
Are you going to sell it yourself?

Seven-day-a-week test

A test question helps separate the wheat from the chaff, the motivated buyer from the non-motivated one. The question is "If you'd like me to help you find a home, I'll be working for you seven days a week. I'll contact you whenever I find a property I think is right for you. How does that suit you?" Serious buyers will be pleased to learn that you want to work diligently for them; prospects who are playing games will not welcome such a commitment from you.

Three follow-up questions

"How long have you been looking for a house?" "Have you looked with any other brokers?" "Which property appealed to you most?"

These questions usually produce better results after you have met your prospects and can discuss their preferences in person. You will find out if they are hard to please, unsure of what they want, confused from having seen so many properties, whether the looking has been haphazard or planned or if they have come close to making an offer on any property. Successful salespeople ask questions to get answers which serve them as beacons, showing them the way to a sale.

Successful residential salespeople say financial qualifying seeks the answer to three questions.

How much cash is available? Is it in the form of cash or equity in property? What jobs will support the purchase and what net income do they produce? How much other debt has been incurred?

Can the buyer write a contract today? Can he make a 10 percent deposit?

Will the deposit be in cash or by a promissory note?

Finances

Finance questions should tell you quickly whether the buyer can invest in another property immediately or whether he must first sell another place. Questioning along this line should reveal his financial situation in general, what down payment is possible, what his outstanding obligations are if he is seeking insured or guaranteed mortgage financing. If you win his confidence as the interview proceeds, he is likely to show no reluctance to share details of his financial situation. Determine the amount of his current mortgage balance and his estimate of the equity he has in his present home. Add these two figures to determine what value the prospect has placed on his present home. This discussion opens the way to explain financing and your firm's guaranteed sales plan, if it has one.

At some point in discussing finance you should explain the costs of settlement on a property. Many buyers have been dismayed to discover on the day of closing that they must put up more cash than planned to cover legal fees, taxes, insurance premiums and other items usually adjusted to the date of closing. If the buyer will be a first-time owner or is coming to your area from another state this discussion is especially important.

Once you've got the facts on a prospect's present financial status, you will want to discuss mortgage financing and monthly payments with him, making full disclosure of all the costs involved in owning the subject property.

Debt limits

There has long been a rule of thumb that the owner should not obligate himself for more than 20 to 25 percent of his adjusted take-home pay to cover principal, interest, taxes, insurance and basic utilities and services (heat, light, water and sewer rent and trash disposal). As inflationary cycles occur, the percentage rate may either be tightened or expanded. The important point is for the buyer to know as accurately as possible the costs involved before obligating himself to meet the monthly payments.

The first-time home buyer may have no concept of what he can afford. The experienced, conservative buyer may not realize his income justifies monthly payments higher than he plans. However, many buyers are knowledgeable in regard to what they will pay or can afford. Housing may be only part of what they are interested in acquiring or enjoying.

If you are reluctant to ask outright what a person's salary is, confirm the loan amount he will need, jot down the principal and interest and add an estimated monthly sum to cover taxes, insurance and the utilities mentioned above and ask if the total monthly payment is in line with his thinking.

The investment property buyer

It is particularly important to qualify buyers of investment property. Many brokers use a counseling session technique to determine what the person in the market for investment real estate needs, wants and can support financially. Is the buyer looking for income today or appreciation? Is he looking for tax benefits? Can he maintain his property himself? Is he really interested in buying? Has he shown enough interest to drive by the property himself before the actual showing?

Your skills in understanding people are also needed to help a confused buyer express his real needs. Many who know what they want appear incapable of expressing their needs until an intelligent, sensitive salesperson helps them formulate their ideas.

Are others involved?

Finally, irrespective of the buyer's age, use the qualifying interview to find out if anyone else will be assisting the buyer in his decision on a new home. Many older people ask the advice of children and relatives; young couples often want parents or a contractor uncle or friend to pass judgment on the place of their choice. When this is the case, you will want to include this person in the showing sequence, particularly if he is not familiar with your market area. To fail to do this could result in lost time and perhaps a lost sale.

The new home

Now you are in a position to begin to discuss the features your prospect wants in a new home. By saving this part of the interview till last, you are in a position to direct the discussion toward the amenities available in homes in the prospect's price range. If you encouraged the prospect in the beginning of the interview to expound on all the things he wants in a new home, you may have to end the discussion by taking away half his dream ideas to fit his realities. You can spare him and yourself that embarrassment by thoughtful guidance. Having established his general price range, ask what features of his present home the family enjoys most and what he feels it lacks. Then listen carefully. This is the time you must learn what he is thinking. Master the art of asking questions, not answering them.

Closing the qualifying interview

As the qualifying interview comes to a close and you are setting an appointment to show properties, you can initiate a positive selling climate by asking, "If we find a home that meets your needs, will you be in a position to make a favorable decision that day?" This is a powerful question, a tested shortcut to success and time and again has prevented the "I want to sleep on it" syndrome.

A well-conducted qualifying interview is expected by today's sophisticated buyer. Common sense dictates a professional approach that gathers information first, fits listings to buyer qualifications and saves the time of buyers, sellers and salespeople.

Showing

Ask questions
From the moment you ask the first question in a qualifying interview until you believe you have all the data you need, your main emphasis in asking questions is to build the buyer's confidence in and reliance on you. Asking questions and listening carefully to the answers will help persuade him that you are genuinely interested in serving his needs.

Sometimes it can be difficult to determine through

qualifying what kind of property is most likely to attract the buyer. There will be times when you simply cannot analyze a buyer's tastes and inclinations or learn in advance what his reaction is likely to be. Taking such a buyer to see property is like shooting in the dark. At such times it may be helpful to send up trial balloons on the way to a showing.

For example, if the house you are going to show has no dining room you might remark enroute, "Dining rooms seem old-fashioned, don't they?" If he agrees, you know that a possible objection has been overcome. If he does not, you think of other houses on your list that have dining rooms. Some salespeople deliberately show homes other than the one they hope to sell. Getting the buyer's reaction to these places gives you a better idea of what to say and show when you finally reach the property where you expect to put your real sales skills to work.

Caveat

It is essential that you keep firmly in mind that every person regardless of race, creed, color, sex or national origin is entitled to equal opportunity in housing. The law in this regard is cited in Chapter 2.

Showing routines

Plan your entire showing routine. Decide the sequence in which you'll show properties, saving till last the one you think fits the buyer's needs best. Call ahead and make showing appointments with the sellers, keeping the arrival time as flexible as possible. If you can get the seller to agree to "sometime this morning" or "afternoon," that's fine. They may ask for a time limit of an hour or two; or you may suggest taking along the key in case the seller is not at home. That's perhaps preferable anyway, giving you total privacy.

As you move from one property to another, ask the buyers what they like about the place they've just seen and how it compares with others you've shown them. Get them talking about their likes and dislikes and use these points as your guide of what to emphasize at the next property.

But say you show a property or two and suddenly realize you've chosen the wrong ones but have other listings you believe will interest the buyers. It's best to be frank, telling them you've thought of a couple other places that might interest them more. If you're near your office, you could say, "Let's go back and call those owners." Remember to cancel out the other appointments. If you're far from your office you might decide to drive by the other places, taking a chance on finding the owners home. (This is a risky second choice for handling the situation.)

Who is coming along?

It is important for you to know in advance who will be coming along. This is especially true in residential sales. Enroute to the property (or even before if possible) you should find out which spouse makes decisions. If the prospective buyer is a widowed or divorced person will a third person "going along for the ride" really decide whether or not the prospect should buy? The third person may be lending money for a down payment or a friend who is an expert in building construction on whose advice the sale may hinge. It is a mistake to ignore this individual, or to express annoyance at his coming along. Instead, direct some leading questions to him. Most salespeople can recall sales they lost because they concentrated on the wrong person.

Try to avoid having the owner of the property accompany you during the showing. If possible obtain the run of the house, since an owner's sales effort may be in direct opposition to yours. Futhermore, if the owner brags about his property, the potential buyer may think the owner is overanxious to sell and conclude that the property can be got at a much lower price.

Showing techniques

Buyer confidence can be won or lost quickly by the salesperson's method of showing a home. No two showings are identical, but the following basic principles can be applied in most cases.

Show the house in relation to the area. Choose your approach route so you take the prospect over pleasant streets passing school, church and park or golf course on the way. If it is impossible to take the buyer in your own car and you must arrange to meet him at the house, give him clear directions and make a point of arriving well ahead of time so you are there to greet him.

Park at a distance to give him a chance to see the house in its entirety. Then walk to the front door with the thought of creating an "at home" feeling, which might not be possible if you enter the house too abruptly.

Point out the exterior features so he will know whether he's in a brick house or a frame building while you are showing him the rooms inside. Explain who the neighbors are and tell about other homes on the street but don't stop for a detailed discussion. Walk directly to the door.

Introduce the prospective buyer to the owners if they are present. Personalize the visit to show that you feel that both the prospect and the owner (or tenant) are important and that you respect them. Introduce them properly by name and add a brief identification (their business connections or other appropriate information) if advisable, to show that you recognize their standing. You might think of yourself temporarily as their host.

Chat briefly but avoid lengthy conversations. Take leave of the owner and proceed with your planned trip through the house as expeditiously as is polite and graceful.

Show the buyer what he wants to see. Guide the way but let your buyer take the lead in selecting the features that interest him most.

When you know what he wants, focus on it. If he has already remarked that he likes a large living room, be sure that he knows the dimensions. Measure it to dramatize your statement that it is 20 feet long. If he mentioned a picture window or a preference for papered walls or hardwood flooring, direct his attention to what he has said he wants to see.

Let him visualize his family right there in the room. Remain quiet and give him an opportunity to mentally place his furniture and get the feeling of the room. Sell the prospect his ideas, not yours. Let him indicate what he is looking for and help him feel he has found it.

Make each room mean something. Have something to say about each room so that if the occasion arises, after the prospect has expressed himself, you can add something convincing. For example, point out that the wall space in the bedroom will accommodate either twin beds or a king size bed.

Suggest new uses especially when the house does not contain facilities he has mentioned as desirable. If a man wants a den or office and no room is fitted for the purpose by the present owners, show him a room that would serve the purpose.

Show the full possibilities of the property to be sure he understands its maximum value. For example, call attention to a dramatic view, an opportunity for a conversational grouping of furniture in the living room or the clear space and headroom for table tennis in the basement.

Handling objections

Keep objections on the positive side. Point out the faults. He will see them himself if you don't and a minor flaw then becomes a major objection. Turn faults into selling benefits by being ready with an intelligent answer. A property fault can become an effective selling point if you know the remedy and particularly when you have a written estimate of the cost of necessary work.

Anticipate objections. Before she says the kitchen is too small, describe it as a step-saving kitchen. Point it out: "You will notice that the kitchen is compact. It gets away from the old barn-size type." Tell why it's good: "The trend today is to have a convenient kitchen, big enough for appliances but with no waste space."

Make him feel at home. Relax, don't hurry. While showing the house, pause when he wants to look at some feature closely. Don't keep the pace at a nervous tempo.

Let him get the feel of the house. After a prospective buyer has been shown through a house, it is an excellent idea to invite him to sit down in the living room, den or a room with an especially attractive view so that he feels that he has been at home there, not just a passerby. Or, let him recheck alone, while you wait. Say something like this: 'If you'd like to go back by yourself, I'll sit down and read the paper. Take your time, I'll be right here to answer any questions you have." Be enthusiastic and your customer will agree. If you have properly screened him, the house should be a good fit and you should be enthusiastic about it as an ideal home for his family. It may be difficult to show the same enthusiasm for a $40,000 house that you feel for a $90,000 home but to the $40,000 buyer, it is equally important. Make him feel he is the only one in the world who should own this home!

Keep his interest and confidence. Listen respectfully and do not argue. He may advance a wrong opinion but you can turn it tactfully or ignore it altogether. Never talk down to a prospect even if he asks questions that seem foolish to you. Meet him on the common ground of confidence and understanding. Be patient and avoid high-pressure tactics. Lead him along until he is ready to make up his mind.

Estimating costs

Paint a true picture. Don't underestimate costs. They'll have to be paid and it's best to prepare the buyer for the correct amounts. If you say that taxes are "about $800" and they turn out to be $850 or that closing costs "may amount to $250" and the actual figure is $300, you are in an adverse position with the buyer.

If you aren't sure of the exact costs, it's better to estimate high. If taxes and settlement costs are lower than you quoted, the buyer may find he has saved a few dollars and will be grateful. If costs run higher, he'll resent your inaccuracy.

99

Know the answers

During a showing, you may be called upon to answer any kind of question about the community in which the property is located. You should be familiar enough with the community to answer such questions. Here are some things a home buyer might want to know.

What elementary and high schools serve the area and where are they located?
The nearest churches, theater, shopping center?
What public transportation is available; how close is the nearest stop?
What are the annual taxes? Are there any special assessments?
Is the house completely insulated and with what material?
When was the house built and by whom; the kind and condition of the heating system; annual fuel bills?
Why is the owner selling?
Who are the neighbors?

A commercial or investment buyer will want to know these things.

Rental information on a building—when leases will be up; what rent increases are in order?
Structural information—when was a new roof put on? Is the plaster still good, etc.?
What is the character of the business district or residential area in which the property is located?
What mortgages are on the property?
What financial options are available for the purchase?
What improvements have been made in recent years?

Answering questions like these quickly and with confidence strengthens your position as the salesperson. They cannot be answered unless you have researched them in advance. Your sales kit should contain maps, charts and reports on all phases of the community's economic, political and social life.

Tie-downs

The idea behind tie-downs is to obtain a yes answer from the buyer to questions or statements that reaffirm his needs or wants. Four techniques are suggested for using tie-downs.

Ask only those questions the yes answer to which will remind the prospect of something he likes about this property. Be specific.

End your statements with tie-down phrases such as "Don't you?" "Can't you?" "Isn't that right?" "Don't you agree?" "Wouldn't you?"

Keep your objectives in mind. Ask your questions with the expectation of a certain outcome. Don't just rattle out irrelevant questions to keep the conversation going. Be selective.

Avoid glibness; don't sound like you're making a pitch. It's easy to sound phony and mechanical. Think about this and develop your skill in tie-down conversation to a natural way of speaking.

Salespeople have a duty to help the buyer overcome normal fears and resistance to change that could prevent his buying the home he really wants. Be sure to help him overcome his objections tactfully, logically and firmly but not in a high-pressure way.

Moving toward a decision

Minor objections should be dismissed by quickly agreeing with the buyer and just as quickly suggesting an advantage. This technique plays down the negative. No home is 100 percent perfect; there are always some disadvantages and a degree of compromise is always necessary. If you are helping the prospect buy a home that meets his requirements, it is sometimes necessary to keep reminding him of the positive features.

If you remind the buyer, point by point, of all that he found to his satisfaction, you have calmed his fears and restored a measure of confidence. You have preserved the negotiation. The purchase agreement is ready for signature. What do you do if he balks again, saying he wants to think it over? Some of the following techniques for meeting final objections may work for you.

As always, do not argue or challenge. Accept the objection and offer a benefit. If you can offer the benefit as a tie-down question, it will be stronger.

Between married couples, the preferences of one may outweigh the objections of the other. Keep the individual preferences of each in mind and see that both are fairly represented. Ask a question to stimulate their thinking.

There is often a "hot button," some unusual feature that is particularly attractive to the buyers. If there is such a button, push it hard. Describe its rarity or uniqueness. Dwell on the pleasure and satisfaction it promises. If they want it badly enough, they will usually compromise on other issues.

If price is the problem and your research among comparables shows it to be fair, emphasize the fact as many times as necessary. If you are in a rising real estate market make the significance of this clear to the buyer.

It is not wise to recommend haste through fear of other imminent offers unless you actually know of any. It is legitimate to point out that while the buyer thinks things over, the house remains on the market and may be sold at any time. Most salespeople recall clients who missed a property through delay, to their subsequent and genuine regret. It will strengthen the point made above if you can relate such a third party experience that you know occurred.

It's impossible to say when to begin closing a sale. Actually, you're closing every step of the way. There is no magical moment when salespeople know the prospect wants a property but there are some signals. The buyer may introduce new objections simply to give himself time to think, so he won't make an unwise decision. That's why many objections are insincere or self-defensive in nature. Such objections are easy to counter.

Use Institute brochures

REALTORS NATIONAL MARKETING INSTITUTE® publishes a sales leaflet "Advantages of Home Ownership" that has proved helpful to salespeople working with first-time buyers. It lists eight reasons to own a home and five ways a REALTOR® can help buyers. The advantages include security, equity investment, tax advantage, financial independence, choice of environment, cash equity and personal satisfaction. The five ways a REALTOR® helps include qualifying the buyer, choosing location, technical information and good value, all available when the buyer selects a REALTOR®. Copies of the brochure may be ordered from the Institute.

The closing

Closing is a series of agreements, exchanges and discussions during which you should be ready to ask for the buyer's offer. Now is the time to keep your mouth closed and your ears open, listening for the signals that the customer is ready to buy. Most customers buy; they are not sold. Stop talking and start listening when the buyer agrees with your sales talk, begins to boost the property and says his family likes it. Nod in agreement and move to close the transaction. Be content to answer questions but stay on track. Don't introduce strange subjects or wander off on a tangent. The buyer has begun to make an important decision. Let him.

Many successful salespeople like to involve the buyer in the calculations of the sale by giving them paper and pencil and having them make their own notes of financial details along with the salesperson. This not only requires concentration on the purchase, it prevents the buyer's mind wandering, perhaps generating new objections while the salesperson's attention is diverted.

Closing the sale is a matter of doing the right thing at the right time. If you have taken care of all the factors leading up to the close, the close itself should be a natural end to the transaction.

To successfully control the closing, the salesperson should know when to stop talking and ask for an offer and how to apply the closing technique.

Timing is extremely important for the close. Trying to close too early, before there is reasonable evidence that a closing technique will work, can make the prospect feel unduly pressured. He will either shy away or question your motives.

On the other hand, talking too much can bore the prospect and make him suspicious of the value of your product. If he has reached the point of decision, further efforts on your part can sometimes bring up subjects which will create objections or doubts that will make your task more difficult.

The good salesperson observes the prospect, watching for signs that the time has come to close. The time to employ a closing technique is when those signs are revealed, whether early or late in the presentation.

Many prospects are concerned with their willingness and ability to pay the price being asked and with the comparative value of the particular house and its community in relation to others.

When you feel the time has come to ask the prospect to make an offer, you can use any of several effective closing techniques. In each case, choose the one that seems most suitable for your particular prospect.

Closing techniques

One approach to closing is the "ideo-motor." The principle of this approach is that if you put an idea in a prospect's mind and keep it there against all extraneous and opposing ideas, it will produce action.

The minor point close is another approach. One sales associate who is very successful uses this method. After he and the prospective buyers have finished inspecting the house and are walking down the front walk, he stops, turns and silently observes the front door of the house. Soon the prospects look to see what he is staring at. When he feels that their curiosity is at a peak, he asks: "Don't you think the door would look better painted black?" If the people say that they like the color as it is, he says, "All right, we'll leave it that color." He has sold the people the front door and the home that goes with it. He has closed on a minor point and a major point is carried.

Another very effective close is the assumptive close. One way to initiate this is to make sure the buyer comes to the office so that the salesperson can drive him to see the house. After the showing, the buyer can't say that he'll think it over and get in his car and leave. As they approach the office upon their return, the salesperson uses an assumptive close by saying, "Let's go into the office and see if we can work this out." If the buyer accepts the invitation, he is getting close to buying.

One technique is the by-pass close. Making a final decision is a painful and difficult process for many people because they fear making a mistake in something as important as buying a house.

The by-pass close breaks the big decision into little ones. Find out which property the prospect likes best, how many bedrooms he will need and whether he would like the house to face the east or west. By getting the answers to these and other questions, you can select the proper location for your prospect, match its features with his preference and leave him with no sensible alternative but to buy.

Some prospects are so lacking in confidence in their own decisions that they need someone to lean on for advice, someone in whom they have confidence and respect. This calls for the advisor technique. To use this closing method effectively, you must gain confidence and respect from the prospect in the early stages of the presentation. You must convince the prospect that you understand and appreciate his needs and desires in housing. If you can establish this rapport, the prospect will be inclined to accept your advice and to let you help him make the decision. He is, in effect, deferring to an expert in whom he has confidence.

When using the advisor technique, be sure to tell the prospect what would be wrong for him as well as what would be right. Help him exclude those houses or locations which would not suit his needs and then show him why another would suit his needs. This will convince him that you are advising and not just selling.

The urgency close is one of the most effective tools for closing a sale and one which can be used with a little imagination in almost any situation. Any excellent or unusual feature of the property, such as proximity to shopping centers or schools, can be used to emphasize the quality of the house and the urgency of making an offer.

It would help in these cases to have a map or diagram indicating availabilities. This makes it easier to show the prospect why one location is superior to another. If your prospect wants some special feature such as a patio or corner location, point out that the number of such houses is limited and that they sell quickly.

Urgency can also relate to price. When prices are rising fast, the safest way to get what you want is to make an offer without delay.

Ask for the offer

You cannot approach the sellers without a viable offer in your hand. At the point when you know the potential buyer is very likely to become the buyer, ask him to make an offer. If you do not get an answer immediately, ask him again. If the offer he makes is almost certain to be unacceptable, don't tell him you can bring it to the owner. Discourage the offer by saying that it will only anger the seller who might then not accept a later, better offer from him. Or explain that you simply cannot honestly advise the seller to consider such an offer and that you must have a more reasonable offer. Never suggest an offering price. However, discourage unrealistic offers that will be of no use to your client, the seller.

Ask him to buy

Ask him to buy and perhaps he will. Whenever it seems logical in the course of your conversation, let the prospect know that you want him to have this house. This can be done without undue pressure and it is flattering to a customer who may never have made such a big purchase before.

Reach an understanding and part as friends. You may not be able to sign a contract on the spot but you can make the sale. If you have done your job well and the house really fits, arrange to talk with the buyer again as soon as he has checked whatever details he feels are necessary. You should have something tangible to leave with him. A card filled out with pertinent facts will serve the purpose; a property brief is still more effective. It should contain an exterior picture, floor plans, description, all financial data and, on costly homes, a few interior views. The property brief will keep on selling and answering questions and as you will want to recover it, you have a good reason for a return call.

Advise the buyer realistically

No sale is really good unless both seller and buyer benefit. If a buyer's income doesn't qualify him for a property that interests him, resist the temptation to sell it to him. It is a trait of human nature for some people to be overoptimistic about their ability to meet financial obligations. As the salesperson, you need to look beyond your immediate profit from such 'a sale and consider what can happen when an unwise buyer over-extends himself. You will naturally be blamed by the seller if the sale fails. You'll be blamed by the buyer if he bogs down in debt.

On the other hand, some buyers arbitrarily set a price limit on a real estate purchase that is lower than they can really afford. Good salespeople sense this and point out the advantages of a higher quality investment that is within the buyer's reach.

Warranty programs

If your firm has subscribed to a warranty program both the buyer and seller should be apprised of it.

Go over the contract section by section with those who will sign it, to be sure they understand and agree to it.

In most states, a real estate salesperson may draw the initial document or fill in standard contract forms even if an attorney is required to finalize the settlement. You should know the exact limits of your authority as identified by the laws of your state. Your broker can help you in this understanding.

Avoid contract problems

A law professor once told his class that if ever real estate salespeople started to write good contracts, half his students would have to start looking for another profession! He was being facetious, of course, but the fact remains that most legal disputes in real estate have their origins in contract flaws, errors that could have been avoided easily when the contract was drafted. To avoid trouble, have everything in writing, including personal items of relatively low value. When left to oral agreement, they can be the basis of future controversy.

Written clauses should express the intent of the parties in as few words as possible. You should adapt standard clauses you have used before to make them fit the immediate need.

If you find it necessary to delete printed matter or paragraphs in a contract which do not apply, have all contracting parties initial the cross-outs since the changes originate with the offer to buy.

If you are not sure of the interest rate a lending institution will apply to a loan assumption or a new loan, you should write in the highest interest rate that the buyer is willing to pay, using the phrase, "not to exceed ____ percent per annum."

If there is not enough space on the form to include the personal property list included in the transaction, itemize the personal property in the form of an addendum and have all parties initial this addendum.

If the deposit seems too small because the buyer's

checking account balance will not cover the appropriate amount, accept the buyer's check for the smaller amount but write the contract so that an increase to the full amount is required within 24 hours of the seller's acceptance.

If a husband and wife are buying property and are unsure how they should take title, refrain from advising them and insert the words "instructions to follow" in the appropriate space on the contract form. If you advise people on title matters you may find you are inadvertently offering legal recommendations.

When the sale seems to be lost

If you've shown a house that you believe meets the qualifications of your buyer and he responds at first then seems to go limp, showing no sign of reaction, your instinct may tell you this is a house he'll never buy.

Don't trust such instinct. Don't despair. Call the buyer later. He may be a person who believes a poker face will keep the price down or it may simply be his nature to not show enthusiasm. If yours is one of the first properties this buyer saw, he may have decided not to respond until he's seen some others. After he has looked at them, he may appreciate the qualities of the place you showed him.

Make that follow-up call. That buyer may still not buy the place you showed him but your continued interest may elicit the response you need to help you suggest other properties.

Have you ever wondered why you didn't sign a prospective buyer? You may find the answer in these reasons.

neglected the prospective buyer too long—he became friendly with another salesperson and gave him his business
became involved in an argument—won the argument and lost the sale
lost the buyer's respect because I failed to know enough to answer his questions
tried too hard to get his signature before I had sold him on his need
talked too much about the great buy he would get and too little about what it would do for him and his family
kept waiting for him to say he would take the property but our interview was interrupted before he ever got around to doing that
talked myself into a sale but kept talking and talked myself out of it
over-stressed my technical knowledge of the contract—I realize now that the buyer wasn't interested in knowing all I know about it
accepted the buyer's objections too readily
pressed for a sale without knowing enough about the buyer's actual needs
failed to call

Telephone courtesies

Good telephone manners are not only important in dealing with clients, they also affect your relationships with other sales associates. Here's a checklist of questions to remind you what not to do:

Do you let the phone ring three or four times before answering?

Do you forget to take a message or take a garbled, incomplete one?

Do you interrogate the caller with questions like Who's calling? and What do you want?

Do you leave the caller hanging several minutes while you look up some fact without asking him if he would prefer you call back?

Do you carry on a conversation in your office while talking to someone on the telephone?

Do you talk with a cigar, cigarette, gum or pencil in your mouth?

Do you fail to have handy the information you are likely to be called about?

Do you repeatedly interrupt your caller in mid-sentence?

Do you speak so indistinctly that you are asked to repeat yourself several times?

Do you sign off abruptly without giving the caller a chance to finish?

Do you bang down the receiver?

9 Negotiating and Closing

With an offer from a potential buyer, a good salesperson doesn't rush head first to the seller. First, think the offer over. Is it a reasonable one? Do you understand all the financial terms? Do you honestly believe this offer will benefit the property owners? If you have been conscientious you will be able to answer these questions affirmatively and you have a reasonable offer that will mutually satisfy buyer and seller.

Do your homework

If the offer is reasonable, now is the time to do your homework so you take as much information as possible to the seller along with the signed offer. Have data on comparable sales as well as other benefits besides price that this particular offer has to its credit. For example, if the suggested possession date fits in perfectly with the seller's plans, this may be a good reason to accept an offer that is slightly below price expectations. Point out that a convenient moving date could save your client money in the long run. Whatever good reasons you give the client for accepting an offer, back them up with solid facts.

Prepare your own financing analysis, showing what the seller will net with this offer. What would he net with other types of financing? How is the seller likely to regard this offer? Remember, the main items of concern usually are price, terms, closing, possession and personal property. A concession on one of these items on one side may bring about a concession on a different item on the other side.

When you have analyzed the positive and negative points in the offer, planned your presentation accordingly and are satisfied that the transaction will be fair and beneficial to both parties, you're in the right frame of mind to make a convincing presentation. As a final thought, recall the buyer's motivations. Think of trade-offs that could be developed that would help bring buyer and seller into agreement.

Set up an appointment quickly

Meantime, if you're not the listing salesperson, get in touch with him and ask him to set up an appointment with the sellers. If you are the lister, have someone in your office call to make the appointment promptly. Having another person arrange the meeting not only allows you time to prepare for it, it helps avoid a premature discussion of the offer with the seller. In either case, you have important preparation work to do prior to the meeting.

Go to the sellers with the thought that you could be bringing them the solution to a series of worries, decisions, apprehensions and sometimes false hopes. Use the first few moments with the sellers to help ease these tensions, engaging in small talk.

Convey the offer

As you settle down for your presentation of the offer, be sure you are seated facing the sellers. This arrangement is important so you can observe their reactions, especially how they respond to each other with both spoken and silent communications.

Try to get the seller to discuss his reasons for selling (if he's a stranger to you) so his motivations will be clearer to you and any urgency in his situation can be reinforced in his mind.

When it's your turn to talk, tell the seller a little about the buyer. First, present his financial qualifications, to demonstrate that this is a sincere contract which can be consummated. Then personalize the buyer briefly. By this time, you're probably able to decide which of the sellers is the dominant one, the decision maker. Now you're ready to proceed with the offer presentation.

This is the time to tell the sellers what's been happening in the market. Keep them involved in the conversation by asking some related questions such as did they know a certain property in the neighborhood has been taken off the market, and why? Now, with the seller's attention and interest locked in, bring out the purchase contract. But don't hand it to the seller just yet!

Explain the offer in plain, simple language. Start out with the positive factors. (Their possession date may fulfill the seller's need to move quickly.) Review the possibly objectionable points but don't stop to defend or even comment on them. Remember they are negative only in your estimation. If you defend them it might create doubts in the mind of the seller that didn't exist before. State the entire offer plainly, then hand it to the seller to read.

Be wary of the seller's first question or comment. It could lead to a rambling discussion of the merits of the offer if you're not careful. For example, the offer may involve a second mortgage and the buyer doesn't want to get involved in that. Acknowledge the comment, but as you do, bring out a scratch pad and use it to resume control of the presentation. You do this by focusing the seller's thinking on how much cash he'll end up with, getting him to check your figures as you note them on the scratch pad.

The next step could be the presentation of the seller's net sheet. He may have seen figures of a general nature when he listed his home; you can now show him exactly what his position will be at the offered price and terms on a certain date.

Diplomacy is important

Throughout this period of presenting an offer, going back to the buyer with a counter offer and perhaps going through it again or starting the whole process over, you must use all your skills to work constructively and diplomatically with people about one of the most crucial topics to anyone: money. You must be sensitive to the feelings of people at the same time that you must be more logical and reasonable than ever before during the selling process. Never show anger, frustration or annoyance with either buyer or seller, no matter what you may feel.

When talking to the owner about the offer, for example, emphasize what the buyers like about the property instead of the negative factors. Explain to your client that the buyer sees one or two drawbacks but on the whole, he is pleased enough with the property to make a reasonable offer. In this way you can explain the buyer's rationale for making his offer without, at the same time, attacking the seller's property. You may also point out the competitive market for similar properties, how many others the buyers have seen and how hard you worked to obtain a reasonable offer.

If you cannot reasonably bring the buyer and seller together on a sale, chances are the buyer does not really want this particular property. It may be too expensive or there may be something about it that does not suit his needs or tastes. Although you should have discovered this well before nearing the closing of the transaction, you can continue working with the prospective buyer until the appropriate property is found for him.

Does he really want to sell?

There are times, however, when the stumbling block is not with the buyer but with the seller. Suspecting this, have an honest talk with the seller and find out what the problem is. Are his objections to price adjustments so rigid that there can be no compromise with any prospective buyer? Has something happened to make the owner change his mind about selling—something he himself does not even realize has happened to make him less serious about the sale? Was he ever really serious about selling? Find these things out before further embarrassing, destructive situations develop with this seller.

The art of negotiation

When the best offer obtainable is lower than the quoted price, the art of negotiation is invoked to bring the buyer and seller together on a mutually agreeable price. Be certain the offer you are writing is the highest obtainable. Present it to the seller, taking pains to explain the rationale of the potential buyer in insisting upon this offer. Avoid saying anything that will make the seller angry with the buyer. Because of the logic of your presentation, you may be pleasantly surprised. The seller may accept.

Frequently, the best you will accomplish is a counteroffer in which the seller agrees to accept a price somewhat above the offer. Be certain this counteroffer is the lowest figure obtainable from the seller at this time before taking it to the potential buyer. Explain to him that he has bought the home conditionally, conveying in depth and unemotionally the rationale of the seller.

Often this will bring the matter to a successful close. However, experienced salespeople tell interesting stories of negotiations requiring several more trips between seller and buyer. Negotiation is truly an art requiring tact, patience and perseverance.

With some stubborn principals it pays to let them sleep on it. Compromises impossible to get tonight are often obtainable tomorrow, after one or both parties have had a chance to cool off and appreciate the significance to them of the loss of the sale or purchase.

If the seller turns down the buyer's first offer, it becomes your challenge to narrow the differences by further negotiation with the buyers. If they understood at the outset that they hadn't bought the house but had only made an offer to buy, they understood from the beginning that their offer might be rejected. They expect you to return either with an acceptance of their offer or with a counteroffer. You should go back to the buyers in person, not try to handle this over the phone.

A short counteroffer may be set forth on the back of the sales contract, written to conform to your own local laws and regulations. However it is written, it must be neat, concise and clear. A lengthy or complicated counteroffer should be written on a separate addendum sheet or, if available, on a form printed for that purpose. Be sure that a reference to the counteroffer is included in the acceptance clause on the face of the contract.

On the way to meeting the buyers again, analyze the counteroffer from their point of view. If you believe it represents a fair solution to their problems your attitude can be positive and constructive.

First, state the points of the original offer you succeeded in getting the seller to accept. Then explain the counteroffer that resulted from hard bargaining. Ask for the buyer's acceptance. If they express reservations, remind them of all the reasons they have for wanting this property. The best way to do this is to have them restate their reasons as responses to your questions. Then reduce the difference between offer and counteroffer to X number of dollars per month. This is the dollar difference technique. Remind them, too, that the house remains on the market while they're thinking about it and could be sold to someone else.

Legal input mandatory

Salespeople should know what goes into a contract for a real estate transaction. However, no contract should be drawn without legal advice. The real estate salesperson is a professional in his field and in his field only. He should never attempt to practice law along with real estate.

Many real estate firms use contract forms or blanks approved by the legal counsel of the local Board of REALTORS® or by the broker's own attorney. Either way, the contract used should be drawn with adequate legal advice and in strict accordance with local laws. All principals in the transaction should have legal counsel. The legal rights of the buyer and seller must be protected throughout the transaction. The salesperson and his firm are largely responsible for this.

Many court controversies over land ownership are the result of rushing transactions through without adequate legal counsel. To be a contributing agent in such cases is gross negligence on the part of the real estate salesperson or the broker. The only way to be sure a sale is properly closed is to have reliable legal counsel. It is never safe to proceed in a closing without the assistance of a good attorney. Both the

REALTOR® and the attorney have important functions in the transaction; there should never be any conflict of interest between them.

To conclude the transaction, when the buyers have accepted the counteroffer, convey the acceptance back to the seller immediately. Give the seller his ratified copy of the agreement at the first opportunity.

If your counteroffer is not accepted

Don't assume the transaction is dead if the counteroffer is not accepted at once. Sometimes buyers regret earlier decisions and phone the next day to close the agreement.

Importance of follow through

Replace the For Sale sign with a Sold sign as soon as all contingencies have been removed from the contract in writing. The sellers are glad to be finished with inquiries and showings.

Follow through with information on what the seller should do in relation to finance payments until closing day. Have the seller get together all the documents and memos that will expedite the closing. Get the current tax bill, the deed to the property and a loan statement or loan payment book. Ask for the title insurance policy, other insurance policies that will be germane to the closing and any other information the seller can provide on encumbrances, unrecorded deeds, reconveyances. These are needed to expedite the settlement and to establish a factual seller's net cash.

The culmination of your successful sales effort should be an exercise in efficiency. Use your desk calendar to note important follow-up details preliminary to the final closing. Keep both buyer and seller fully informed, conforming with uniform settlement practices. Give them copies of settlement papers as far in advance as possible so they can become familiar with them and, if they wish, discuss details with their legal counsel. Do everything in your power to have all parties to the final settlement fully prepared for closing the transaction.

The contract

The initial contract of sale between buyer and seller should set forth, in detail, the entire agreement entered into between these two principals. It should scrupulously conform to the requirements and customary practices of your state and locality. In addition to the standard provisions, you will want to include special provisions covering agreements such as specific mention of all chattels or removable fixtures, warranties or certifications which may cause misunderstandings between the two parties. The contract should also include any other elements legal counsel suggests. It is highly advisable to have available a list of previously drafted and approved clauses, stipulations or provisions necessary to add to or modify your standard form for recurring situations.

Earnest money deposit

As evidence of good faith, the buyer should always make an earnest money deposit when he signs a contract. The amount should be substantial and depends upon the value of the property. Earnest money makes the offer bona fide to the owner. When the time comes to ask for this deposit, the customer usually inquires, "How much do you want?" The reply should be: "It is customary to make an earnest money deposit of 10 percent of the purchase price." Also explain that the deposit is part of the required equity money which will have to be posted soon. It is good to give the buyer a choice between the amount you want and a higher figure. If you want $1,000, you can say, "Do you want to give me $1,000 or $1,500?" The probable answer will be, "Well, I haven't $1,500 right now so I'll give you $1,000." If you say, "Can I have a deposit of $1,000?", you expose yourself to negotiation or acceptance of a lower figure representing what the buyer can give rather than what you need. Both you and your buyer know that he can handle the contract; therefore, the businesslike thing is to ask for a substantial deposit. Too many transactions are lost after contracts have been fully executed, when only nominal earnest money payments are made. Not many people will run the risk of sacrificing a thousand dollars or more.

REALTORS® normally ask for 10 percent as the deposit when an offer is made or when the buyer signs a contract to purchase at the asking price. If the buyer demurs, you can say: "I want a deposit that will show the seller that you really mean business." Or, "If the situation were reversed, you certainly would want to know that the buyer had made a deposit, wouldn't you?" The earnest money deposit might be called "a down payment on the down payment." In paying it the buyer seals his confidence in you just as surely as he shows evidence of his own good faith in the transaction.

You're not through when a sale is made

In most cases, the serious buyer and seller will get together on price, financing and other considerations. You may have to work with buyer and seller through several offers and counteroffers but if the principals are truly interested, an agreement will be reached.

With this agreement, a sale has been made. The prospect has agreed to purchase the property on terms acceptable to the cwner. However, there is a difference between making a sale and closing the transaction. The transaction is not closed until there is payment of full price, the deed is delivered and all technical details of the sale have been handled and completed. Good salesmanship is as important as you close the transaction as at any time in the course of listing, showing and selling the property. Expert procedure during this time can settle any misunderstandings that may develop and can maintain the goodwill of buyer and seller, both of whom may represent future business through referrals. Your legal responsibilities regarding disclosure of settlement costs are covered in a law passed in 1974.

RESPA

The Real Estate Settlement Procedures Act (RESPA) became effective on 20 June 1975. Under this law, a number of new procedures and forms are required for settlements involving most home mortgage loans, including FHA, VA and loans from financial institutions with federally-insured deposits. Most of the RESPA requirements are the responsibility of the lender. Some of them, however, directly affect the REALTOR®. It is important that you become familiar with the law, in terms of both its direct requirements of you as a REALTOR® and the effects it will have on the lending and settlement process in your area.

Following is a summary of the RESPA provisions which are most important for REALTORS® in their roles as brokers and salespeople. If you perform other roles, such as lending and closing, you will need to check further on how the law affects you. For more detailed information, please consult your local board.

Here are the things you should know about RESPA.

the timing—dates on which the new law becomes effective
the coverage—types of transactions affected by the new law
the booklet—settlement cost information booklet
the process—timing and procedure for advance disclosure of closing costs and waiver provisions
unearned fees—prohibition against kickbacks and unearned fees
title insurance—prohibition against sellers requiring buyers to pay for title insurance from a company selected by the seller
seller or agent disclosure requirements—requirement for disclosure of ownership information and, in limited cases, previous sales price on existing homes

Forms for settlement

At the time you have a binding contract your broker will have a form to be filled out and kept in the permanent file of the sale. Closing forms vary from firm to firm but they include most of the following information, depending on the kind of property involved.

purchase price
earnest money deposit
mortgage history
mortgage institution
tax information
closing date
location of property
insurance information
title expense
service charges
sales commission
attorney's fees
escrow fees
rental information
list of tenants
utility information
possession date
guarantees on any equipment
    or improvements

Checklist for settlement

A great many details are involved in a closing. Many real estate offices prepare a printed checklist so that no detail will be overlooked. Such a list may include:

Title
    abstract guarantee
    correcting affidavits
    quit claim deeds
    judgments, liens
    satisfy mortgage
    survey
    estate-guardianship matters
    title insurance

certificate of title
vendor's affidavit
warranty deed
Financing
  lease with option
  payment book
  loan application
  extra propositions
  notes—mortgage to vendor
  second mortgage to vendor
Taxes
  property tax bills
  receipts
  personal taxes paid
  FHA tax credits
  exemption receipts
  state & local taxes (deed)
  intangible tax
  gross income tax
Insurance
  cancelled
  new
  prorate
  endorsements
  assignments—interest
  company consent
  deliver to mortgage
  FHA credits
Statements
  insurance
  loan
  rent
  commission
  proration
  closing
Assignments
  leases
  loan book
  FHA tax-insurance credits
  lease with option
  roof guarantee
  notice to vacate
  letters to tenants
  management contract
  service contracts
  utility contracts
Bill of sale
  refrigerator
  automatic heater
  stoker
  air conditioners
  other equipment
  personal property

The settlement

There are several methods of handling settlement. Some brokers prefer to get buyer and seller together at the same time. Others prefer to have the papers signed in advance by one of the parties and then to obtain the other signature. The closing, whether with both buyer and seller present or done individually, should take place where all the necessary records, facilities and clerical assistance are available. The principals should be able to study the statements without distraction. If the buyer is financing through a mortgage, the closing may take place in the offices of the lending institution. You should follow through to the very end of the transaction, assisting in every aspect of the transaction and seeing things through to a satisfactory conclusion.

The real estate firm, optionally, may perform such services as transfer of utilities to the name of the purchaser, agreement of leases and endorsement of insurance policies. Such services, plus a cooperative, interested attitude on the part of the salesperson and the broker will be remembered by the buyer and seller.

Keep in touch

Even when the transaction is closed, you are not finished in your dealings with both buyer and seller and you never should be. Many salespeople get in touch with the new owner shortly after the transaction is complete. Some bring a gift; some send a congratulatory letter; some just drop in for a friendly talk. Anniversaries of moving into a new home are remembered by real estate firms with a card each year. When you show continued interest you build confidence that pays dividends in additional sales.

Don't forget the seller, either. It may not be long before he has need of a real estate firm and you want him to remember you at that time.

Salespeople who keep the respect and friendship of their buyers and sellers are always a step ahead of the others. They will speak well of you when someone asks them whom to consult on a real estate matter. A satisfied client is a precious asset in the real estate business. At least half, and in most cases more, of the sales made by most real estate firms can be traced to referrals from satisfied buyers and sellers.

Building future sales

Whether he is selling new homes or old ones, the salesperson who does a good job in locating young couples in small homes is building for the future. Before long, as families grow, they will be in a position to buy larger homes. Equity built up in a small home can be the down payment on a larger one. If you render good service for the first home and keep in touch after the sale you can expect to be well received in the future when you offer your services to these clients and their friends.

Make it a point to call on buyers shortly after you sell them a home. In addition to giving leads, many of them will soon be in a better financial position and ready for a better home if they can break even on the sale of their present one. Many first home buyers outgrow their new quarters faster than more seasoned buyers who not only know with certainty what their likes and needs are but know what their income is likely to be in the future. These first homeowners recognize that their own limitations rather than any pressure from their REALTOR® led them to purchase homes that are now inadequate. Some may wish they had waited or bought a different style of home. By showing concern for their welfare, you will make friends who may some day list their homes with you.

10   Financing

Helping the buyer

The sale of real estate generally involves a relatively large financial commitment. The average buyer is seldom in a position to finance his purchase with cash but must borrow the difference between the sales price and whatever cash he has available.

You cannot complete a sale until the buyer is in a position to obtain the funds he needs. Successful salespeople maintain good working relations with several lending institutions in their area and do all they can to be of assistance to a client in obtaining real estate financing. Mortgage information is as near as your telephone and your mortgage banker can be helpful in financial details in advance of the sales offering.

On project or new development home sales your lender will provide you with complete and accurate mortgage information. On income property sales he will furnish you with a mortgage financing description that will answer every question raised by the buyer. While much financing information can be obtained in advance of your offering, it is important that salespeople not try to assume the role of a mortgage banker. Do not be afraid to say, "I don't know, but I will find out." Many loans could be worked out if brought to the lending institution rather than having the problem decided by the salesperson.

The following is a checklist of the ways salespeople can be ready with reliable facts for borrowers and lending institutions.

Assemble all the required data regarding the property involved and have it in concise form for the lender

Take the lender's representative to see the property

Present the facts about the property accurately—show all that is good and bad

Obtain the lender's views on value and mortgage and discuss them thoroughly with him

Learn why one interest rate is obtainable and another is not. Be prepared to give your client the feel of the money market

Discuss amount of loan and number of years for which it is available. Such background information helps you explain to the buyer what financing is available and helps him understand and accept the mortgage situation

Know enough about mortgage costs so you can tell the buyer approximately what amount to expect

In most instances, a client will place considerable trust and confidence in a salesperson who can offer sound and timely counsel on financial arrangements. It pays to be as informed as possible on real estate financing methods and the practices of lending institutions.

The mortgage

The mortgage is the basic instrument in real estate finance. It is what the average person identifies with the field of real estate finance. A mortgage is a pledge of property to secure a loan. In and of itself, it does not represent a promise to pay anything. The promise to pay is contained in the note (often called a promissory note) which usually accompanies the mortgage. Thus the mortgage is comprised of two separate items: a mortgage (pledge of the real estate to secure the loan) and a promissory note (the promise to pay). However, the term "mortgage" has, through frequent usage, come to embrace both the mortgage or deed of trust and the note.

Legal characteristics

A mortgage is essentially a contract. As such, it must possess all the legal characteristics associated with contracts, as follows:

competent parties
an offer and acceptance
valuable consideration
legality of object
a written, signed document

Forms of mortgages

Mortgages fall into two categories: amortized and straight term.

Amortized mortgages provide for payment of the entire principal and accrued interest in level, periodic payments. This type is most common and is generally referred to as a fully amortized loan. A variant of the amortized loan is the partially amortized mortgage, where level, periodic payments (including some principal repayment) are made throughout the term with a single, much larger "balloon" payment at the end. While the partially amortized loans are quite common and acceptable for commercial and investment use, they are generally frowned upon for residential property because of the bad reputation given them by unethical lenders who attract unsuspecting borrowers by illustrating the low monthly payments while glossing over the fact that the final payment or balloon may be a large amount (so large, in fact, that foreclosure is not uncommon).

In a straight term loan the principal is not repaid until the end of the mortgage term. Interest payments may also be deferred until the end of the term or may be paid at specified intervals (monthly, yearly etc.) Few straight term mortgages are negotiated for residential property.

Types of mortgages

The basic mortgage loan can be tailored to fit many needs and serve a variety of purposes. Each type may have advantages or drawbacks with respect to the borrower's needs. You should be familiar with the basic characteristics of each type.

Conventional mortgages

The conventional mortgage is by far the most common type of mortgage loan today. Only the credit standing of the borrower and the property offered as collateral support the promissory note. A lender unwilling to rely on the borrower's credit or the property offered as security may require conservative terms on the loan—usually a large down payment or mortgage insurance. Generally speaking, lenders prefer to write conventional mortgages for several reasons. First, conventionals allow more flexibility in the specific agreements and terms of the loan. Second, conventionals avoid the profusion of paperwork typically associated with insured or guaranteed mortgages. Third, the costs of loan administration are minimized. Last, lenders prefer conventionals because the interest rates are determined by prevailing market conditions. Frequently, insured or guaranteed loans are subject to interest rate ceilings far below current market rates. When an institution is faced with this situation, it charges the borrower discount "points" (each equivalent to one percent of the loan) to bring the interest into line with the conventional rate. This means more administrative problems for the lender and is rarely favored by the borrower who must absorb the points he is charged.

Insured or guaranteed mortgages

Frequently, borrowers without funds to cover the down payment on a conventional mortgage will apply for an insured or guaranteed loan where the equity requirement is minimized. The principal advantage of obtaining insurance (from either a private mortgage insurer or the Federal Housing Administration) or a guarantee (from the Veterans' Administration) is that the lender will generally loan funds equal to a higher percentage of property value since he is protected from possible default losses.

While private mortgage insurance doesn't insure the entire loan (typical practice is the top 20 percent), it is generally the least expensive program of insurance and carries no special requirements with regard to borrower eligibility or property characteristics. Private insurance does, however, require the largest down payment of the available programs.

FHA insurance requires rather stringent borrower eligibility and property requirements. It is more costly than private insurance but sets a ceiling on the interest rate. Although the lender may charge points to compensate for market rates above the ceiling, the borrower is not permitted to pay the points. The seller has to absorb the discount points charged by the lender granting an FHA loan. The property must be appraised by an approved FHA appraiser. The purchase price may be more than the appraised value of the property but the purchase must sign an affidavit stating that he is aware that he is purchasing the property at a price above the appraised FHA valuation. No secondary financing of any kind is permitted when obtaining a new FHA loan. Perhaps the most significant advantage to those who qualify for FHA insurance is the low down payment required.

The VA mortgage guarantee program is only open to qualified veterans. Its eligibility and property requirements are considerably less demanding than the FHA and no premium charge is leveled on the borrower. Veterans may obtain loans up to 100 percent of the selling price, paying only the closing costs.

Each of the three options has particular advantages to the borrower, depending on his situation and eligibility.

Blanket mortgages

Developers of large parcels of land (as in a single-family housing development) frequently utilize blanket mortgages. These allow the borrower to sell subdivided parcels, pay off the portion of the loan that parcel represents and obtain a release from the mortgage. The retention of financing on the remaining unsold parcels makes this type of mortgage perfect for development and subdividing purposes. A usual lender stipulation is that the borrower must pay off more than a pro rata share of the loan. In effect, if a tract of ten parcels is developed, the lender may require that in excess of 10 percent of the loan be paid off as each parcel is sold until the entire loan is retired.

Wraparound mortgages

A wraparound mortgage (sometimes also called an all-inclusive deed of trust) is a mortgage encompassing any existing loans and is subordinate to them. The existing loans remain on the property as unsatisfied, outstanding obligations with the wraparound becoming a second, third or fourth, etc. The face amount of the wraparound is the total of all existing mortgages plus the amount being loaned by the wraparound mortgagee. This type of financing is more fully explained in the article, "What Is a Wraparound Mortgage?" from *real estate today®: Ten Years of the Best*, an anthology of articles from *real estate today®*. It is published by the REALTORS NATIONAL MARKETING INSTITUTE®.

Graduated payment mortgage

The graduated payment mortgage (GPM) is one in which low early payments rise over a period of time before leveling off to a permanent payment amount. In effect, additional money is borrowed through the early years of the mortgage, which money is used to reduce the initial monthly payment amount. The additional loan is added to the outstanding mortgage balance and is repaid slightly by increasing the payments to be made in later years when the borrower's earning power is theoretically increased.

The Department of Housing and Urban Development through its Housing and Community Development Act of 1977 made the government-insured GPM program permanent under Section 245 of the National Housing Act.

Variable interest rate mortgage

The variable interest rate mortgage (VIRM) is one in which the interest rate increases or decreases either at specified periods of time and rate or in relation to the prime rate or by any formula agreeable to the mortgagee and mortgagor. This type of financing is more generally used by developers for interim financing during the construction period, and the rate floats at a percentage above the prime rate.

Purchase money mortgages

When there is a ready, willing but not quite able buyer, the seller may offer to sell the property and take a purchase money mortgage as partial payment. The buyer's equity or cash down payment makes up the difference. The urgency to make the sale may encourage the seller to offer mortgage terms below the current market. Purchase money mortgages are subordinate to any existing mortgages on the property.

Second mortgages

If a lender is unwilling to lend the amount a borrower needs, the borrower may seek additional funds from other sources if his credit standing is good. Funds obtained in this manner are subordinate to the original mortgage which represents the first lien on the property. Loans obtained subsequent to and in addition to the primary mortgage are called second, third or junior mortgages. Any number of these lower level liens may exist but it is unlikely that a borrower will negotiate more than a second or perhaps a third mortgage.

A point to keep in mind, however, is that because of the added risk, the interest rates borne by these junior mortgages run considerably above loans which represent first liens on a property.

As can be easily seen from the preceding comments, the basic mortgage instrument can be varied and adapted to suit the needs of a purchaser/investor. One variation on the mortgage loan concept is the land contract.

Land contracts

Land contracts, also called "installment sales" or "articles of agreement for warranty deed," generally incorporate all the elements of the traditional mortgage/promissory note arrangement. This type of financing is used by land speculators and investors who wish to minimize the amount of equity outlay. Essentially, the buyer assumes possession and the seller retains title until a specific portion or all of the purchase price is paid. The buyer might have to pay anywhere from 50 to 75 percent of the sales price before title passes to him.

While the land contract minimizes the equity outlay, the resultant sales price reflects this. Benefits accrue to both parties in the contract. The seller has the opportunity to divest himself of the property slowly through an installment sales schedule thus avoiding the tax consequences of a single large sale. Both buyer and seller trade off risk to capitalize on alternative financial benefits or the potential thereof. Although the land contract is similar to the mortgage loan concept, it requires detailed negotiations to develop the contract provisions.

The mortgage market

The mortgage market is comprised of an array of lenders (institutional and individual), borrowers and both public and private regulatory and financing agencies. The transactions and interactions between these participants in the market dramatically affect the viability and very nature of real estate finance.

Savings and loan associations

These institutions are among the most important sources of financing for housing and home ownership. Also known as building associations, homestead associations and cooperative banks, S&Ls are generally considered to be thrift type institutions. While their primary financing is in one- to four-family residential mortgages, some S&Ls (particularly the large ones) finance large apartment and condominium developments and, to a lesser degree, commercial and industrial properties.

S&Ls may be either stock or mutual institutions and either state or federally chartered. Their lending policies and practices are closely regulated by either state banking commissions or the Federal Home Loan Bank System.

S&Ls write about one-third of all new mortgages on one- to four-family homes annually. The local nature of their operations and relatively small asset size vis-a-vis large financial institutions tend to restrict the geographic scope of their lending area and contribute to their image as the local savings and home-financing institution. In 1978, more than 4,700 S&Ls controlled over $700 billion in assets. (For additional data and statistics, see annual edition of *Savings and Loan Factbook* published by U.S. League of Savings Association.)

S&Ls specialize in conventional home mortgages and maintain relatively small proportions of their loan portfolios in either FHA-insured or VA-guaranteed loans. Their terms are the most liberal of the thrift institutions (high loan to value ratios and longer maturities) but their interest rates are typically higher than other institutions. The present S&L trend seems to be to invest funds in higher yielding loans (income-producing property and consumer installment loans). This is the result of tight money market conditions and partly a reaction to institutional reform and realignment.

Mutual savings banks

MSBs are perhaps the most conservative thrift-type financial institution. While the average MSB holds somewhere between 60 to 70 percent of its loan portfolio in one- to four-family home mortgages, conservative attitudes toward risk management have produced portfolios containing much higher proportions of government-insured or -guaranteed loans than are found in other financial intermediaries. Real estate financing at MSBs takes place under low loan to value ratios and maturities of the most conservative while still practicable length. However, as an offset to these conservative terms, MSBs generally offer to lend at rates below those of institutions offering more liberal terms. Thus, MSBs offer an interesting complement to the policies of S&Ls.

Commercial banks

Commercial banks are primarily lenders of short- to medium-term business loans. While they hold approximately 14 to 15 percent of outstanding mortgage loans, the mortgage lending business is not nearly as important to them institutionally as it is to thrift institutions. During periods of easy credit, high yields tend to attract commercial banks into the mortgage market. This slackens off during periods of severe monetary restraint.

The impact of commercial banks on real estate finance as a source of credit to other financial institutions is of a secondary or indirect nature. Banks serve as "warehouses" for mortgages by holding blocks of real estate loans under short-term repurchase agreements with other lending institutions and are extremely important in the short-term construction loan area. Trusts held by commercial banks represent another funnel into the real estate mortgage market.

Lending policies at commercial banks are regulated by state banking commissions and the Federal Reserve System. Commercial banks, on a scale from liberal to conservative, fall somewhere near mutual savings banks with respect to mortgage lending terms. An added advantage to commercial banks is the broader lending area within which they are permitted to operate and thus lend.

Life insurance companies

Although life insurance companies were at one time a substantial force in the residential mortgage market, they have since relinquished heavy involvement in real estate in favor of the securities markets. Life insurance companies' greatest involvement came at the time government insurance and guarantee programs became available. The combination of low risk and relatively high yield proved an attractive package to them until the late 1960s when securities (particularly private placements) began to offer even more attractive yields. Life insurance companies have minimum loan requirements, often five hundred thousand dollars to one million dollars. This virtually eliminates them as lenders for single-family housing except when the companies acquire large blocks of loans in a subdivision or portfolio.

Mortgage companies

Mortgage bankers and brokers are an indirect source of funds for real estate finance but because the task they perform is so inextricably interwoven with the operations of other major institutional sources, they cannot be overlooked or their importance denied.

Mortgage companies do not hold large portfolios of mortgage loans for investment purposes. Some specialize in originating mortgages, sell large blocks of them to other financial institutions and retain the servicing of them for a small fee. The task of servicing mortgages includes the collection of interest and principal payments and frequently involves arranging for payment of taxes and insurance premiums on the mortgaged property. Other mortgage companies act in a "mortgage correspondent" capacity, placing funds of lenders they represent. In general, these companies serve to facilitate movement of funds between primary and secondary mortgage markets. Additionally, they act as a bridge between short- and long-term capital markets.

Other institutional sources

Real estate investment trusts have become important lenders in the real estate mortgage market in the last decade, particularly with large developments such as apartment complexes and shopping centers. Federal tax laws allow REITs preferential tax treatment similar to that of mutual funds. REITs provide a funnel for individuals' funds into the real estate mortgage market. Although not very important in the one- to four-family home mortgage market, their importance as a lender in other categories of long-term mortgages and construction financing has become quite noticeable despite recent credit shortages and industry problems.

Credit unions and pension funds are substantial sources of real estate finance. Neither has a particularly large impact on the mortgage market but their potential merits warrant including them.

Credit unions are a relatively accessible source of home improvement loans. Some of the large credit unions are involved in the mortgage market but their impact is all but insignificant.

The size of pension fund assets and their importance in the financial market is substantial. One would expect pension funds to be active in nearly all investment areas (particularly those which meet the safety of principal, liquidity and yield requirements), but a survey of distribution of these assets reveals that investments in mortgages are insignificant.

Over the past two decades, pension funds have experienced a shift in investment policy. In the transition from archconservative to moderately liberal, mortgages have gained some favor but there has been no overwhelming conversion from stocks and bonds into mortgages. Some of this can be attributed to legal restrictions but the major portion is due to extra- or non-legal considerations.

The difficulty and cost of administering mortgage portfolios, the small size of the average fund and (in the case of government pension funds) political policy decisions all contribute to the narrow scope of pension fund activity. In comparison to other financial institutions pension funds are relative newcomers. They are, however, the single most important institution with regard to potential in the mortgage market. The next decade should see increasing competition among pension funds and other financial intermediaries as pensions become more active participants in mortgage finance.

Noninstitutional sources

Individuals and trust funds are two major noninstitutional sources of real estate financing. Because individuals constitute such a disorganized and unstructured lending force only generalized comments can be made about them.

They have always represented an alternative source. In many cases, individuals are willing to assume much greater risk than institutional financiers and are more apt to engage in noneconomic lending policies.

Trust funds, mentioned briefly in conjunction with commercial banks, are a second noninstitutional source. Although they account for less than 1 percent of outstanding mortgage loans, they go largely unnoticed by the market because mortgages acquired in the exercise of a trust do not usually appear on the asset breakdown of the institution administering the funds.

Availability of mortgage funds

Real estate financing is not always readily available on terms and conditions one might wish. Government regulation and agency activities, fluctuations in the capital market, attitudes toward risk and a variety of other considerations affect the availability of mortgage funds.

Government influences

While the importance of the FHA and VA have been discussed, other important government agencies also affect the mortgage market. Some of these, such as the Federal Reserve System (FRS) and the Federal Home Loan Bank System (FHLBS) are primarily regulatory agencies and oversee the operations of commercial banks and federally chartered savings and loan associations. The Federal Reserve Board (FRB) established the "discount rate," an important monetary policy control of the interest rate at which members may borrow from their local district Federal Reserve Bank.

Other government and quasi-government agencies, such as the Government National Mortgage Association (GNMA), the Federal Home Loan Mortgage Corporation (FHLMC) and the Federal National Mortgage Association (FNMA), operate an extensive secondary mortgage market. These secondary mortgage market activities extend primarily to FHA and VA loans and, on a limited basis, to conventional mortgages. By increasing and decreasing their purchase of mortgages from institutional lenders, these government agencies are able to contract or expand the amount of mortgage funds available in the market.

The Department of Housing and Urban Development (HUD), of which the FHA and GNMA are parts, additionally affects the housing and mortgage markets through its housing subsidy and urban renewal programs.

Many other smaller agencies also have an impact on the availability of funds for real estate financing. The Farmer's Home Administration (FmHA), the Small Business Administration (SBA) and even the Department of Transportation have noticeable, however small, effect on mortgage and capital markets. The general credit policies of the U.S. government can have persuasive effects on interest rates and overall economic conditions as well. Perhaps the best that can be said is that government influence on and over the availability of mortgage money is, while indirect, both widespread and of great magnitude.

Lending risks

Both institutional and noninstitutional lenders of funds must face and assume various types of risks. Institutional lenders, in particular, have developed rather formal and definite policies and procedures in evaluating the risks associated with real estate mortgage loans.

Both the borrower and the lender assume risk in financing arrangements. The borrower risks the property he pledges as security and perhaps other assets as well. The lender faces the potential loss of his principal and the attendant yield on it. Thus the risk in lending is not borne exclusively by any single party to the contract.

125

Risk in lending stems from several sources. Both borrower and lender face interest rate and purchasing power risks. Rates may rise, making the lender's yield below market or they may fall, making the cost of borrowing higher than necessary. Inflation affects the purchasing power of the dollar to the benefit of the borrower; deflation to the benefit of the lender. From the lender's standpoint, the borrower and property also represent sources of risk. Thus, the lender will always conduct a careful check of the borrower's credit standing and have an appraisal of the property to make sure that it represents adequate security given the size of the loan. If risks for the lender seem too great, he may deny the loan or request that mortgage insurance (either private or FHA/FA) be provided. Most lenders have standardized guidelines concerning the acceptability of mortgage applications. If the risks associated with the proposed mortgage do not conform to these standards, the application is usually denied.

Other areas of risk involve the legality of ownership interest, zoning and subdivision prohibitions and a host of legal considerations. Thus, risk in lending affects the overall availability of mortgage funds—particularly with respect to the individual's circumstances. As with other counsel the broker may give his clients, information concerning the risks associated with mortgage financing is of great importance and should be understood clearly from the outset.

Special financing arrangements

There are occasions when standard mortgage financing provisions do not provide the borrower with the incentives or investment return he is seeking. In these situations, special types of financing have evolved to cope with unique needs and circumstances. The needs of the borrower often demand that special lending packages be constructed to provide for these needs. The following are some of the more common special arrangements. Sale-leasebacks are discussed on page 134.

Condominiums

Condominiums have become popular as a way to combine the ease of apartment living with the tax and equity-building benefits of home ownership. They have also created a need to structure financing tailored to the special nature of condominium development. The condominium arrangement varies from the usual real estate ownership arrangement insofar as it involves a single property divided into units (such as apartments, offices, etc.) with each being owned by a different person. The buyer of a condominium may elect to mortgage his interest and pay property taxes and other operating expenses. He is also liable for management and maintenance expenses on those portions of the property he owns in common with the other owners.

Construction loans

Because of their short-term maturity, construction loans are not generally considered to be mortgages. Unlike a typical mortgage in which proceeds are paid out in a lump sum and repaid over a 20- to 30-year term, a construction loan is disbursed slowly as the construction proceeds, requires a seasoned lender to administer the disbursement properly and is rarely written for maturities in excess of three years. Because of the high risk involved in speculative construction, lenders typically require high interest rates on these loans.

Commercial banks and, to a lesser extent, savings associations and REITs are the most common sources of construction loans. In many cases the construction lender may also pick up the permanent loan on the property since his early involvement with the project necessitates little added expense to underwrite the final mortgage.

While these special lending/financing situations can hardly be considered an exhaustive listing, they represent methods likely to be used by the average broker. Land leases in lieu of purchase, syndications, the use of non-realty collateral for mortgage security, mortgage bonds and wrap-around mortgages are other special types and methods of real estate financing not discussed here but with which you may at some point become involved.

11 Expanding Your Services

As the real estate industry broadens its scope, brokers are challenged to develop and/or enter new services and fields of selling.

Improving existing properties

The shortage of vacant land within city limits has increased the value of ground under existing homes. Unearned increment of land value in many cases actually increases the sale price of used homes. A study of land values under older homes in districts where streets are paved, sewer, water and other utilities are in and paid for will reveal their sales advantage over unimproved lots in a subdivision.

Rehabilitation and redevelopment, not demolition, may be the most practical way to renew old neighborhoods. Present owners may be persuaded to modernize for profit. Their activities may be part of a broad program backed by the local Board of REALTORS®, the local government and, in some cases, the individual entrepreneur working single-handedly to get such campaigns under way.

Guaranteed sales plan

A cash down payment on a new property is often a major problem for home buyers who have substantial equity in another home. Many firms offer a buy-and-sell plan in which the broker pledges to buy the prospect's property at a specific price if it does not sell within a stated time period. The idea of trading in a home is attractive to a prospective buyer who understands it will give him the cash he needs for down payment on a new home. Without it, he might have to defer buying until the older property is sold. Meanwhile, he could lose a chance for a good buy and the salesperson loses his chance to make a sale.

Equity advances

The equity advance is a program by which money is advanced against the equity in the existing home to provide for the purchase of a new home without the broker guaranteeing the sale or taking the existing home in on trade. Usually sufficient money will be loaned to ensure that money will be available for moving costs and mortgage payments during the holding period until the property is eventually sold.

Selling for builders

Most new homes are the products of builders who make their living supplying housing to meet public demand. To complete their program of development, construction and sale, builders must either have salespeople in their organization or use the services of REALTORS®. Some brokers work with builders from the start of a subdivision project. They help find the site, handle the purchase, arrange financing, handle advertising, marketing and the sale and settlement of the finished properties. And when buyers have old homes to dispose of, the brokers sell them too, sometimes offering a trade-in.

While some large firms have new home specialists sell builders' houses, many treat new home sales like other listings and their salespeople sell both new and pre-owned homes.

Referrals

A number of commercial referral firms serve residential brokers throughout the country. These contract programs not only refer individual buyers to member firms but also serve industries transferring employees from city to city. In a less structured form, inter-market referrals are made between individual firms, many as the result of contacts made through national real estate professional organizations.

Brokerage of investment or income-producing properties

While the great majority of real estate brokers in the United States today are involved with the sale of single family homes, one other area of real estate brokerage has grown tremendously in the past decade, the field of commercial and investment brokerage.

Although most home buyers are primarily concerned with the amenities associated with the home they live in, many have found over the past several decades that their residence is also one of the best investments they have made. For this reason and others to be discussed in greater detail, increasing numbers of investors are turning to real estate as an outlet for their investment capital.

Investment by individuals is the very foundation of the private enterprise economic system of the United States and a great majority of our population is involved in some form of investment. Since World War II, disposable personal income has risen as has the number of individuals who are both able and willing to invest their excess funds in one of many investment alternatives available to them. Indeed, the number of investors has grown at a rate much higher than the population growth rate since 1940 and investment capital is flowing in at an ever-increasing rate from the large and growing middle-income families and individuals.

Trend toward real estate investments

Although there is a wide variety of alternative investments for the typical small investor, the trend in recent years has been into income-producing real estate. Perhaps the most obvious reason for this is the decreasing purchasing power of the dollar because of inflation. In addition, real estate offers some unique tax advantages not available in many other forms of investment. Finally, investment in real estate offers broad financing possibilities that are not present with most other forms of investment.

Inflation

The United States has been plagued by inflation since the end of World War II. Since the early 1970s the rate of inflation has increased at even a greater annual rate than in previous decades. Many investors have turned from fixed income investments which provide no protection against inflation to investments in common stocks and real estate. Real estate, in particular, has shown relatively steady increases in value as population and wealth have increased without accompanying increases in the supply of real estate resources.

Tax advantages

A variety of federal income tax impacts may provide advantages to the typical real estate investor. It is not within the scope of this discussion to provide an exhaustive discussion of such impacts. Two excellent sources for complete information on the financing and taxation of commercial-investment real estate are *Marketing Investment Real Estate—Finance, Taxation, Techniques,* published by the REALTORS NATIONAL MARKETING INSTITUTE®, and the courses offered by the Institute.

Two major potential advantages, however, should be recognized. The first is the tax advantage associated with the ownership of income-producing real estate through depreciation. Ownership of real estate is treated for tax purposes like the ownership of a small business. As such, the owner may charge depreciation expenses on the improvement portion of the property. The importance of the depreciation deduction from an investment standpoint is simple: it allows the investor to charge depreciation expenses that in reality have required no cash outlay; in doing so he reduces the income from the property subject to the federal income tax. More importantly, the depreciation taken on a given property may exceed the real depreciation in the property and create tax-free dollars through income tax savings to the extent that the depreciation expenses exceed the actual income from the property. The excess expenses may be applied to reduce other taxable income of the property owner. This tax savings is, in effect, a form of income generated by the real estate since a tax dollar that does not have to be paid is a form of cash return.

Suppose an investor purchases an apartment property for $95,000 and obtains an $80,000 mortgage loan at the time of purchase. If the property has the income during the first year shown in the example, it would appear that the investor incurs a substantial loss during the first year of ownership. This is shown under the column heading "Income Tax Accounting" which depicts the normal treatment of property income and expense for the purpose of determining income tax liability. In this case, it may be seen that the "paper" loss during the first year was $2,366. However, this accounting of income (or loss in this case) reflects $5,047 of "non-cash" expenses for depreciation. The accounting loss in income for tax purposes may be used to offset other earned income and save the taxes that would have been paid on this other income. The savings would be measured by the tax rate that would have been paid by the investor on $2,366. If

The following numerical example explains the concept.

Sample first year statement Annual Operating Property Data	Income tax Accounting	Cash flow Accounting
Scheduled gross income	$15,000	$15,000
Less: vacancy & credit losses (5%)	− 750	− 750
Effective gross income	$14,250	$14,250
Less: gross operating expense	− 5,250	− 5,250
Net operating income	$ 9,000	$ 9,000
Less:		
interest expense*	− 6,319	− 6,319
principal payment		− 1,709
depreciation**	− 5,047	
Cash flow before taxes		$ 972
Net profit or loss	($ 2,366)	
Tax savings***		$ 946
		$ 1,918

* Financing Data: $80,000 mortgage at 8% for 20 years; annual payments—$8,028.
** Depreciation charged based upon improvement value of $80,750, 20-year life with 125% declining balance depreciation.
***The marginal tax rate of the investor is 40%. At this tax rate, he would pay $946 on $2,366 of income at the 40% marginal tax bracket. If a similar amount of income is sheltered from the income tax, the taxes saved would be $946.

the investor were in a 40 percent tax bracket, this would amount to a saving of $946. When this tax saving is added to the "cash flow before taxes," the investor actually receives $1,918 during the first year of the ownership of property whereas his income tax property accounting indicates a loss of $2,366. Note that the cash flow after taxes of $1,918 was generated by an equity investment of only $15,000. Of course, the tax shield from depreciation will decline in subsequent years but the first year property statement shows the concept of tax shield quite clearly and suggests why individuals, even middle income investors, are being attracted to real estate as an investment.

Exchange

Investment real estate can be exchanged on a tax deferred basis, an advantage not afforded many other investments. Briefly, Section 1031 of the Internal Revenue Code provides that no gain or loss is to be recognized for tax purposes if investment property is exchanged solely for property of a like kind which is also to be held as an investment. Even though the exchange is not solely for like kind property, only a portion of the gain might be recognized while the balance can be deferred to a later date.

Exchanging has become an important tool to the real estate investment broker. It requires clear understanding of the federal income tax code as well as an awareness of investor objectives. In the real market, exchanges may be a simple trade of one property for another, but more likely they involve complex multiple holdings involving many owners and lenders.

Financing

When real estate is purchased, it is generally financed jointly by the equity owner and a mortgage lender. Because real estate is fixed in location and site improvements have long physical and economic lives, real estate represents excellent collateral for loans. As the residential broker well knows, it is common to find 90 percent and above mortgage loans on owner-occupied homes. It is not as common to find such high loan-to-value ratios on commercial and investment property; nevertheless such property is typically financed with as large a loan as the investor can possibly obtain. The loan-to-value ratio will vary considerably by type of property but it is not uncommon to find commercial property financed so that the loan represents between 50 and 75 percent of value.

Since real estate provides such excellent security for loans, it is clear why lenders are willing to make sizable loans on real estate investments. There are two fundamental reasons why investors are likewise anxious to borrow on real estate investments. The first is simply that the value of most investment properties makes it impossible for the small investor to purchase the property outright without the loan. In addition, however, the factor of "financial leverage" explains the primary reason why real estate investors borrow.

Leverage is the use of borrowed funds that utilize a fixed or limited borrowing cost to finance income properties. When an investor purchases a property, he acquires the rights to both the income generated by the property through its rent plus any appreciation that might occur over the time he owns it. Take, for example, the case illustrated earlier of a $95,000 apartment building in which the equity owner borrowed $80,000 and invested only $15,000 of his own capital. Here, the "overall rate of return" on the property is $9,000 + $95,000 or 9.5 percent. That is, an investor who purchased the property for $95,000 without debt financing would earn $9,000 per year on his total investment before taxes. If, on the other hand, he financed the purchase with an $80,000, 8 percent loan, he would pay $6,319 of his $9,000 income on interest cost but have $2,681 as a return on his initial investment of $15,000. This represents a before-tax return of $2,681 + $15,000 or nearly 18 percent.

Role of the real estate investment broker

When dealing with income-producing properties, the real estate broker plays a number of highly specialized roles for which he may be paid a commission, a fee for services rendered or a combination of both. Inceasingly, investment brokers are serving as real estate analysts and investment counselors to the ever-growing number of investors who seek out and rely upon their expertise. For the smaller investors, the investment broker may provide assistance in first acquiring and then managing a portfolio of real estate holdings. During this process, he works closely with the investor's accountant and attorney in identifying the tax consequences of the acquisition of the investment program. For the larger investor or group of investors, the broker may act as a leasing agent, a mortgage broker and a feasibility consultant. He often works closely with investors in identifying feasible developments, presenting the loan package to potential mortgage lenders on the project, obtaining tenants, and later in managing the property.

Clients

The clients and/or prospects of the investment property broker range from the owner of a very small duplex apartment property to the syndicated ownership of a larger shopping center or office building. At times, the investment broker represents the seller but often he represents someone who seeks to acquire an investment property by purchase, exchange and/or lease. Some commercial and investment brokers are paid a counseling retainer by large corporations.

Types of investment properties

Investment property may be categorized into eight general types.

One-tenant realty

In this category, there is fee interest in an income-producing property which is leased to one tenant with a "AAA" credit rating for periods of between 15 to 25 years with the tenant paying property taxes and all other operating and fixed charges. This is usually referred to as a net lease. The parcel may be of the retail business, commercial or industrial type; its location may be in the central or outlying business area or, in the case of a manufacturing plant, an established industrial area. This form of acquisition has appeal to insurance companies, colleges, investment trusts and endowment and pension funds. Purchasers of this kind of real estate are usually content with a lower rate of return, depending upon the location, length of lease, the stability of the lessee and special conditions or privileges contained in the lease.

Multiple-tenant realty

This category is typically represented by the well-located, one-story multiple retail building, to be leased to national or local chains or to substantial independent operators. Assuming proper location, these parcels offer enhancement opportunities and are in great demand, especially if leased on a percentage basis with equitable minimum annual guarantees. As a rule, this type of property is sold to an individual investor or to a syndicate that assumes payment of taxes and cost of exterior repairs.

Shopping centers

Shopping centers are almost a specialty unto themselves. They vary from the small neighborhood centers with four to six local tenants (usually including a drugstore, a dry cleaner and possibly a package store), to the large million-square-foot or more closed mall regional shopping centers which offer 40 to 50 types of merchandise and include competing stores in several categories. This type of property is usually sold to a syndicate or institutional investor and requires a great deal of experience to analyze and document its return and potential.

Mixed-use improvements

The multiple-story building usually has stores on the ground floor and offices or apartments on the upper floors. Such a property is attractive to those who seek to combine speculation with investment. The hazards usually involve the income to be derived from upper-floor tenants. This type of property, if well situated and depending upon the ratio of the first floor income to the total, usually sells on the basis of a higher yield.

Multi-family housing

Apartment buildings of four units or more provide standard service to tenants. Well-located parcels of this kind find a ready market, especially on an equity basis, among those seeking large depreciation shields for income. While many are sold for permanent investments, it must be recognized that because of the vast number that have been erected in recent years and the continued change in design, size of units and services to be furnished, a greater risk is assumed.

Condominium housing responds to a number of socio-economic trends involving high building costs, maintenance chores and the permanence and cost of occupancy. They offer the buyer some of the conveniences of tenancy and the power of ownership. The condominium concept also presents the broker with several income opportunities. In addition to making a sales commission for selling an existing rental project that will be converted, the broker can coordinate the entire conversion process: arrange for interim and permanent financing, supervise the rehabilitation, handle the resale of units and manage the condominium after conversion.

Industrial

Industrial structures have undergone greater change in design than almost any other form of building. At one time most industrial or manufacturing structures were multi-story. The lack of operating efficiency in such buildings led to the modern plant that is in most cases only one story high except for perhaps the office portion. The ground area is much larger to provide adequate parking. The advent of trucking facilities and superhighways in a great many cases made railroad service unnecessary. If it can be turned into a substantial leaseback, it is salable at a fairly low return. Otherwise, the buyer is confronted with the possibility of single purpose obsolescence and will show interest only if the return is high.

Office buildings

The well-located office building was once subject to a

higher vacancy ratio than was the case with business or apartment parcels. However, the picture has changed and the occupancy record is more satisfactory, though it still varies. The office building has a ready market depending primarily on the size of the property and character of tenancy as a determinant of the type of investor.

Transient housing

Hotel and motel buildings have an appeal to many investors. New construction techniques make them adaptable to market conditions. Motels affect the occupancy rate of some older hotels. This kind of investment is speculative. The net percentage yield which will attract capital varies greatly.

Specialized sales tools

Sale-leaseback

Large corporations that operate numerous stores or agencies in cities across the nation sell and lease back their local buildings to increase their working funds. The common pattern is for the corporation to sell their buildings to local investors and then to occupy the same premises as tenant under a long-term lease. Frequently, they furnish exact specifications for a building in a new location and the owner has the structure built specifically for the corporation which will move in as lessee.

Sale-leaseback is, in truth, a single transaction. The property owner agrees to sell all or part of his holding with the stipulation that the buyer lease it back to him. On the other hand, the buyer agrees to buy only on the condition that the seller will lease the property over a given number of years. If this reciprocity is absent the transaction, by definition, is not a sale-leaseback.

The owner's relationship to his property is relatively unimportant. The holding could be a factory, office building, apartment, commercial strip shopping center, warehouse or free-standing store. He could be the sole tenant, one of several tenants or physically absent.

What is implied, of course, is that he owns the property (usually with mortgage), that he operates it (presumably at a profit) or that he occupies it and accepts a self-imposed obligation for its maintenance, repair and upkeep. In seeking the sale-leaseback he normally will not anticipate relief from these obligations. In other words, the owner will generally agree to execute a net lease.

Motivations for pursuing a sale-leaseback may vary but certain patterns are easily discerned: the need for long-term working capital; a shifting tax posture with regard to capital gains; mergers, acquisitions and consolidations can set the stage for tax shelters; and opportunities which necessitate immediate improvement in the ratio of current assets to current liabilities.

But what of the reverse side of this coin? The buyer has negotiated for valuable real estate with a guaranteed net income computed to yield an equitable return on his investment. Through experience he predicates the acceptable lease-rental during the primary term on (1) the prevailing interest rate and (2) the depreciation and amortization rates.

Ground lease

The ground lease has a history running to ancient times. The use of another's unimproved land for a farm, a home or a business can often prove profitable for both landowner and tenant. The technique is most prevalent in Hawaii and is starting to see a lot of use in Florida and other areas. Most homes in Hawaii are sold on leasehold land, the most common application of the ground lease on residential property. In this case, a person buys a home but not the land under it. Instead, he signs a lease for the land which is usually a long-term lease covering the expected life of the house.

The downtown office building owner might well prefer a ground lease because he then would not have the tremendous expense of buying land at rates which may be $100 per square foot or more. There are also some tax advantages for the commercial developer or firm. They can expense the rental while they could not depreciate the land as it is a non-wasting asset.

An increasing number of applications of the ground lease theory is being used in many areas. Among them is the procedure by which air rights over a piece of property are leased from the owner.

Percentage leases

REALTORS® and property managers frequently negotiate leases under which the rental is determined on the basis of the tenant's potential earnings and modified on the basis of his actual earnings, a percentage of gross receipts.

The modern version of percentage leases is a relatively recent development, although the concept of sharing between lessor and lessee is centuries old.

In the past, some percentage leases failed to accomplish the desired result. In the late 1920s, for example, the minimum guarantee in many leases was the same amount the tenant would have paid on a straight rental. The percentage feature did not become operative until the tenant had succeeded beyond normal expectations and at that point it provided little benefit for the tenant.

To correct earlier inequities, real estate experts, owners and tenants developed the principle that any minimum guaranteed rental should be somewhat less than the market value with the exact difference depending upon the property involved and the type of tenant. Since then thousands of leases have been negotiated on this principle, providing a basis of equality for both tenants and owners despite fluctuating economic conditions. This method provides a hedge against mounting inflation for the landlord. The tenant is benefited by contracting to pay a lower guaranteed rent plus a small percentage of average receipts.

Though percentage leases have been made covering many kinds of property, the dominant use is in rentals for retail spaces. The percentage lease has come to be preferred in practically all downtown lease transactions, in neighborhood shopping areas and many suburban shopping centers.

Increasing use of the principle of percentage leases has enabled commercial property specialists to develop a scientific approach based on a growing body of knowledge. However, the rule of reason remains the only yardstick for determining the appropriate percentage rental rate in each separate case and local factors which have a direct bearing on the lease must be judged in the light of professional experience.

136 Legal and tax counsel

Since every real estate transaction is contractual, salespeople need to be aware of matters that will concern their clients' lawyers. Legal considerations can range from the wording of a listing contract to the dower interest of a widow. No salesperson should undertake to act as a lawyer but should always recommend that buyers and sellers seek legal counsel. An agreement between the NATIONAL ASSOCIATION OF REALTORS® and the American Bar Association has recommended that REALTORS® insert in their standard contract forms the following statement: "This is a legally binding contract. If not understood, seek competent advice."

Tax matters are also relevant to all real estate transactions; yet the salesperson's job is to sell property, not to offer tax counsel. You should understand possible tax costs and savings and so inform your clients. But it is your function as a salesperson to point the way and then suggest that a lawyer or C.P.A. be consulted as competent authority.

Glossary

This is one of the most significant chapters in the Handbook because the Glossary contains important information, not only for everyone in the real estate field, but also for those in allied professions. The reader, therefore, would do well to master the definitions so that he can make accurate descriptions, analyze transactions succinctly and communicate with REALTORS® and other sales associates by using exact terminology; he must also be able to clarify clients' problems by explaining precisely the terms that may be confusing to them.

Definitions included in this Glossary are original or are from standard textbooks: *Houses: The Illustrated Guide to Construction, Design and Systems* by Henry Harrison (REALTORS NATIONAL MARKETING INSTITUTE®); *Appraisal Terminology* (AMERICAN INSTITUTE OF REAL ESTATE APPRAISERS); *Advanced Principles of Real Estate Practice* by Ernest M. Fisher (Macmillan); *Real Estate,* Fifth Edition, by Arthur M. Weimer and Homer Hoyt (John Wiley).

abandonment
The voluntary relinquishment or surrender of possession of property.

abatement
Reduction in degree, worth, amount or intention.

abstract of title
A summary of all conveyances, such as deeds or wills and legal proceedings, giving the names of the parties, the description of the land and the agreements, arranged to show the continuity of ownership. (See also "title.")

abuttment
Touching or joining.

acceleration clause
A clause in a mortgage, lease or land purchase contract providing for the balance of the obligation to become due and payable at once when a payment due is in default.

access
The right to enter and leave a tract of land from a public way.

accession
Addition to property by such methods as accretion or annexation.

Accredited Farm and Land Member (AFLM)
Designation awarded by the FARM AND LAND INSTITUTE.

ACCREDITED MANAGEMENT ORGANIZATION® (AMO®)
Designation awarded by the INSTITUTE OF REAL ESTATE MANAGEMENT.

ACCREDITED RESIDENT MANAGER® (ARM®)
Designation awarded by the INSTITUTE OF REAL ESTATE MANAGEMENT.

accretion	An addition to land through natural causes (opposite of erosion). Generally the mineral deposits left on riparian lands by movement of waters.
accrued depreciation	See "depreciation, accrued."
acknowledgment	The act by which a party executing a legal document goes before an authorized officer or notary public and declares the same to be his voluntary act and deed.
acre	A measure of land, consisting of 43,560 square feet.
adjacent	Close but not touching.
administrator	A person appointed by a probate court to settle the affairs of an individual dying without a will.
administrator's deed	Type of deed used in conveying the real property of an intestate when authorized by the court. It is executed by an administrator and should recite the proceeding under which he is directed to sell.
ad valorem	Designates an assessment of taxes against property. Literally, according to value; based on the "ability to pay" theory.
advance fee	Fee paid in advance for services rendered.
adverse possession	The actual, exclusive, open notorious, hostile and continuous possession and occupation of real property under an evident claim of right or title. The time required legally to obtain title by adverse possion varies from state to state.
affidavit	A sworn statement in writing.
affirm	To make a formal judicial statement but not under oath.
after-acquired property	Property acquired after a certain event takes place.
agency	A contract by which the agent undertakes to represent the principal in business transactions, using some degree of discretion.
agent	One who represents another who has given authority to do so.
agency coupled with an interest	An agency relationship in which the agent has an estate or interest in property handled by the agency.
air rights	The rights vested by a grant (fee simple, lease agreement, or other conveyance) of an estate in real property to build upon, occupy, or use, in the manner and degree permitted, all or any portion of space above the ground or any other stated elevation within vertical planes, the basis of which corresponds with the boundaries of the real estate described in the grant.
alienation	Transfer of property from one owner to another.
alienation clause	Provides that the balance of the debt be paid upon transfer of title.
alloidal system	Absolute ownership of land, free from rent or service.
allotment	A body of land which has been divided into small parts; an allotment may be marketed with or without any substantial improvements, such as sidewalks and public utilities having been installed, although the most common practice now is to provide for their installation. In England, an allotment is a small tract of land which is rented to an artisan or laborer for cultivation.

138

alluvion	Increase of land by water flowing by and depositing soil on a shore or river bank.
amenities	The qualities and state of being pleasant and agreeable. In appraising, those qualities that attach to property in the benefits derived from other than monetary. Satisfactions of possession and use arising from architectural excellence, scenic beauty and social environment.
AMERICAN INSTITUTE OF REAL ESTATE APPRAISERS (AIREA)	(See Chapter 2, p. 20.)
American Land Title Association	Association of land title companies, created to aid in safe transfer of title and property and educate consumers.
AMERICAN SOCIETY OF REAL ESTATE COUNSELORS (ASREC)	(See Chapter 2, p. 21.)
amortization	The act or process of extinguishing a debt, with equal payments at regular intervals over a specific period of time.
ancillary	Designating or pertaining to a document, proceeding, officer or office, etc., that is subordinate to, or in aid of another primary or principal one; as, an ancillary attachment, bill or suit presupposes the existence of another principal proceeding.
annuity	A sum of money or its equivalent that constitutes one of a series of periodic payments. Any advantage that may be interpreted in terms of money and answers the requirements of regularity may be considered an annuity.
appraisal	An estimate of quantity, quality or value. The process through which conclusions of property value or property facts are obtained; also commonly the report setting forth such estimate and conclusion. (See also "valuation.")
appraiser	One who is authorized to appraise property.
appreciation	An increased conversion value of property or mediums of exchange due to economic or related causes which may be either temporary or permanent. Appreciation is the antonym of depreciation where the latter is used to denote shrinkage in conversion value. Also, the excess of appraisal value over book value of property. Also, the process of developing appraised value by the application of price indices to actual costs or estimated cost of another date and of lower price levels. Also, as applied to gain in condition of physical property such as in railroad property where roadbeds, for instance, are increased in value by solidification and grassing of slopes. (See also "depreciation.")
appreciation rate	The index figure used against the actual or estimated cost of a property in computing its cost of reproduction new as of a different date or under different conditions of a higher price level.
appurtenance	That which has been added to another thing; that which has been added or appended to a property and which becomes an inherent part of the property and passes with it when it is sold, leased or devised.

assemblage	The act of bringing two or more individuals or things to form an aggregate whole; specifically, the cost or estimated cost of assembling two or more parcels of land under a single ownership and unit of utility over the normal cost or current market price of the parcels held individually.
assessed value	A value set upon real estate by governmental assessors for the purpose of assessing taxes.
assessment	A non-recurring charge levied against property to meet some specific purpose portioned either by benefit derived to property or based on value of property. The valuation of property for taxation; also the value so assigned. (See also "taxable value.")
assessor	A public official who evaluates property for the purpose of taxation.
assets	Property of all kinds under a single ownership. (See also "current assets.")
assignee	One to whom a transfer of interest is made.
assignment	The transfer of an interest in a bond, mortgage, lease or other instrument, by writing.
assignor	One who makes an assignment.
assumption of mortgage	When a buyer takes ownership to real estate encumbered with a mortgage, he may assume the responsibility as the guarantor for the unpaid balance of the mortgage. Such a buyer is liable for the mortgage repayment.
attachment	Legal seizure of property to force payment of a debt.
attorney-in-fact	One who is authorized to perform certain acts under a power of attorney.
auction	A public sale of property to the highest bidder where successive increased bids are made.
avulsion	Loss of land by sudden action of nature, as a flood.
balloon mortgage payment	Payment that is a great deal larger than earlier payments; frequently the last payment which pays the mortgage in full.
bankrupt	A person who through a court proceeding is relieved from the payment of all debts after surrender of all assets to a court appointed trustee is bankrupt.
bargain and sale deed	Conveys title; does not include warranties of title.
base line	Imaginary line used by surveyors to locate and describe land.
basis	Original cost of property plus value of any improvements put on by the seller and minus the depreciation taken by seller.
beneficiary	One entitled to the proceeds of property held in trust; also proceeds of wills, insurance policies or trusts.
bequeath	To give personal property to another by will.
bilateral contract	Parties exchange reciprocal contracts; i.e. each party agrees to perform an act for the other.
bill of sale	Written agreement transferring personal property from one person to another.
binder	An agreement to cover a down payment as evidence of good faith on the part of the purchaser of real estate.

blanket mortgage	A mortgage that has two or more properties pledged or conveyed as security for a debt, usually for subdividing and improvement purposes.
blight	A reduction in the productivity of real estate from a wide variety of causes and having a multitude of visible effects on the physical appearance and condition of the property or area affected.
blighted area	Area in which property values have decreased appreciably.
blockbusting	Illegal practice in which owners in a specific neighborhood are persuaded to sell because they are told minorities moving in will reduce neighborhood housing values.
bona fide	In good faith.
bond	Originally any obligation under seal. A real estate bond is a written instrument promising to pay a specified sum of money to the bearer at a specified date. Attached to the bond are small coupons, which consist of promises to pay, at stated times, an amount representing interest on the amount of the bond. Bonds are usually issued on the security of a mortgage or a trust deed.
book depreciation	The amount reserved upon books or records to provide for the retirement or replacement of an asset.
boot	That with which the exchangor "sweetens the pot": cash, note, mortgage, car, a boat—anything other than the prime article which is being exchanged that is needed to balance equities.
broker	An agent who buys or sells for a principal for a fee without having title to property.
brokerage	The buying and selling business of a broker.
building code	Government regulations specifying minimum construction standards.
building restrictions	Limitations on the use of property or the size and location of structures, established by legislation or by covenants in deeds.
bundle of rights theory	An undivided ownership of a parcel of real estate embraces a great many rights, such as the right to its occupancy and use, the right to sell in whole or in part, the right to bequeath, the right to transfer by contract for specified periods of time, the benefits to be derived by occupancy and use of the real estate. These rights of occupancy and use are called beneficial interests. An owner who leases real estate to a tenant transfers one of the rights in his bundle, namely, the beneficial interest or the right to use or occupancy, to the tenant in accordance with the provision of the lease contract. He retains all the other rights in the bundle. As compensation for temporary relinquishment of the beneficial interest in the real estate, the owner receives rent.
capital	Accumulated wealth. A portion of wealth which is set aside for the production of additional wealth; specifically, the funds belonging to the partners or shareholders of a business, invested with the expressed intention of their remaining permanently in the business.
capital asset	All property except that which is for sale in the ordinary course of business, such as stock, place of residence, and equipment used in conducting business.

capital charges	Sums required to satisfy interest upon and amortization of monies invested in an enterprise.
capital expenditures	Investments of cash or other property or the creation of liability in exchange for property to remain permanently in the business; usually land, buildings, machinery and equipment.
capital gain	A profit from sale of a capital asset.
capital loss	A loss from the sale of a capital asset.
capital requirements	The total monetary investment essential to the establishment and operation of an enterprise; usually the appraised investment in plant facilities and normal working capital. May or may not (for certain purposes) include appraised cost of business "rights", such as patents, contracts, etc.
capital surplus	Capital surplus comprises paid-in surplus, donated surplus and revaluation surplus that is surplus other than earned surplus; surplus not arising from profits of operation but from such sources as sale of capital stock at premium, profit on dealings in a corporation's own stock, donated stock, appraisal valuations and surplus shown by the accounts at organization.
capitalization	The act or process of converting (obtaining the present worth of) future incomes into current equivalent capital values; also the amount so determined. Commonly referring to the capital structure of a corporation.
capitalization rate	The rate of interest or return adopted in the process of capitalization; ordinarily assumed to reflect factor of risk to capital so invested.
carrying charges	Expenses necessary for holding property, such as taxes on idle property or property under construction.
cash out	The selling out of one property in an exchange prior to, during the escrow or immediately thereafter.
certificate of reasonable value (CRV)	Certificate issued by the Veterans Administration showing the property's current market value estimate.
certificate of title	A document usually given to the home buyer with the deed stating that title of the property is clear; it is prepared by a title company or an attorney and is based on the abstract of title; sometimes an opinion of title serves the same purpose.
Certified Commercial-Investment Member (CCIM)	The CCIM designation is awarded by the REALTORS NATIONAL MARKETING INSTITUTE® to the REALTOR® or REALTOR-ASSOCIATE® who is primarily active in providing services to the public in selling, exchanging, leasing, managing, developing and syndicating commercial and investment real estate and further, who has (1) achieved a superior level of knowledge through the successful completion of certain prescribed courses; (2) proved his competence in the application of that knowledge through documented practical experience as approved by the Admissions Committee; and (3) demonstrated and maintained a high standing of character, ethical practice and financial responsibility in his community and marketplace.
CERTIFIED PROPERTY MANAGER® (CPM®)	Designation awarded by the INSTITUTE OF REAL ESTATE MANAGEMENT.

142

Certified Real Estate Brokerage Manager (CRB)	The CRB designation is awarded by the REALTORS NATIONAL MARKETING INSTITUTE® to the REALTOR® or REALTOR-ASSOCIATE® who has proven competence in the management of a real estate brokerage firm and who has (1) achieved a superior level of knowledge through the successful completion of certain prescribed courses; (2) proved his competence in the application of that knowledge through documented practical experience as approved by the Admissions Committee; and (3) demonstrated and maintained a high standing of character, ethical practice and financial responsibility in his community and marketplace.
Certified Residential Specialist (CRS)	The CRS designation is awarded by the REALTORS NATIONAL MARKETING INSTITUTE® to the REALTOR® or REALTOR-ASSOCIATE® who has demonstrated expertise in the field of residential marketing and who has (1) achieved a superior level of knowledge through the successful completion of certain prescribed courses; (2) proved his competence in the application of that knowledge through documented practical experience as approved by the Admissions Committee; and (3) demonstrated and maintained a high standing of character, ethical practice and financial responsibility in his community and marketplace.
chain, engineer's	A series of 100 wire links each of which is one foot in length.
chain, surveyor's	A series of wire links each of which is 7.92 inches long; the total length of the chain is four rods or 66 feet. Ten square chains of land is one acre.
chain of title	The succession of conveyances from some accepted starting point whereby the present holder of real property derives his title.
chain store	One of a number of retail stores under the same ownership, under a central management, selling uniform merchandise and following a uniform policy.
chattel	Any item of movable or immovable property other than real estate.
chattel mortgage	A mortgage on personal property; now known as a security agreement, under the Uniform Commercial Code.
chattel, personal	An item of movable property.
chattel, real	An estate annexed to or concerned with real estate.
circuit breaker	A device in the electrical system to interrupt the circuit when an overload occurs; an automatic switch which can be reset is used instead of a fuse to protect each circuit.
clear title	A title which is not encumbered or burdened with defects.
client	Person who employs the agent. Typically the client is the seller and the buyer is the customer.
closing	Point of a real estate transaction when the seller transfers title to the buyer in exchange for the purchase price.
closing statement	A listing of the debits and credits of the buyer and seller to a real estate transaction for the financial settlement of the transaction.
cloud on the title	An outstanding claim or encumbrance which, if valid, would affect or impair the owner's title.
code of ethics	Standards subscribed to by members of the NATIONAL ASSOCIATION OF REALTORS®.

codicil	Addition to a will.
color of title	Condition in which title appears to be valid and actually is not because of some defect.
commercial acre	What is left of an acre after areas for streets, sidewalks, alleys are deducted.
commercial property	Property intended for use by all types of retail and wholesale stores, office buildings, hotels and service establishments.
commission	Payment for the performance of specific duties; in real estate, usually payment measured by a percentage of another sum—as a percentage of the sales price paid for selling a property.
common law	Rules based on usage as demonstrated by decrees and judgments from the courts.
common property	Land or a tract of land considered as the property of the public in which all persons enjoy equal rights; a legal term signifying an incorporeal hereditament consisting of a right of one person in the land of another; property not owned by individuals or government, but by groups, tribes or informal villages.
common wall	Wall separating two housing units.
community property	Property owned jointly by husband and wife.
comparables	Properties which are similar in value to a particular property and are used to indicate fair market value for that property.
compound interest	Interest paid both on the original principal and on interest accrued from the time it fell due.
condemnation	The taking of private property for public use through the exercising of due process of law. (See also ''eminent domain'' and ''expropriation.'')
conditional sales contract	A contract in which the seller retains title of the property until paid in full, while allowing buyer use of that property, as long as he obeys all conditions of the contract.
condominium	A form of property ownership providing for individual ownership of a specific apartment or other space not necessarily on the ground level together with an undivided interest in the land or other parts of the structure in common with other owners.
conformity, principle of	Holds that the maximum of value is realized when a reasonable degree of homogeneity, sociological as well as economic, is present. Thus conformity in use is usually a highly desirable adjunct of real property since it creates and/or maintains maximum value and it is maximum value which affords the owner the maximum returns.
consequential damage	The impairment of value which does not arise as an immediate result of an act but as an incidental result of it. The impairment of value to private property caused by the acts of public bodies or neighboring property owners. The term ''consequential damage'' applies only in the event no part of land is actually taken. The damage resulting from the taking of a fraction of the whole (that is, over and above the loss reflected in the value of the land actually taken) is commonly known as severance damage. (See also ''severance damage.'')

consideration	The price or subject matter which induces a contract; may be in money, commodity exchange or a transfer of personal effort. In appraising, usually the actual price at which property is transferred.
constant payment mortgage	Systematic loan reduction plan by which the borrower pays a fixed amount each month, part to be applied to repayment of principal and part to payment of interest.
construction loan	A loan to finance the improvement of real estate.
contiguous	Adjacent; in actual contact; touching; near.
contingencies	Possible happenings which are conditioned upon the occurrence of some future event which is itself uncertain or questionable, i.e., an offer to purchase conditioned upon a termite inspection or the commitment of a mortgage loan.
contingent fees	Remuneration based or conditioned upon future occurrences, conclusions or results of services to be performed.
contract	An agreement entered into by two or more parties by the terms of which one or more of the parties, for a consideration, undertakes to do or to refrain from doing some act or acts in accordance with the wishes of the other party or parties. A contract to be valid and binding must (1) be entered into by competent parties, (2) be bound by a consideration, (3) possess mutuality, (4) represent an actual meeting of minds and (5) cover a legal and moral act.
contract for deed	Similar to a mortgage but different in its use as evidence of equity of the seller of a piece of property when he does not receive the entire purchase price either in cash or a purchase-money mortgage.
control data	A method of using transactions of real properties to adjust the market data utilized in the comparative approach to valuation. Such control data is necessary in order to segregate certain influences which have caused changes in real estate values, either generally or specifically. Control data is also useful where it is necessary to identify and segregate causes affecting values in specific areas due to a public improvement, such as a freeway.
conversion value	Value created by changing from one state, character, form or use to another.
convey	The act of deeding or transferring title to another.
conveyance	A written instrument that passes an interest in real estate from one person to another, including land contracts, leases, mortgages, etc.
cooperative apartment	An apartment owned by corporations, either for or not for profit, or by trusts, in which each owner purchases stock to the extent of the value of his apartment, title being evidenced by a proprietary lease.
corner influence	The effect of street intersections upon adjacent property—the cause of a different value for real estate adjacent to a corner, as compared with property away from the corner.
corporeal	Pertaining to a right or group of rights of a visible and tangible nature.
correction deed	A deed which corrects a previous erroneous deed.

145

cost approach to value	Valuation set by estimating cost of reproduction of the building plus the value of the property on which it stands.
cost of reproduction	The normal cost of exact duplication of a property with similar materials.
counteroffer	A new offer made as a result of another offer, which cancels the original offer.
Counselor of Real Estate (CRE)	Designation awarded by the AMERICAN SOCIETY OF REAL ESTATE COUNSELORS.
covenant	An agreement written into deeds and other instruments promising performance or nonperformance of certain acts or stipulating certain uses or nonuses of the property.
creative selling	The creation of a market for a property; creating a property from bare land or underimproved land which suits the particular needs of prospects and selling it to them.
creditor's position	That portion of the market price of a property which is represented by or can be obtained through a prime first mortgage.
cubical content	The actual space within the outer surfaces of the outside or inclosing walls and between the outer surfaces of the roof and the finished surface of the lowest basement or cellar.
cul de sac	The terminus of a street or alley. Usually laid out by modern engineers to provide a circular turnaround for vehicles.
current assets	Assets that are readily convertible into cash, usually within one year, without loss of value.
current liability	Indebtedness maturing within one year.
curtesy	The estate to which, by common law, the husband is entitled in the land of his deceased wife. The extent varies with statutory provision.
custodian	One who has care or custody, as of some public buildings; a keeper.
damages	The estimated reparation in money for injury sustained; e.g. by the taking of a portion of property (in condemnation) for street widening. (See also "consequential damage" and "severance damage.")
datum plane	The horizontal plane from which heights and depths are measured.
d/b/a	Abbreviation for "doing business as usual"; used as an assumed name.
debentures	Certificates of obligation and promise to pay; commonly, loans to limited companies issued on the general credit of the company without any specific pledged security and bearing a fixed rate of interest, the principal either being repayable after a certain number of years or unredeemable during the existence of the company. Unredeemable debentures are generally issued by railway and like companies.
debtor's position	That portion of the market price of property which is in excess of a prime first mortgage, or mortgageable interest; the equity holder's position.
debt service	Sum of money needed to pay mortgage obligations.
decentralization	Dispersion from a center, as the outward growth or movement of a retail center.

146

dedication	The voluntary giving of private property to some public use by the owner, as the dedication of land for streets, schools, etc., in a development.
deed	An instrument in writing which, when executed and delivered, conveys an estate in real property.
deed money escrow	An agreement where money is deposited with a third party to be delivered to a seller of real estate upon the receipt of the deed to the property sold.
deed of trust	(See "trust deed.")
deed restrictions	Limitations placed on use of real property by written deed.
deed, quit claim	(See "quit claim deed.")
deed, warranty	(See "warranty deed.")
default	Failure to meet an obligation when due; thus a mortgagor is in default when he fails to pay interest or principal on his mortgage when due.
defeasance	A provision or condition in a deed or in a separate instrument which, being performed, renders the instrument void.
defects in title	Title impaired by outstanding claim.
defendant	Person being sued in a lawsuit.
deferred maintenance	Existing but unfulfilled requirements for repairs and rehabilitation.
deferred payments	Money payments to be made at some future date.
delivery	The final and absolute transfer of a deed from seller to buyer in such a manner that it cannot be recalled by the seller. A necessary requisite to the transfer of title.
demise	A transfer of an estate to another for years, for life or at will.
deposit, earnest money	A sum of money or other consideration tendered in conjunction with an offer to purchase rights in real property.
depreciation	A loss from the upper limit of value. An effect caused by deterioration and/or obsolescence. Deterioration is evidenced by wear and tear, decay, dry rot, cracks, encrustations or structural defects. Obsolescence is divisible into parts. Functional obsolescence may be due to poor plan, functional inadequancy or overadequacy of size, style, age or otherwise. It is evidenced by conditions with the property. Economic obsolescence is caused by changes external to the property such as neighborhood infiltrations of inharmonious property uses, legislation and the like. (See also "appreciation.")
depreciation, accrued	The actual depreciation existing in a property at a given date.
depreciation allowance	Amounts claimed or allowed for depreciation. The term is often used in income tax cases but should always be qualified or explained.
depreciation, combination of 200 percent declining balance and straight-line	Depreciation deductions can be computed on the 200 percent declining balance method and later be switched to computation under the straight-line depreciation method without any necessity for obtaining the permission of the Commissioner of Internal Revenue. This switch may be beneficial in the latter part of the life of an asset where the depreciation deduction will be greater under the straight-line method than under the 200 percent declining balance method.

depreciation, declining balance	An accounting term designating the deduction of cost or other basis of property over the estimated useful life of the property, according to certain formulae.
depreciation, 150 percent declining balance	Deduction computed by applying 150 percent of the straight-line depreciation rate to a figure derived by adjusting the cost or other basis of property by previously allowed or allowable depreciation and other basis adjustments.
depreciation, 200 percent declining balance	Deduction computed by applying 200 percent of the straight-line depreciation rate to the cost or other basis of the property after adjustment for prior years' allowed or allowable depreciation and other basis adjustments.
depreciation methods	Methods used to measure loss in value of an improvement through depreciation. In appraising, the methods generally used are annuity, sinking fund and straight-line. In accounting, relates to various methods by which capital impairment is computed. In addition, accountants also use declining balance (and variations thereof), weighted rate and accelerated.
depreciation rate	The periodic amount of percentage at which the usefulness of a property is exhausted, especially the percentage at which amounts are computed to be set aside as accrual for anticipated depreciation.
depreciation reserve	The capital amount which summarizes the annual charges to operations by reason of depreciation. In accounting, the account on the books of a concern wherein the accruals for depreciation are recorded.
depreciation, straight-line	An accounting term designating the deduction of the cost or other basis of property, less estimated salvage value, in equal amounts over the estimated useful life of the property.
depreciations, sum-of-the-years'-digits	Annual depreciation allowable computed by applying changing fractions to the cost or other basis of property reduced by estimated salvage. The numerators of the fraction change each year to the estimated remaining useful life of the asset and the constant denominator is the sum of all the years' digits corresponding to the estimated useful life of the asset. For example, the fraction for the first year's depreciation on a five-year asset is 5/15. The 5 is the estimated useful life remaining and 15 is computed adding together each year's remaining useful life, i.e. $5+4+3+2+1=15$.
depth tables	Tabulations of factors or coefficients representing the rating of value per front foot between a lot of a selected "standard" depth and of other lots of greater or lesser depth.
descent	Acquisition of an estate by inheritance.
deterioration	Impairment of condition. One of the causes of depreciation and reflecting the loss in value brought about by wear and tear, disintegration, use in service and the action of the elements. (See also "depreciation.")
devise	A gift of real property by last will and testament.
disposal field	A drainage area, not close to the water supply, where waste from a septic tank is dispersed, being drained into the ground through tile and gravel.
documentary stamp	A revenue stamp issued for the payment of a tax on documents, as deeds, checks or wills.

domicile	Permanent home.
donor	One who gives a gift.
dower	That portion of, or interest in, the real estate of a deceased husband which the law gives for life to his widow. The extent varies with statutory provisions. Cannot be cut off without wife's consent.
downzoning	Change in zoning to a lower classification than the area previously held.
duress	Unlawful pressure placed on a person to force him to do something against his will.
earnest money	Advance payment of part of the purchase price to bind a contract for property.
easement	The right to use or enjoy certain privileges that appertain to the land of another such as the right of way, or the right to receive air and light by reason of an agreement of record with the owner of adjacent property.
easement appurtenant	An easement that goes with the property being sold.
economic life	The period over which a property may be profitably utilized. The period during which a building is valuable.
economic obsolescence	Impairment of desirability or useful life arising from economic forces, such as changes in optimum land use, legislative enactments which restrict or impair property rights and changes in supply-demand relationships. Loss in the use and value of property arising from the factors of economic obsolescence is to be distinguished from loss in value from physical deterioration and functional obsolescence. (See also "obsolescence.")
economic rent	The base rental justifiably payable for the right of occupancy of vacant land.
effective age	Statement of amount of depreciation suffered by property, stated in terms of the property's condition as opposed to its actual age.
effective gross revenue	Total income less allowance for vacancies, contingencies and sometimes collection losses but before deductions for operating expenses.
emblements	That which grows on the land and can be harvested, e.g. crops.
eminent domain	The power to appropriate private property for public use. If public welfare is served, the right of eminent domain may be granted by the state to quasi-public or even private bodies such as railroad, water, light and power companies (See also "condemnation" and "expropriation.")
enabling act	State statute to provide a legal base for zoning codes.
encroachment	The act of trespassing upon the domain of another. Partial or gradual invasion or intrusion; e.g., encroachment of "low value" district upon high property value residential section.
encumbrance	An interest or right in real property which diminishes the value of the fee but does not prevent conveyance of the fee by the owner thereof. Mortgages, taxes, judgments are encumbrances known as liens. Restrictions, easements, reservations are encumbrances although not liens.
equipment	That portion of fixed assets other than real estate; usually qualified as "office equipment," "automotive equipment,"

etc.; to be distinguished from assets that are included under the category of "fixtures" by virtue of their attachment to realty, either in a physical sense or by legal interpretation.

equitable title	The right to obtain ownership to property when legal title is in someone else's name.
equity	In finance, the value of the interest of an owner of property exclusive of the encumbrances on that property; also, justice.
erosion	The wearing away of land through natural causes as by running water, glaciers and winds.
escalator clause	Clause permitting adjustment of payments either up or down.
escheat	Reversion of property to the state by reason of failure of persons legally entitled to hold or lack of heirs. State must try to find heirs.
escrow	A deed or other instrument placed in the hands of a disinterested person (sometimes called the escrowee) for delivery upon performance of certain conditions or the happening of certain contingencies.
escrow holder	One who receives a deed or item from a grantor to be delivered to his grantee upon the performance of a condition or the occurrence of a contingency.
estate	A right in property. An estate in land is the degree, nature or extent of interest which a person has in it.
estate at will	Possession of property at the discretion of owner.
estate for years	Tenant has rights in real property for a designated number of years.
estate in reversion	The residue of an estate left in the grantor, to commence possession after the termination of some particular estate granted by him. Not to be confused with "remainder estate."
estoppel	An impediment to a law of action, whereby one is forbidden to contradict or deny one's own previous statement or act.
estoppel certificate	Certificate which shows the unpaid principal sum of a mortgage and the interest thereon, if the principal or interest notes are not produced or if the seller claims that the amount due under the mortgage which the purchase is to assume is less than that shown on record.
et al.	And others.
et ux.	And wife.
et vir.	And husband.
eviction	Physical removement of tenant from property.
exchange	The trading of an equity in a piece of property for the equity in another piece of property.
exchangor	The broker or salesperson who performs the exchange.
exclusive agency	A contract to sell property as an agent which gives the agent the exclusive right to sell the property. The owner reserves the right to sell the property and not pay the commission. The term is also applied to the property so listed.
exclusive right to sell	Contract, for a specific time period, between owner and broker which gives broker sole and exclusive right to sell

the property. The broker is entitled to the commission regardless of who sells the property.

execute	Making a document legally valid, as by signing a contract.
executor	Person appointed in will to carry out requests in that will.
executor's deed	A deed given by an executor.
existing mortgage	Mortgage contract in which the seller of a house is mortgagor and which is to be assumed by the purchaser.
expropriation	The act or process whereby private property is taken for public use or the rights therein modified by a sovereignty or any entity vested with the necessary legal authority; e.g., where property is acquired under eminent domain. (See also "condemnation" and "eminent domain.")

facade	The principal face of a structure.
fair value	Value that is reasonable and consistent with all of the known facts.
FARM AND LAND INSTITUTE (FLI)	(See Chapter 2, p. 20.)
feasibility survey	An analysis of the cost-benefit ratio of an economic endeavor.
Federal Deposit Insurance Corporation	Agency of the federal government that insures deposits at commercial banks and savings banks.
Federal Home Loan Bank	A district bank of the Federal Home Loan Bank System that lends only to member financial institutions such as savings and loan associations.
Federal Home Loan Bank Board	The administrative agency that charters federal savings and loan associations and exercises regulatory authority over members of the Federal Home Loan Bank System.
Federal Home Loan Bank System	The network of Federal Home Loan Banks and member financial institutions.
Federal Housing Administration (FHA)	An agency of the federal government that insures mortgage loans.
Federal National Mortgage Association (Fannie Mae)	An agency of the federal government that buys and sells FHA insured and VA guaranteed mortgage loans. It provides the primary market, banks and savings and loan associations, with a ready market for mortgages to permit a greater turnover of money for loans.
Federal Savings and Loan Association	A savings and loan association with a federal charter issued by the Federal Home Loan Bank Board. A federally chartered savings and loan association as opposed to a state-chartered savings and loan association.
Federal Savings and Loan Insurance Corporation	An agency of the federal government that insures savers' accounts at savings and loan associations.
fee	Remuneration for services. When applied to property, an inheritable estate in land.
fee simple	The most complete form of ownership of real property.
fee simple absolute	Highest and most complete ownership or enjoyment in real estate: (1) Ownership of unlimited duration; (2) Do as one pleases with land as long as one obeys the law; (3) Upon owner's death, real estate will go to his heirs.

fee tail	An estate of inheritance limited to some particular class of heirs of the person to whom it is granted.
fiduciary	The relationships between a person charged with the duty of acting for the benefit of another, as between guardian and ward. The person so charged.
financing statement	A document prepared for filing with the register of deeds or secretary of state, indicating that personal property or fixtures are encumbered with a debt.
finder's fee	A fee or commission paid to a broker to obtain a mortgage or to refer a loan to a mortgage broker; also refers to a commission paid for locating a property.
first mortgage	A mortgage which has priority as a lien over all other mortgages.
fixed charges	The regular, recurring costs or charges required in the holding of a property or for the guarantee of the unimpairment of capital invested therein, as distinguished from the maintenance of the condition or utility of the property and other direct expenses of operation.
fixtures	Appurtenances affixed to structures or land, usually in such manner that they cannot be independently moved without damage to themselves or the property housing supporting or pertinent to them. Variable under state laws.
flashing	Metal used in waterproofing the joint between chimney and roof or used similarly in roof valleys and hips.
floor load	As commonly used, the live weight-supporting capabilities of a floor, measured in pounds per square foot; the weight, stated in pounds per square foot, which may be safely placed upon the floor of a building if uniformly distributed.
footing	A concrete support under a foundation, chimney or column that usually rests on solid ground and is wider than the structure being supported.
forced sale	The act of selling property under compulsion as to time and place. Usually a sale made by virtue of a court order, ordinarily at public auction.
forced sale value	Amount that may be realized at a forced sale. That price that could be obtained at immediate disposal. Actually an improper use of the word "value." The term "forced sale value" is used erroneously to designate "forced sale price."
foreclosure	The legal process by which a mortgagee, in case of default by the mortgagor, forces sale of the property mortgaged in order to recover his loan.
forfeiture	The means by which the property of the citizen inures to the benefit of the state through the violation of law and occurring in the United States only in case of seizure for taxes.
franchise	A privilege or right conferred by governmental grant or contractually by a business enterprise upon an individual or group of individuals. Usually, an exclusive privilege or right to furnish public services or sell a particular product in a certain community.
freehold	A tenure of land held in fee simple absolute, fee simple limited or in fee tail unencumbered by lease.

front foot	A measure (one foot in length) of the width of lots applied at their frontage upon a street.
front foot cost	Cost of a parcel of real estate expressed in terms of front foot units.
functional obsolescence	Impairment of functional capacity or efficiency. (See also "obsolescence.")
general mortgage bond	A written instrument representing an obligation secured by a mortgage but preceded by senior issues.
gift deed	Deed with no consideration.
GI loan	A mortgage loan for which veterans are eligible and which is guaranteed by the Veterans Administration, subject to VA regulations similar to FHA loan.
girder	A heavy wood or steel structural member supporting beams, joists and partitions.
good faith	Bona fide.
good will	Intangible asset derived from good public business reputation and expectation of continued good business.
Government National Mortgage Association (Ginnie Mae)	A division of the United States Department of Housing and Urban Development (HUD) that operates the special assistance section of federally aided housing programs. GNMA guarantees payment on securities issued and sold by FNMA and on securities issued and sold by private offerers (such as banks) if these securities are backed by pools of VA, FHA, or FmHA mortgages.
government survey	System of land description used in the United States.
grade	The ground level at the foundation.
grading	The process of plowing and raking a lot to effect desired contour and drainage.
graduated lease	A lease which provides for a certain rent for an initial period, followed by an increase or decrease in rent over stated periods.
GRADUATE REALTORS® INSTITUTE (GRI)	Designation awarded by the individual State Board of REALTORS®.
grant	Transferring title to real property.
grantee	One who receives a transfer of real property by deed.
grantor	One who transfers real property by deed.
gross earnings	Revenue from operating sources, before deduction of the expenses incurred in gaining such revenues.
gross income	Total receipts during a given period. The total revenue which, although not necessarily actually received, has accrued from all sources during a specified time.
gross income multiplier	A figure which, times the gross income of a property, produces an estimate of value of that property. It is obtained by dividing the selling price by the monthly gross rent (gross income).
gross lease	A lease of property under the terms of which the lessor is to meet all property charges regularly incurred through ownership.

gross profits	Profits computed before the deduction of general expenses.
gross revenue	Total revenue from all sources before deduction of expenses incurred in gaining such revenue.
gross sales	The total sales as shown by invoices, before deducting returns, allowances, etc.
ground rent	The net rent paid for the right of use and occupancy of a parcel of unimproved land; or that portion of the total rental paid that is considered to represent return upon the land only.
guarantee (of sale)	The written commitment by a broker that within a certain period of time he will, in absence of a sale, purchase a given piece of property at a specified sum.
guaranteed mortgage	A mortgage in which a mortgage company buys the mortgages with its own funds and in turn sells these mortgages to its clients, who receive all of the papers in connection with the mortgage, including the bond, the mortgage and the assignment, together with the company's policy of guarantee. The company guarantees the payment of both principal and interest and assumes the responsibility of complete supervision of the mortgage, for which it receives a fee out of the interest, as it is collected.
habendum clause	A clause in a real estate document which specifies the extent of the interest (as life or fee) to be conveyed.
hard money mortgage	A mortgage loan given in exchange for cash, instead of to finance a real estate purchase.
height density	A zoning regulation designed to control the use or occupancy within a given area by designating the maximum height of structures.
heir	One who might inherit or succeed to an interest in lands under the rules of law, applicable where an individual dies without leaving a will.
hereditaments	Every sort of inheritable property, such as real, personal, corporeal and incorporeal.
highest and best use	The use of, or program of utilization of, a site which will produce the maximum net land returns in the future. The optimum use for a site.
holographic will	Will written in testator's handwriting and not witnessed.
homestead	Tract of land occupied as a family home.
Horizontal Property Acts	Laws pertaining to condominiums. They permit ownership of layers of air space, as opposed to the traditional vertical ownership.
house style	The design of a house based on historic or contemporary fashions.
house type	The structural configuration of the house. Common types are one-story, one-and-one-half story, two-story, two-and-one-half story, three or more stories, bi-level (split entry or raised ranch), split level, etc.
Housing and Urban Development (HUD)	A federal cabinet department that administers federal funds for public housing programs, including rehabilitation loans, urban renewal, public housing, model cities, new FHA-subsidy programs and water and sewer grants.
hundred percent location	The location or site in a city which is best adapted to carrying on a given type of business.

154

hypothecate	To pledge property as security, to mortgage.
improper improvement	(See also "misplaced improvements.")
improvements	Valuable additions to property which raise the value of the property.
improvements on land	Structures, of whatever nature, usually privately rather than publicly owned, erected on a site to enable its utilization; e.g., buildings, fences, driveways, retaining walls, etc.
improvements to land	Usually publicly owned structures such as curbs, sidewalks, street lighting system and sewers, constructed so as to enable the development of privately owned land for utilization.

155

income	A stream of benefits generally measured in terms of money as of a certain time; a flow of service. It is the source of value.
income approach	Method of valuation of property determined by the future income of the property.
income price ratio	Obtained by dividing the net income of a property by the selling price.
income property	A property in which the income is derived from commercial rentals or in which the returns attributable to the real estate can be so segregated as to permit direct estimation. The income production may be in several forms; e.g., commercial rents, business profits attributable to real estate other than rents; etc.
incompetent	One who is incapable of managing his affairs because he is mentally deficient or underdeveloped; as, children are incompetents in the eyes of the law.
incorporeal rights	Non-possessory rights in real property, such as easements.
increment	An increase; most frequently used to refer to the increase in the value of land that accompanies population growth and increasing wealth in the community. The term "unearned increment" is used in this connection since values are supposed to increase without effort on the part of the owner.
incurable depreciation	Depreciation to the extent that it is not practical to restore or replace that which is depreciating.
independent contractor	One who is hired to perform an act but is only subject to control as to the end result, not how it was reached.
industrial park	A controlled, park-like development, designed to accommodate specific types of industry, and providing the required appurtenances such as public utilities, streets, railroad sidings, water and sewage facilities, etc.
industrial property	Land zoned and suited for the use of factories, warehouses and other similar industrial purposes.
injunction	Judicial order requiring the party enjoined to take or not take a specific action.
installment contracts	A contract between the buyer and the seller whereby the purchase price is paid in installments. The buyer has possession of the property and equitable title to it while the seller has legal title. (Also called "contract for deed.")

INSTITUTE OF REAL ESTATE MANAGEMENT (IREM)	(See Chapter 2, p. 19.)
institutional lender	Banks, insurance companies, savings and loans and any lending institution whose loans are regulated by law.
instrument	Any formal legal document.
insurance coverage	The total amount of insurance carried against a specified risk(s).
insurance rate	The ratio of the insurance premium to the total amount of insurance carried thereby usually expressed in dollars per 100 dollars or per 1,000 dollars or sometimes in percent.
insurance risk	A general or relative term denoting the hazard involved in the insuring of property. The premium or cost of insurance is predicated upon the relative risk or hazard considered to be involved.
intangible property	The elements of property in an enterprise that are represented in the established organization, doing business, goodwill and other rights incident to the enterprise; as distinguished from the physical items comprising the p ant facilities and working capital.
interchange	A system of underpasses and overpasses for routing traffic on and off highways without interfering with through traffic and for linking two or more highways.
interest rate	The percentage of the principal sum charged for its use.
INTERNATIONAL REAL ESTATE FEDERATION (FIABCI)	(See Chapter 2, p. 21.)
intestate	Someone who has died without leaving a valid will.
inventory	A tabulation of he separate items comprising an assembled property.
investment	Monies placed in a property with the expectation of producing a profit assuming a reasonable degree of safety and ultimate recovery of principal; especially for permanent use, as opposed to speculation.
investment property	That property which a person would invest to get a return on his money acceptable to him.
joint and several liability	More than one signer of a note of contract is liable for a debt and a creditor çan obtain payment either individually or jointly from the parties.
joint tenancy	A tenancy shared equally by two or more parties with the right of survivorship.
joint venture	An arrangement under which two or more people or businesses go into a single venture as partners.
judgment	Formal decision of a court as to the rights and claims of parties to a suit.
junior lien	A lien placed on property after a previous lien has been made and recorded.
laches	Unreasonable and inexcusable delay in asserting a right, so that the court is justified in refusing to honor that right.
land	In a legal sense, the solid part of the surface of the earth, as distinguished from water; any ground, soil or earth

whatsoever regarded as the subject of ownership and everything annexed to it, whether by nature, e.g., trees and everything in or on it, such as minerals and running water, or annexed to it by man; e.g., buildings, fences, etc. In an economic sense, land consists of all those elements in the wealth of a nation which are supposed to be furnished by nature as distinguished from those improvements which owe their value to the labor and organizing power of man.

land contract
Sometimes called "contract for deed"; a contract given to a purchaser of real estate who pays a small portion of the purchase price when the contract is signed but agrees to pay additional sums at intervals and in amounts specified in the contract until the total purchase price is paid and the seller gives a deed. 157

land economics
The study of land from the standpoint of its ability to meet the needs or desires of man.

land improvements
Physical changes in or construction of a more or less permanent nature attached to or appurtenant to land, of such character as to increase its utility and/or value.

land trust certificate
A certificate of beneficial ownership in real estate, title to which is held in trust by the trustee who issues the certificate.

latent defect
Hidden structural defect.

lease
A transfer of possession and the right to use property to a tenant for a stipulated period during which the tenant pays rent to the owner; the contract containing the terms and conditions of such an agreement.

lease, graded or step-up
A lease with a rental payment that increases to specified amounts at specified periods of time.

lease, ground
A lease for vacant land upon which the tenant may erect improvements.

lease, index
A lease in which the rental payment varies in accordance with variation of an agreed-upon index of prices or costs.

lease, net
A lease in which the tenant pays certain agreed-upon property expenses such as taxes or maintenance.

lease, percentage
A lease in which the rental is based on a percentage of the lessee's sales income.

lease, reappraisal
A lease in which an arrangement is made for determination of the amount of rent at some future period by independent appraisers.

lease, tax participation clause (in a lease)
An agreement in a lease where the lessee agrees to pay all or a stated portion of any increase in real estate taxes.

lease with option to purchase
A lease in which the lessee has the right to purchase the real property for a stipulated price at or within a stipulated time.

leased fee
A property held in fee with the right of use and occupancy conveyed under lease to others. A property consisting of the right to receive ground rentals over a period of time and further right of ultimate repossession.

leasehold, leasehold estate
An estate held under a lease.

legal description
A statement containing a designation by which land is identified according to a system set up by law or approved by law.

less than freehold estate	Land held by person who rents or leases property.
lessee	One who possesses the right to use or occupy a property under lease agreement.
lessee's interest	A leasehold estate. (See also "leasehold.")
lessor	One who holds title to and conveys the right to use and occupy a property under lease agreement.
leverage	The use of borrowed funds in financing with the anticipation that the property acquired will increase in return so that the investor will realize a profit not only on his own investment but also on the borrowed funds.
levy	To impose or collect by authority or force.
license	Permission or authority to engage in a specified activity or perform a specified act.
lien	A charge against property whereby the property is made security for the payment of a debt.
life estate	A freehold interest in land, the duration of which is confined to the life of one or more persons or contingent upon certain happenings.
limited partnership	An arrangement in which some partners have no say in the management of the business and are liable only for the sum of their investment.
line fence	A common expression for a fence placed on a boundary line.
liquidated damages	A predetermined amount to be the compensation in case of breach of contract by one of the parties.
lis pendens	Legal document indicating that action is pending on a specific property.
listing	A record of property for sale by a broker who has been authorized by the owner to sell. Also used to denote the property so listed.
littoral	A shore and the area contiguous to it. The zone comprised between high and low water marks.
load-bearing wall	An integral part of the house which helps to support the floors or roof and cannot be moved readily, if at all, as distinguished from a partition which carries no load and can be removed.
load center	Electrical distribution center for a house, either the main center or a branch distribution point equipped with circuit breakers instead of a main switch and fusebox.
loan discount fee	(See "points".)
loan relief	When the principal walks away via a cash or an exchange deal from an encumbrance that he had on a particular piece of property.
louver	Slats set at an angle to provide ventilation without admitting rain or direct light.
maintenance	The act of keeping or the expenditures required to keep a property in condition to perform adequately and efficiently the service for which it is used.
maintenance reserve	An amount reserved to cover costs of maintenance.
marginal land	That which barely pays the cost of working or using. Land whereon the costs of operating approximately equal the gross income.

158

marketable title	Clear title with no undisclosed encumbrances, has no serious defects and will not expose the buyer to litigation.
marketing	The management process through which efforts to conceive, develop and deliver goods and services are integrated to satisfy the needs and wants of selected customers as a means of achieving company objectives.
market price	The price paid for a property; the amount of money that must be given or which can be obtained at the market in exchange under the immediate conditions existing at a certain date. To be distinguished from market value.
market value	The quantity of other commodities a property would command in exchange; specifically the highest price estimated in terms of money which a buyer would be warranted in paying and a seller justified in accepting, provided both parties were fully informed, acted intelligently and voluntarily and, further, that all the rights and benefits inherent in or attributable to the property were included in the transfer. At any given moment of time, market value connotes what a property is actually worth and market price that it can be sold for. The amounts may or may not coincide, since current supply and demand factors enter strongly into market price. (See also "market price" and "value.")
Master's deed	(See "Sheriff's deed.")
maturity	Date when an indebtedness comes due.
maximum rent	Rent established by any maximum rent regulation or order for the use of housing accommodations within any defense-rental area. Regulations from rent control administrator.
mechanic's lien	Lien given statute to those who perform labor or furnish materials in the improvements of real property.
megalopolis	Urban complex encompassing several major cities.
Member Appraisal Institute (MAI)	Designation awarded by the AMERICAN INSTITUTE OF REAL ESTATE APPRAISERS.
merger	Combining of one or more smaller interests into one.
metes and bounds	The lengths and direction of the boundaries of a tract of land, usually irregular in shape.
metropolitan districts	Areas which include, according to the U.S. Department of Commerce, in addition to the central city or cities, all adjacent and contiguous civil divisions having a density of not less than 150 inhabitants per square mile and also, as a rule, those civil divisions of less density that are directly contiguous to the central cities or are entirely or nearly surrounded by minor civil divisions that have the required density.
misplaced improvements	Improvements (on land) which do not conform to the best utilization of the site.
misrepresentation	False statement made to or concealment of knowledge from another party with the intent to provoke action from that party.
month to month tenancy	Tenant rents for a month at a time.
monument	A stone or other fixed object used to establish real estate boundaries.
mortgage	A conditional conveyance of property contingent upon failure

159

of specific performance such as the payment of a debt; the instrument making such conveyance.

mortgage certificate	Mortgages are sometimes divided up among many investors through the use of the certificate. Such certificates are not obligations to pay money, as is a bond or note, but are merely a certification by the holder of the mortgage (generally a corporate depository) that he holds such mortgage for the beneficial and undivided interest of all of the certificate holders. The certificate itself generally sets forth a full agreement between the holder and the depository, although in some cases a more lengthy document known as a depository agreement is executed.

mortgage guarantee policy	A policy issued on a guaranteed mortgage.
Mortgage Guaranty Insurance Corp. (MGIC)	Independent insurance company that will insure a percentage of the principal of a loan made by approved lenders to qualified buyers.
mortgagee	The source of the funds for a mortgage loan and in whose favor the property serving as security is mortgaged.
mortgagor	The owner of property who borrows money and mortgages the property as security for the loan.
mud room	A vestibule or small room used as the entrance from a play yard or alley and frequently containing a washer and dryer.
multiple exchange	Three or more principals involved with various pieces of property.
multiple listing service	A means of making possible the orderly dissemination and correlation of listing information to its members so that REALTORS® may better serve the buying and selling public.
NATIONAL ASSOCIATION OF REALTORS®	(See Chapter 2, p. 12.)
natural resource property	A property involving primarily recoverable or adaptable resources of nature which may be or are susceptible to being commercially exploited.
net earnings	Revenue from operating sources, after deduction of the operating expenses, maintenance, uncollectable revenues and taxes applicable to operating properties or revenues but before deduction of financial charges and generally before deduction of provision for depreciation and retirements.
net income	In general, synonymous with net earnings but considered a broader and better term; the balance remaining after deducting from the gross income all operating expense, maintenance, taxes and losses pertaining to operating properties, except interest or other financial charges on borrowed or other capital.
net income multiplier	A figure which, times the net income of a property, produces an estimate of value of that property. It is obtained by dividing the selling price by the monthly net rent (net income).
net lease	Lessee pays rent plus maintenance and operating expenses.
net listing	Broker receives as commission all monies received above minimum sales price agreed to by owners and broker.

net profits	Used without qualifying expression to describe only the profits remaining after including all earnings and other income or profit and after deducting all expenses and charges of every character including interest, depreciation and taxes.
net worth	Assets left after subtracting liabilities.
nonconforming use	A use which was lawfully established and maintained but which, because of the application of a zoning ordinance to it, no longer conforms to the use regulations of the zone in which it is located. A nonconforming building or nonconforming portion of a building is a nonconforming use of the land upon which it is located. Such uses preclude additions or changes without municipal approval.
note	An instrument of credit given to attest a debt.
novation	Substitution of a new obligation for an old one.
nuisance value	This is not a true value but is the amount that someone, other than the owner of a property, will pay for it, not for its own sake but because in its present hands it is an annoyance or is actually damaging to the prospective buyer.
obligee	One to whom debt is owed.
obligor	One who owes a debt.
obsolescence	Impairment of desirability and usefulness brought about by changes in the art, design or process or from external influencing circumstances that make a property less desirable and valuable for a continuity or use. (See also "depreciation," "functional obsolescence" and "economic obsolescence.")
offer	A promise by one party to do a specified deed as the other party in turn performs a specific deed.
open-end mortgage	A mortgage with a clause giving the mortgagor the privilege of borrowing additional money after the loan has been reduced without rewriting the mortgage.
open listing	A listing available for sale from more than one packer
operating expenses	Generally, all expenses occurring periodically which are necessary to produce net income before depreciation.
operating income	Income derived from the general operation of a business. It is not synonymous with net profit but rather indicates a stage in the profit and loss account where all direct costs of operation and all direct income from operation have been taken into the account and nothing else.
operating profit	Profit arising from the regular operation of an enterprise engaged in performing physical services (public utilities, etc) excluding income from other sources and excluding expenses other than those of direct operation.
opinion of title	Legal opinion stating that title to the property is clear and marketable; serves the same purpose as a certificate of title.
option	An agreement granting the exclusive right during a stated period of time, without creating any obligation, to purchase, sell or otherwise direct or contract the use of a property.
orientation	Siting, or the positioning of a structure on its lot, with regard to the points of the compass, prevailing winds, privacy from street and protection from outside noises.

original cost	The actual cost of a property to its present owner; not necessarily the first cost at the time it was originally constructed and placed in service.
over-improvement	An improvement which is not the highest and best use for the site on which it is placed by reason of excess in size or cost.
overall property tax limitation	A constitutional or statutory limitation on the total amount of taxes which may be levied for all purposes against any parcel of real estate within any one year, such overall limit to be a fixed percentage of the true value of such parcel of real estate. It is so called to distinguish it from the limitations on separate portions of the real estate tax in effect in nearly all states.
ownership	The right to possess and use property to the exclusion of others.
package mortgage	Mortgage finances purchase of real estate and specific household appliances.
parol evidence	Legal rule which prevents previous oral or written negotiations to a signed contract from changing the contract.
participation mortgage	Lender participates in venture beyond a fixed return, or received a yield on the loan above and beyond the straight interest loan.
partition	Act of dividing property among the several owners who may hold either in joint tenancy or as tenants in common.
partition proceedings	A legal procedure by which an estate held by tenants in common is divided and title in severalty to a designated portion passed to each of the previous tenants in common.
partnership	"An association of two or more persons who carry on a business for profit as co-owners." (from Uniform Partnership Act)
party wall	A dividing wall erected upon and over a line separating two adjoining properties and in which the owners of the respective parcels have common rights to its use.
patent	Government grant or franchise of land.
percentage lease	Lease whose rental is based on a percentage of the gross income of the tenant.
percolation test	A soil test to determine if it will handle water seepage from a septic tank.
performance bond	A bond to guarantee specific completion of an undertaking in accordance with an agreement, such as that supplied by a contractor guaranteeing the completion of a building or a road.
perimeter heating	Baseboard heating or any system in which registers or radiators are located along the outside walls of a room, particularly under the windows.
perpetual easement	An easement constantly maintained. (See also "easement.")
perpetuity	Going on for an unlimited time.
personalty	Property which is movable. All property is either personalty, realty or mixed.
physical depreciation	A term that is frequently used when physical deterioration is intended. In a broad concept it may relate to those elements contributing to depreciation that are existent or inherent in

162

the physical property itself, as distinguished from other and external circumstances that may influence its utilization. Not a clear or proper term without qualification and explanation.

plat	A plan or map of certain piece or pieces of land.
plat book	A record showing the location, size and name of owner of each plot of land in a stated area.
plenum	A chamber in a warm air furnace in which the air is heated and from which the ducts carry the warm air to the registers.
plottage increment	The appreciation in unit value created by joining smaller ownerships into one large single ownership.
points	One percent of the amount of the loan. A service charge of the lender.
police power	Authority of a state to adopt and enforce laws to promote public health and safety.
potable	Suitable for drinking; said of water.
potential value	A loose term signifying a value which would or will exist if and when future probabilities become actualities.
power of attorney	Written instrument authorizing a person to act for another.
power of sale	A clause inserted in a will or deed of trust agreement authorizing the sale or transfer of land in accordance with the terms of the clause.
prefabricated house, prefab	A house manufactured, and sometimes partly assembled, before delivery to the site.
preliminary title report	Title report which reports only on documents having an effect on the title.
prepayment privilege	Right of a debtor to pay off a loan before maturity.
presumption	Inference of a fact from circumstances that usually attend such a fact.
price level	A relative position in the scale of prices as determined by a comparison of prices (of labor, materials, capital, etc.) with prices as of other times.
principal	(1) A sum lent or employed as a fund or investment, as distinguished from its income or profits; (2) the original amount (as of a loan) of the total due and payable at a certain date; (3) a party to a transaction, as distinguished from an agent; (4) head of real estate firm.
principal meridian	Line used in surveying.
probate	Judicial proceeding to prove validity of will.
profit and loss statement	Statement which shows total financial condition of business.
property	The exclusive right to control an economic good. The recognized attribute that human beings may have in their relation with wealth. A "property" refers to units capable of being used independently in a single ownership. A "property" may consist of the rights to a single parcel of land, a house and lot, a complete manufacturing plant or any one of the items assembled together to constitute such a plant. It may also consist of the rights developed and inherent in the attached business of an enterprise or any one of the elements reflected therein, such as the rights to a patent, a trademark, a contract or the proven "goodwill" of the public.

property brief	A description of a property for sale with complete details and pictures in a form suitable for presentation to a prospect.
property management	The operation of real property including the leasing of space, collection of rents, selection of tenants and the repair and renovation of the buildings and grounds.
prorate	To allocate between seller and buyer their proportionate share of an obligation paid or due. For example, to prorate real property taxes or fire insurance.
punitive damages	Damages assessed against someone because of malicious acts that person has done.
public property	A property the ownership of which is vested in the community.
purchase money mortgage	A mortgage that is executed by the purchaser at closing as a part or all of the purchase price. The same as a second mortgage held by the seller.
quit claim deed	A deed of conveyance whereby whatever interest the grantor possesses in the property described in the deed is conveyed to the grantee without warranty.
quantity survey	Method of estimating building costs by estimating all raw materials, labor and installation costs.
quiet enjoyment	Right of the owner to enjoy his property with no interference.
quiet title action	Court action to settle the title of a property when there is a cloud on the title.
real estate	Land and hereditaments or rights therein and whatever is made part of or is attached to it by nature or man.
real estate broker	Any person, firm, partnership, copartnership, association or corporation which for a compensation sells or offers for sale, buys or offers to buy, negotiates the purchase or sale or exchange of real estate, leases or offers to lease or rents or offers for rent any real estate or the improvements on real estate for others as a whole or partial vocation.
real estate investment trust	An unincoporated trust or association set up to invest in real property and which has centralized management, issues beneficial interest to 100 persons or less and meets other strict requirements of the income tax laws; 90 percent of income must come from real property rentals, dividends, interests or gains from sale of securities or real estate.
real estate salesperson	A salesperson who is responsible to a real estate broker and who assists him in his business of buying, selling, exchanging, appraising and managing property.
REAL ESTATE SECURITIES AND SYNDICATION INSTITUTE (RESSI®)	(See Chapter 2, p. 21.)
Real Estate Settlement Procedures Act (RESPA)	Federal law ensures that buyer and seller both know all aspects of settlement costs when a residence is financed by a federal mortgage loan.
real estate syndicate	Partnership where members join in order to participate in real estate ventures.
real estate tax	A pecuniary charge laid upon real property for public purposes.

real property	Property and what is on it (immovable).
realtist	A member of the National Association of Real Estate Brokers.
REALTOR®	A professional in real estate who subscribes to a strict Code of Ethics as a member of the local and state boards and of the NATIONAL ASSOCIATION OF REALTORS®
REALTOR-ASSOCIATE®	An individual engaged in the real estate profession other than as a principal, partner, corporate officer or trustee who is associated with an Active Member of a Board and who holds Associate membership in a Board, its respective State Association and the NATIONAL ASSOCIATION OF REALTORS®
REALTORS NATIONAL MARKETING INSTITUTE® (RNMI)	(See Chapter 2, p. 15 to 19.)
realty	A synonym for real estate.
recapture clause	A clause in an agreement providing for retaking or recovering possession. As used in percentage leases, to take a portion of earnings or profits above a fixed amount of rent.
reciprocity	Mutual agreement between state for recognizing licenses of salespeople.
reconciliation	Appraiser brings all information together to arrive at the estimate of market value for the property.
recording	The entering or recording of a copy of certain legal instruments or documents, as a deed, in a government office provided for this purpose; thus making a public record of the document for the protection of all concerned and giving constructive notice to the public at large.
rectangular survey	Government survey method using principal meridians and base lines to form quadrangles, townships, and ranges.
redemption	The recovery, by payment of all proper charges, of property which has been lost through foreclosure of a mortgage or other legal process.
regulation "z"	Regulation developed by the Federal Reserve System for aiding in reinforcement of the Truth in Lending Act.
release clause	A clause relinquishing a right or claim by the person in whom it exists to the person against whom it could be enforced, such as a clause in a mortgage deed reconveying the legal title to the mortgagor upon payment of the mortgage debt.
remainder	A future interest in an estate that matures at the end of another estate.
remainder estate	An estate in property created simultaneously with other estates by a single grant and consisting of the rights and interest contingent upon and remaining after the termination of the other estates.
rent	Payment made to the owner of property in return for use of that property.
rent control	Control by a government agency of the amount to be charged as rent.
rental value	A term of specifically limited significance and application; the worth for a stated period of the right to use and occupy property; the rent which a prospective tenant is warranted in

paying for a stated period of time, i.e., a month, a year, etc., for the right to use and occupy certain described property under certain prescribed or assumed conditions.

replacement cost	(1) the cost that would be incurred in acquiring an equally desirable substitute property; (2) the cost of reproducing new, on the basis of current prices, a property having a utility equivalent to the one being appraised; it may or may not be the cost of a replica property; (3) the cost of replacing unit parts of a structure to maintain it in its highest economic operating condition.
reproduction cost	(See "cost of reproduction.")
rescission	Cancelling or repealing a contract by mutual consent of the parties and the returning of parties to their original positions.
reservation	A right reserved by an owner in the grant (sale or lease) of a property.
reserves	Capital set aside for payment of future taxes or maintenance.
Residential Member (RM)	Designation awarded by the AMERICAN INSTITUTE OF REAL ESTATE APPRAISERS.
restrictions	A limitation upon the use or occupancy of real estate placed by covenant in deeds or by public legislative action.
reversion	The right of a lessor to recover possession of leased property upon the termination of the lease with all the subsequent rights to use and enjoyment of the property.
reversionary right	The right to receive possession and use of property upon the termination or defeat of an estate carrying the rights of possession and use and vested in another.
right of occupancy	A privilege to use and occupy a property for a certain period under some contractual guarantee, such as a lease or other formal agreement.
right of way	The term has two significances: As a privilege to pass or cross, it is an easement over another's land; it is also used to describe that strip of land which railroad companies use for a roadbed or as dedicated to public use for roadway, walk, or other way. However, the best thought appears to be toward a fine distinction in usage as follows: (1) a single right or easement for several independent or combined uses, e.g., in a right for a pipe line for the combined use of pipes, poles, sewers, etc.; (2) two or more rights or easements from different parties and over different parcels but for a single use (rights of way); (3) two or more rights or easements from different parties or for different parties and over different parcels for several independent or combined uses (rights of ways).
riparian	Pertaining to the banks of a river, stream, waterway, etc.
riparian grant	The conveyance of riparian rights.
riparian lease	The written instrument setting forth the terms, conditions and date of expiration of the rights to use lands lying between the high water mark and the low water mark.
riparian rights	All phases of right and title of the upland owner in and to the water and land below high water mark; he is entitled to have water wash his land and rights to construct on or over it to the extent it does not interfere or injure another's riparian rights.

166

rod	A measure of length containing 5½ yards or 16½ feet; also, the corresponding square measure.
row houses	A series of individual houses having architectural unity and a common wall between each unit.
sale-leaseback	A financing technique in which the owner sells property to an investor and then leases it back.
sales contract	A contract embodying the terms of agreement of a sale.
salvage value	Value of a property after full depreciation.
sandwich lease	A leasehold in which the interest of the sublessor is inserted between the fee owner and the user of the property. For example, the owner of a fee simple "A" leases to "B" who in turn leases to "C." The interest of "A" may be called the leased fee, that of "B" the sandwich lease and that of "C" the leasehold.
satisfaction of mortgage	Document issued by mortgagee when mortgage is paid off.
second mortgage	Mortgage made on top of another and subordinate to the first. (Also called a "junior mortgage.")
section (of land)	One of the portions, of one square mile each (640 acres), into which the public lands of the United States are divided; one thirty-sixth part of a township.
seisin	A feudal term defining possession of property by one who claims rightful ownership. Generally accepted today as synonymous with ownership.
septic tank	An underground tank in which sewage from the house is reduced to liquid by bacterial action and drained off.
service property	A property devoted to or available for utilization for a special purpose but which has no independent marketability in the generally recognized acceptance of the term, such as a church property, a public museum or a school.
setback	The distance a structure must be set back from the street in accordance with local zoning rules.
settlement	(See "closing".)
severalty	A holding by individual right; separate state or character.
severance damage	The impairment in value caused by separation. Commonly, the damage resulting from the taking of a fraction of the whole property, reflected in a lowered utility and value in the land remaining and brought about by reason of the fractional taking.
sheriff's deed	An instrument drawn under order of court to convey title to property sold to satisfy a judgment at law.
simple interest	Interest computed only on principal balance.
sill	The board or stone at the foot of a door or the woodwork or masonry on which a window frame stands.
site	Lands made suitable for building purposes by dividing into lots, laying out streets and the like.
siting	Site planning; placement and orientation of a house on its lot.
SOCIETY OF INDUSTRIAL REALTORS® (SIR)	(See Chapter 2, p. 19.).

167

soil bank	A program administered by the Commodity Stabilization Service of the Department of Agriculture in which farmers contract to divert land from production of unneeded crops to conservation uses and for which they receive an annual rent.
special assessment (improvements)	A charge laid against real estate by public authority to defray the cost of making public improvements from which the real estate benefits.
Specialist in Real Estate Securities (SRS)	Designation awarded by the REAL ESTATE SECURITIES AND SYNDICATION INSTITUTE.
special warranty deed	A warranty only against the acts of the grantor himself and all persons claiming by, through or under him. (See also "warranty deed.")
specific performance, specifically enforceable	The requirement that a party must perform as agreed under a contract in contrast to compensation or damages in lieu of performance; the arrangement whereby courts may force either party to a real estate contract to carry out an agreement exactly.
specimen tree	A tree of particular interest because of shape or species, placed in a position of prominence in the yard, often a silver spruce, weeping birch, magnolia or other outstanding ornamental tree.
spot survey	Survey that shows size and location of structures on property.
spot zoning	Change in zoning that allows a non-conforming use in an area zoned for another purpose.
square foot method	One of the methods of estimating construction, reproduction or replacement costs of a building by multiplying the square foot floor area by an appropriate square foot construction cost figure.
squatter's rights	The rights to occupancy of land created by virtue of long and undisturbed use but without legal title or arrangement; in the nature of right at common law.
standard depth	The depth of the typical neighborhood lot, usually applied to lots in particular use categories such as central business lots, outlying commercial lots and lots in different-priced residential neighborhoods.
standard metropolitan statistical area (SMSA)	City or cities and their suburbs with a minimum population of 50,000 that constitutes a metropolitan area by Bureau of Census standards.
statute of frauds	Law that requires certain contracts, such as agreements of sale, to be in writing in order to be enforceable.
statutory warranty deed	A warranty deed form prescribed by state statutes.
straight-line depreciation	(See "depreciation, straight-line.")
step-up lease	Lease that allows for increases and decreases in rent on a predetermined basis.
subdivision	Area of land consisting of subdivided land suitable for building.

sublease	An agreement conveying the right of use and occupancy of a property in which the lessor is the lessee in a prior lease.
subordination	The relegation to a lesser position, usually in respect to a right or security.
supply and demand, law of	Holds that price or value varies directly, but not necessarily proportionately, with supply.
survey	The process of ascertaining the quantity and/or location and boundaries of a piece of land; it may include physical features affecting it, such as grades, contours, structures, etc. A statement of the courses, distance and quantity of land.
survivorship	All rights of a joint tenant passes to the surviving joint tenant.
sweat equity	Equity created by labor of purchaser or borrower that increases the value of the property.
switch site	A property which has railroad switching facilities or is so located that such facilities can be installed.
syndication	A combining of persons or firms to accomplish a joint venture which is of mutual interest.
tacking	Combining successive periods of occupation of property so one can establish a claim of adverse possession.
tangible property	Property that by its nature is susceptible to the senses. Generally the land, fixed improvement, furnishings, merchandise, cash and, in actual practice, including other items of working capital used in carrying on an enterprise.
tax	A charge or burden, usually pecuniary, laid upon persons or property for public purposes; a forced contribution of wealth to meet the public needs of a government.
tax abatement	Reduction in taxes assessed.
tax penalty	Forfeiture of a sum because of non-payment of taxes.
tax receivership	The office or function of a receiver appointed by a court or under a statute upon default of taxes.
tax sale	A sale of property for delinquent payment of taxes assessed upon its owner.
tax shelter	Taxable loss to apply against taxable income.
tax title	A title, acquired by the purchaser, at a forced sale of property for non-payment of taxes.
taxable value	The total amount or base upon which taxes are computed under predetermined tax rates. May cover all or any part of the assets represented in tangible and/or intangible property and may be for ad valorem or other forms of taxation. (See also "assessment.")
taxpayer	(1) One who pays a tax; (2) a building erected for the primary purpose of producing revenues to meet the taxes on the land.
tenancy	A holding, as of land, by any kind of title, occupancy of land, a house or the like under a lease or on payment of rent or tenure.
tenancy at sufferance	A tenancy which arises when a tenant holds over after expiration of his lease.
tenancy at will	A tenancy which may be terminated at the will of either the lessor or lessee.

tenancy by the entirety	A joint estate equally owned by husband and wife, with the survivor receiving the entire estate. Each party must consent to its termination.
tenancy in common	A tenancy shared by two or more parties.
tenant	Any person in possession of real property with the owner's permission.
tenement	Term describing buildings and structures on property.
testate	Having made a will before death.
title	The union of all the elements which constitute proof of ownership. (See also "abstract of title.")
title company	A corporation organized for the purpose of issuing or insuring title to real property.
title guarantee	(See "title insurance.")
title guarantee policy	Title insurance furnished by the owner, provided as an alternative for an abstract of title. Also called Torrens certificate.
title insurance	An agreement binding the insurer to indemnify the insured for losses sustained by reason of defects in title to the real estate.
title theory	System in which mortgagee has legal title to the mortgaged property and mortgagor has equitable title.
topography	The contour of land, its elevation, surface variations and location of physical features.
Torrens certificate	A document, issued by the proper public authority called a "registrar" acting under the provisions of the Torrens law, indicating the party in whom title resides.
Torrens system	A system of land registration used in some jurisdictions in which the sovereign issues title certificates covering the ownership of land which tend to serve as title insurance.
tract book	(See "plat book.")
trade	(See "exchange.")
trade fixtures	Articles of personal property attached to property that is necessary to owner's business and can be removed.
trader	(See "exchangor.")
trust	A fiduciary relationship, and instrument thereof, which places the legal title to and the control of property in the hands of a trustee for the benefit of another person. A trust may be temporary, conditional or permanent.
trust account	Bank account set up by broker to deposit funds entrusted to him by his principals.
trust deed	A deed which established a trust. It generally is an instrument which conveys legal title to property to a trustee and states his authority and the conditions binding upon him in dealing with the property held in trust. Frequently trust deeds are used to secure lenders against loss. In this respect they are similar to mortgages.
trustee	One who holds title to property for the benefit of another.
trust indenture	An instrument evidencing a trust arrangement.
under-improvement	An improvement which is not the highest and best use for the site on which it is placed by reason of being smaller in size or

	less in cost than a building which would bring the site to its highest and best use.
unimproved	As relating to land—vacant or lacking in essential appurtenant improvements required to serve a useful purpose.
urban renewal	The process of rehabilitating city areas by demolishing, remodeling or repairing existing structures and buildings, public buildings, parks, roadways and individual areas on cleared sites in accordance with a more or less comprehensive plan.
use density	The number of buildings in a particular use per unit of area; sometimes represented by a percentage of land coverage or density of coverage.
valuation	The act or process of estimating value; the amount of estimated value. (See also "appraisal.")
value	The quantity of one thing which can be exchanged for another. In real estate valuation it is the amount of money deemed to be the equivalent in worth of the property being appraised.
warranted value	A term erroneously used in place of warranted price. Value is always warranted inasmuch as it is dependent on services or benefits which will or could actually be received by the owner. Price paid or asked, however, may or may not be warranted.
warranty deed	Conveyance of title that contains certain assurances and guarantees by the grantor that the deed conveys a good and unencumbered title. Conveyances vary from state to state but generally assume: (1) a good title to land; (2) no encumbrances except stated in deed; (3) that grantee will not be evicted or disturbed by person having a better title or lien.
waterpower right	A property consisting of the rights to the use of water as power, developed or undeveloped.
water rights	A property consisting of the rights to a water supply.
WOMEN'S COUNCIL OF REALTORS® (WCR)	(See Chapter 2, p. 21.)
working capital	The readily convertible capital required in a business to permit the regular carrying forward of operations free from financial embarrassment. In accounting, the excess of current assets over current liabilities as of any date.
working drawing	A sketch of a part or a whole structure, drawn to scale and in such detail as to dimensions and instructions as is necessary to guide the workmen on a construction job.
writ of execution	A legal order which directs a proper agent of a court (frequently a sheriff) to carry out an order of that court.
yield	The ratio of the dividends per share in dollars to purchase price per share in dollars. Income of a property is the ratio of the annual net income from the property to the cost or market value of the property.
zoning	Government regulation of land use; regulation by local government under police power of such matters as height, bulk and use of buildings and use of land intended to accomplish desirable social and economic ends.

| zoning map | A map depicting the various sections of the community and the division of the sections into zones of permitted land uses under the zoning ordinance. |
| zoning ordinance | A law to regulate and control the use of real estate for the health, morals, safety and general welfare. |

Appendix

General Information Tables

Metric Equivalents

Linear Measure

1 centimeter = 0.3937 in.
  1 in. = 2.54 centimeters.
1 decimeter = 3.937 in. or 0.328 feet.
  1 ft. = 3.048 decimeters.
1 meter = 39.37 in. or 1.0936 yards.
  1 yard = 0.9144 meter.
1 decimeter = 1.9884 rods.
  1 rod = 0.5029 decimeter.
1 kilometer = 0.62137 mile.
  1 mile = 16.093 kilometers.

Square Measure

1 sq. centimeter = 0.1550 sq. in.
  1 sq. in. = 6.452 square centimeters.
1 sq. decimeter = 0.1076 sq. ft.
  1 sq. ft. = 9.2903 square decimeters.
1 sq. meter = 1.196 sq. yds.
  1 sq. yd. = 0.8361 sq. meter.
1 acre = 3.954 sq. rods.
  1 sq. rod = 0.2529 acre.
1 hectare = 2.47 acres.
  1 acre = 0.4047 hectare.
1 sq. kilometer = 0.386 sq. mile.
  1 sq. mile = 2.59 sq. kilometers.

Measurements in General Use

7.92 inches make 1 link.
25 links make 1 rod.
16.50 feet make 1 rod.
4 rods make 1 chain.
10 chains make 1 furlong.
8 furlongs make 1 mile.
320 rods make 1 mile.
5,280 feet make 1 mile.
10 square chains make 1 acre.
160 square rods make 1 acre.
640 acres make 1 square mile.
43,560 square feet make 1 acre.
1,728 cubic inches make 1 cubic foot.
27 cubic feet make 1 cubic yard.
A Gunter's chain is 22 yards of 100 links.
A section is 640 acres.
A township is 36 sections, each 1 square mile.
A span is 9 inches.
A hand (horse measurement) is 4 inches.
A degree is 60 geographical miles.
A nautical mile is 6,076 feet.
A league is 3 miles.
A fathom (nautical) is 6 feet
A stone is 14 pounds.
A square acre is $208^7/_{10}$ feet on each side.

Computing Square Feet

Sq. Ft.	Acres	Sq. Ft.	Acres	Sq. Ft.	Acres	Sq. Ft.	Acres
1,742,400	40	217,800	5	26,136	0.6	3,049.2	0.07
1,306,800	30	174,240	4	21,780	0.5	2,613.6	0.06
871,200	20	130,680	3	17,424	0.4	2,178	0.05
435,600	10	87,120	2	13,068	0.3	1,742.4	0.04
392,040	9	43,560	1	8,712	0.2	1,306.8	0.03
348,480	8	39,204	0.9	4,356	0.1	871.2	0.02
304,920	7	34,848	0.8	3,920.4	0.09	435.6	0.01
261,360	6	30,492	0.7	3,484.8	0.08		

Calendar of The Numerical Day of The Year

The table below shows, opposite each day of the month, the day of the year. For instance: 8 January is the 8th day of the year, 10 April is the 100th day of the year, and 23 October is the 296th day of the year.

To determine the number of elapsed days from one given date to another given date of a calendar year, subtract the smaller number opposite the earlier date from the larger number opposite the later date. For instance: to determine the time elapsed from 10 April to 23 October, subtract 100 from 296 which equals 196, the correct number of elapsed days.

January		February		March		April		May		June	
1	1	1	32	1	60	1	91	1	121	1	152
2	2	2	33	2	61	2	92	2	122	2	153
3	3	3	34	3	62	3	93	3	123	3	154
4	4	4	35	4	63	4	94	4	124	4	155
5	5	5	36	5	64	5	95	5	125	5	156
6	6	6	37	6	65	6	96	6	126	6	157
7	7	7	38	7	66	7	97	7	127	7	158
8	8	8	39	8	67	8	98	8	128	8	159
9	9	9	40	9	68	9	99	9	129	9	160
10	10	10	41	10	69	10	100	10	130	10	161
11	11	11	42	11	70	11	101	11	131	11	162
12	12	12	43	12	71	12	102	12	132	12	163
13	13	13	44	13	72	13	103	13	133	13	164
14	14	14	45	14	73	14	104	14	134	14	165
15	15	15	46	15	74	15	105	15	135	15	166
16	16	16	47	16	75	16	106	16	136	16	167
17	17	17	48	17	76	17	107	17	137	17	168
18	18	18	49	18	77	18	108	18	138	18	169
19	19	19	50	19	78	19	109	19	139	19	170
20	20	20	51	20	79	20	110	20	140	20	171
21	21	21	52	21	80	21	111	21	141	21	172
22	22	22	53	22	81	22	112	22	142	22	173
23	23	23	54	23	82	23	113	23	143	23	174
24	24	24	55	24	83	24	114	24	144	24	175
25	25	25	56	25	84	25	115	25	145	25	176
26	26	26	57	26	85	26	116	26	146	26	177
27	27	27	58	27	86	27	117	27	147	27	178
28	28	28	59	28	87	28	118	28	148	28	179
29	29	29	See	29	88	29	119	29	149	29	180
30	30		above	30	89	30	120	30	150	30	181
31	31		—	31	90	—	—	31	151	—	—

To determine the number of elapsed days from one given date to another given date in consecutive years, subtract the number appearing opposite the earlier date from 365 and add this result to the number appearing opposite the later date. For instance: to determine the time elapsed from 23 October of one year to 8 January of the following year, subtract 296 from 365 which equals 69 and add this to 8 which equals 77, the correct number of elapsed days.

Leap Year. It must be remembered that each Leap Year has an extra day, 29 February. Therefore, if 29 February is included in the period of time to be determined, one day must be added to the result obtained by the use of this table.

July		August		September		October		November		December	
1	182	1	213	1	244	1	274	1	305	1	335
2	183	2	214	2	245	2	275	2	306	2	336
3	184	3	215	3	246	3	276	3	307	3	337
4	185	4	216	4	247	4	277	4	308	4	338
5	186	5	217	5	248	5	278	5	309	5	339
6	187	6	218	6	249	6	279	6	310	6	340
7	188	7	219	7	250	7	280	7	311	7	341
8	189	8	220	8	251	8	281	8	312	8	342
9	190	9	221	9	252	9	282	9	313	9	343
10	191	10	222	10	253	10	283	10	314	10	344
11	192	11	223	11	254	11	284	11	315	11	345
12	193	12	224	12	255	12	285	12	316	12	346
13	194	13	225	13	256	13	286	13	317	13	347
14	195	14	226	14	257	14	287	14	318	14	348
15	196	15	227	15	258	15	288	15	319	15	349
16	197	16	228	16	259	16	289	16	320	16	350
17	198	17	229	17	260	17	290	17	321	17	351
18	199	18	230	18	261	18	291	18	322	18	352
19	200	19	231	19	262	19	292	19	323	19	353
20	201	20	232	20	263	20	293	20	324	20	354
21	202	21	233	21	264	21	294	21	325	21	355
22	203	22	234	22	265	22	295	22	326	22	356
23	204	23	235	23	266	23	296	23	327	23	357
24	205	24	236	24	267	24	297	24	328	24	358
25	206	25	237	25	268	25	298	25	329	25	359
26	207	26	238	26	269	26	299	26	330	26	360
27	208	27	239	27	270	27	300	27	331	27	361
28	209	28	240	28	271	28	301	28	332	28	362
29	210	29	241	29	272	29	302	29	333	29	363
30	211	30	242	30	273	30	303	30	334	30	364
31	212	31	243	—	—	31	304	—	—	31	365

Widths Times Depths Equaling One Acre

1 Acre Equals		1 Acre Equals		1 Acre Equals	
Length	Width	Length	Width	Length	Width
16.5 ft.	2640. ft.	66. ft.	660. ft.	132. ft.	330. ft.
33.	1320.	75.	580.8	150.	290.4
50.	871.2	100.	435.6	208.71	208.71

Price per Acre Produced By Certain Prices Per Square Foot

Cents per Sq. Ft.	Dollars per Acre	Cents per Sq. Ft.	Dollars per Acre	Cents per Sq. Ft.	Dollars per Acre	Cents per Sq. Ft.	Dollars per Acre
1¢	$ 435.60	9¢	$ 3,920.40	30¢	$13,068	70¢	$30,492
2	871.20	10	4,356.00	35	15,246	75	32,670
3	1,306.80	12	5,227.20	40	17,424	80	34,848
4	1,742.40	14	6,098.40	45	19,602	85	37,026
5	2,178.00	16	6,969.60	50	21,780	90	39,204
6	2,613.60	18	7,840.80	55	23,958	95	41,382
7	3,049.20	20	8,712.00	60	26,136	100	43,560
8	3,484.80	25	10,890.00	65	28,314		

The Rent You Pay

Rent money, figured on a 5 percent interest basis, amounts to large sums in a few years.

Per Month	10 Years	15 Years	20 Years	25 Years
$ 25	$ 3,773.34	$ 6,473.55	$ 9,919.77	$ 14,318.10
30	4,528.00	7,768.26	11,903.72	17,181.72
35	5,282.68	9,062.97	13,887.68	20,045.34
50	7,546.68	12,947.10	19,839.54	28,636.20
60	9,056.02	15,536.52	23,807.45	34,363.44
75	11,320.02	19,420.65	29,759.31	42,954.30
85	12,829.36	22,010.07	33,727.22	48,681.54
100	15,093.36	25,894.20	39,679.08	57,272.40
150	22,640.04	38,841.30	59,518.62	85,908.60
200	30,186.72	51,788.40	79,358.16	114,544.80
300	45,280.08	77,682.60	119,037.24	171,817.20
400	60,373.44	103,574.80	158,716.32	229,089.60
500	75,466.80	129,471.00	198,395.40	286,362.00

Rent Prorating Table

Rent per Year	Rent per Month	Rent per Day (30 Days)	Rent per Day (31 Days)	Rent per Year	Rent per Month	Rent per Day (30 Days)	Rent per Day (31 Days)
$1	$ .09	$ .003	$ .0029	$ 1,025	$ 85.42	$ 2.847	$ 2.756
2	.17	.0056	.0054	1,050	87.50	2.917	2.823
3	.25	.0083	.008	1,075	89.59	2.986	2.890
4	.34	.011	.01	1,100	91.67	3.056	2.958
5	.42	.014	.013	1,125	93.75	3.125	3.025
6	.50	.016	.016	1,150	95.84	3.195	3.092
7	.59	.019	.019	1,175	97.92	3.264	3.159
8	.67	.022	.021	1,200	00.00	3.334	3.226
9	.75	.025	.024	1,225	102.09	3.403	3.293
10	.84	.028	.027	1,250	104.17	3.472	3.36
20	1.67	.056	.054	1,275	106.25	3.541	3.428
25	2.09	.070	.068	1,300	108.34	3.611	3.495
30	2.50	.084	.081	1,325	110.42	3.681	3.562
40	3.34	.111	.108	1,350	112.50	3.75	3.629
50	4.17	.139	.134	1,375	114.59	3.82	3.697
60	5.00	.166	.161	1,400	116.67	3.889	3.764
70	5.84	.195	.189	1,425	118.75	3.958	3.831
75	6.25	.208	.202	1,450	120.84	4.028	3.898
80	6.67	.222	.215	1,475	122.92	4.098	3.965
90	7.50	.25	.242	1,500	125.00	4.167	4.033
100	8.34	.278	.269	1,525	127.09	4.236	4.10
125	10.42	.347	.336	1,550	129.17	4.306	4.167
150	12.50	.417	.403	1,575	131.25	4.375	4.234
175	14.59	.486	.470	1,600	133.34	4.445	4.301
200	16.67	.556	.538	1,625	135.42	4.514	4.369
225	18.75	.625	.605	1,650	137.50	4.584	4.436
250	20.84	.695	.672	1,675	139.59	4.653	4.503
275	22.92	.764	.740	1,700	141.67	4.723	4.570
300	25.00	.834	.807	1,725	143.75	4.792	4.638
325	27.09	.903	.874	1,750	145.84	4.861	4.705
350	29.17	.972	.941	1,775	147.92	4.931	4.772
375	31.25	1.042	1.009	1,800	150.00	5.00	4.84
400	33.34	1.112	1.076	1,825	152.09	5.07	4.906
425	35.42	1.181	1.143	1,850	154.17	5.139	4.973
450	37.50	1.25	1.21	1,875	156.25	5.209	5.04
475	39.59	1.32	1.277	1,900	158.34	5.278	5.108
500	41.67	1.389	1.344	1,925	160.42	5.347	5.175
525	43.75	1.458	1.412	1,950	162.50	5.417	5.242
550	45.84	1.528	1.479	1,975	164.59	5.487	5.31
575	47.92	1.598	1.546	2,000	166.67	5.56	5.377
600	50.00	1.667	1.613	3,000	250.00	8.334	8.065
625	52.09	1.737	1.68	4,000	333.34	11.111	10.753
650	54.17	1.806	1.748	5,000	416.67	13.889	13.441
675	56.25	1.875	1.815	6,000	500.00	16.667	16.13
700	58.34	1.945	1.882	7,000	583.34	19.445	18.818
725	60.42	2.01	1.950	8,000	666.67	22.223	21.506
750	62.50	2.084	2.017	9,000	750.00	25.00	24.194
775	64.59	2.153	2.084	10,000	833.34	27.778	26.882
800	66.67	2.223	2.151	11,000	916.67	30.556	29.57
825	68.75	2.292	2.218	12,000	1,000.00	33.34	32.259
850	70.84	2.361	2.286	13,000	1,083.34	36.111	34.947
875	72.92	2.431	2.352	14,000	1,166.67	38.889	37.635
900	75.00	2.50	2.420	15,000	1,250.00	41.667	40.323
925	77.09	2.57	2.487	16,000	1,333.34	44.445	43.011
950	79.17	2.639	2.554	17,000	1,416.67	47.223	45.699
975	81.25	2.708	2.621	18,000	1,500.00	50.00	48.388
1,000	83.34	2.778	2.689	19,000	1,583.34	52.778	51.076

To Value Deep Lots

This table, known as the Cleveland Standard, in which a number of existing methods are adapted, may be used to determine the percentage of value in lots of varying depth. Assuming the land to be worth $100 per front foot, 100 feet deep, it may be seen that a lot 200 feet in depth is worth $122 per front foot for that depth. Any value and depth may be secured. 100 feet depth = 100%.

Percentage of Unit Value for Lots from 1 to 700 Feet Deep

1 ft.	3.10%	51	73.25	101	100.41	151	115.19	201	122.10
2	6.10	2	74.00	2	100.85	2	115.38	2	122.20
3	9.00	3	74.75	3	101.27	3	115.57	3	122.30
4	11.75	4	75.50	4	101.70	4	115.76	4	122.40
5	14.35	5	76.20	5	102.08	5	115.95	5	122.50
6	16.75	6	76.90	6	102.48	6	116.12	210	122.95
7	19.05	7	77.55	7	102.88	7	116.29	15	123.38
8	21.20	8	78.20	8	103.25	8	116.46	20	123.80
9	23.20	9	78.85	9	103.62	9	116.62	30	124.60
10	25.00	60	79.50	110	104.00	160	116.80	240	125.35
1	26.70	1	80.11	1	104.36	1	116.96	50	126.05
2	28.36	2	80.77	2	104.72	2	117.13	60	126.75
3	29.99	3	81.38	3	105.08	3	117.30	70	127.40
4	31.61	4	82.00	4	105.43	4	117.47	80	128.05
5	33.22	5	82.61	5	105.78	5	117.64	90	128.65
6	34.92	6	83.21	6	106.13	6	117.79	300	129.25
7	36.41	7	83.82	7	106.47	7	117.94	10	129.80
8	37.97	8	84.42	8	106.81	8	118.09	20	130.35
9	39.50	9	85.01	9	107.15	·9	118.24	30	130.90
20	41.00	70	85.60	120	107.50	170	118.40	340	131.40
1	42.50	1	86.15	1	107.80	1	118.54	50	131.90
2	43.96	2	86.70	2	108.11	2	118.70	60	132.40
3	45.30	3	87.24	3	108.43	3	118.85	70	132.85
4	46.61	4	87.78	4	108.75	4	119.00	80	133.30
5	47.90	5	88.30	5	109.05	5	119.14	90	133.75
6	49.17	6	88.82	6	109.35	6	119.28	400	134.20
7	50.40	7	89.35	7	109.65	7	119.41	10	134.60
8	51.61	8	89.87	8	109.93	8	119.54	20	135.00
9	52.81	9	90.39	9	110.21	9	119.67	30	135.40
30	54.00	80	90.90	130	110.50	180	119.80	440	135.80
1	55.05	1	91.39	1	110.76	1	119.92	50	136.15
2	56.10	2	91.89	2	111.02	2	120.05	60	136.50
3	57.15	3	92.38	3	111.28	3	120.18	70	136.85
4	58.20	4	92.86	4	111.55	4	120.31	80	137.20
5	59.20	5	93.33	5	111.80	5	120.43	90	137.55
6	60.30	6	93.80	6	112.05	6	120.55	500	137.85
7	61.25	7	94.27	7	112.28	7	120.66	10	138.15
8	62.20	8	94.73	8	112.52	8	120.77	20	138.45
9	63.10	9	95.17	9	112.76	9	120.88	30	138.75
40	64.00	90	95.60	140	113.00	190	121.00	540	139.05
1	64.95	1	96.04	1	113.20	1	121.10	50	139.30
2	65.90	2	96.50	2	113.43	2	121.21	60	139.55
3	66.75	3	96.95	3	113.64	3	121.32	70	139.80
4	67.60	4	97.40	4	113.85	4	121.43	80	140.05
5	68.45	5	97.85	5	114.05	5	121.53	600	140.55
6	69.30	6	98.30	6	114.25	6	121.62	20	140.95
7	70.10	7	98.74	7	114.45	7	121.71	40	141.35
8	70.90	8	99.17	8	114.64	8	121.80	60	141.75
9	71.70	9	99.58	9	114.82	9	121.90	80	142.05
50	72.50	100	100.00	150	115.00	200	122.00	700	142.35

Housing and Depreciation Tables

Home Ownership, by States, 1970
(Number of Units in Thousands)

State	No. of Occupied Dwelling Units	Percentage Owner-Occupied	Percentage Renter-Occupied	State	No. of Occupied Dwelling Units	Percentage Owner-Occupied	Percentage Renter-Occupied
Alabama	1,034	66.6%	33.4%	Nebraska	474	66.4	33.6
Alaska	79	50.3	49.7	Nevada	160	58.5	41.5
Arizona	539	65.3	34.7	New Hampshire	225	68.2	31.8
Arkansas	614	66.6	33.4	New Jersey	2,218	60.9	39.1
California	6,574	54.9	45.1	New Mexico	289	66.4	33.6
Colorado	691	63.4	36.6	New York	5,893	47.3	52.7
Connecticut	933	62.5	37.5	North Carolina	1,509	65.3	34.7
Delaware	165	68.0	32.0	North Dakota	182	68.4	31.6
D. C.	263	28.2	71.8	Ohio	3,289	67.7	32.3
Florida	2,282	68.5	31.5	Oklahoma	850	69.2	30.8
Georgia	1,369	61.1	38.9	Oregon	692	66.1	33.9
Hawaii	203	46.9	53.1	Pennsylvania	3,705	68.8	31.2
Idaho	219	70.1	29.9	Rhode Island	292	57.9	42.1
Illinois	3,502	59.4	40.6	South Carolina	734	66.1	33.9
Indiana	1,609	71.7	28.3	South Dakota	201	69.6	30.4
Iowa	896	71.7	28.3	Tennessee	1,212	66.7	33.3
Kansas	727	69.1	30.9	Texas	3,432	64.7	35.3
Kentucky	983	66.8	33.2	Utah	298	69.3	30.7
Louisiana	1,052	63.1	36.9	Vermont	132	69.1	30.9
Maine	303	70.1	29.9	Virginia	1,390	62.0	38.0
Maryland	1,175	58.7	41.3	Washington	1,106	66.8	33.2
Massachusetts	1,760	57.5	42.5	West Virginia	546	68.9	31.1
Michigan	2,653	74.4	25.6	Wisconsin	1,329	69.1	30.9
Minnesota	1,154	71.5	28.5	Wyoming	105	66.4	33.6
Mississippi	637	66.3	33.7				
Missouri	1,521	67.2	32.8	Entire U. S.	63,417	62.9%	37.1%
Montana	217	65.7	34.3				

Source: U. S. Bureau of the Census.

All-Occupied Year-Round Housing Inventory by Tenure (in Millions)

Year	Occupied Units	Owner-Occupied Units	Renter-Occupied Units	Percentage Owned	Percentage Rented
1940	34.9	15.2	19.7	43.6%	56.4%
1950	42.9	23.6	19.3	55.0	45.0
1960	53.0	32.8	20.2	61.9	38.1
1970	63.5	39.9	23.6	62.9	37.1
1973	69.3	44.6	24.7	64.4	35.6
1974	70.8	45.8	25.0	64.6	35.4
1975	72.5	46.9	25.7	64.6	35.4
1976	74.0	47.9	26.1	64.7	35.3

Source: 1960 and 1970 Census of Housing, and Annual Housing Survey—1976

Percentage Distribution of Existing Homes Sold, By Sales Price

Price Class	1973	1974	1975	1976	1977
Under $30,000	53.5	45.1	37.2	31.6	24.7
$30,000-$39,999	22.1	23.9	24.1	22.6	20.4
$40,000-$49,999	11.7	14.1	16.3	17.6	17.3
$50,000-$59,999			9.4	11.2	12.9
$60,000-$69,999	12.7	16.9	5.5	6.7	9.0
$70,000 and over			7.5	10.3	15.7
Total	100.0	100.0	100.0	100.0	100.0
Median	$28,900	$32,000	$35,300	$38,100	$42,900

Source: NATIONAL ASSOCIATION OF REALTORS®

Housing Units Started

	1970	1972	1974	1976	1978
Units Started (1,000)					
Total	1433.6	2356.6	1337.7	1537.5	2019.5
Metropolitan	1017.9	1720.4	922.5	1043.5	1431.7
Nonmetropolitan	415.7	636.2	415.3	494.1	587.8
Region:					
Northeast	217.9	329.5	183.2	169.2	200.2
North Central	293.5	442.8	317.3	400.1	451.2
South	611.6	1057.0	552.8	568.5	823.4
West	310.5	527.4	284.5	399.6	544.6
Type of Structure:					
1-unit	812.9	1309.2	888.1	1162.4	1432.8
2-4 units	84.8	141.3	68.1	85.9	125.1
5 + units	535.9	906.2	381.6	289.2	461.7

Percentage Distribution of New Homes Sold, By Sales Price

Price Class	1973	1974	1975	1976	1977
Under $30,000	42	29	20	12	7
$30,000-$39,999	31	35	32	26	21
$40,000-$49,999	16	19	23	26	24
$50,000-$59,999	6	9	12	15	18
$60,000-$69,999	3	5	6	9	11
$70,000 and over	3	4	6	11	18
Total	100	100	100	100	100
Median	$32,500	$35,900	$39,300	$44,200	$48,800

Sources: Dept. of Commerce, Bureau of Census.

Percentage Distribution of Financing of New Homes Sold

Financing	1973	1974	1975	1976	1977
Conventional	73.4	72.9	66.1	70.9	72.3
FHA	9.9	8.5	9.8	8.8	8.9
VA	11.2	13.1	12.4	11.9	11.4
FmHA	*	*	7.8	3.6	2.9
Cash	5.4	5.4	4.0	4.8	4.6
Total	100.0	100.0	100.0	100.0	100.0

*included in conventional

Source: U.S. Department of Commerce, Bureau of the Census.

Annual Depreciation Rates
Annual percentage of property values at beginning of schedule

Useful Life	Straight Line	150% Declining Bal.	200% Declining Bal.	Sum-of-the Years-Digits
50 years	2.0%	3.0%	4.0	3.9%
45 "	2.2	3.3	4.4	4.3
40 "	2.5	3.8	5.0	4.9
35 "	2.9	4.3	5.7	5.6
30 "	3.3	5.0	6.7	6.4
25 "	4.0	6.0	8.0	7.7
20 "	5.0	7.5	10.0	9.5
15 "	6.7	10.0	13.3	12.5
10 "	10.0	15.0	20.0	18.2

Building Depreciation and Annual Straight Line Rates

	Life in Years	Rate
Apartments	40%	2.5%
Banks	50	2.5
Dwellings	45	2.2
Factories	45	2.2
Farm Buildings	25	4.0
Garages	45	2.2
Grain Elevators	60	1.6
Hotels	40	2.5
Land Improvements	20	5.0
Loft Buildings	50	2.0
Machine Shops	45	2.2
Office Buildings	45	2.2
Stores	50	2.0
Theatres	40	2.5
Warehouses	60	1.6

Amortization and Capitalization Tables

Payment Differential Finder

Difference In Monthly Payment	Daily Difference (31 Days)	Annual Difference
$ 1	$ .03	$ 12
2	.06	24
3	.10	36
4	.13	48
5	.16	60
6	.19	72
7	.23	84
8	.26	96
9	.29	108
10	.32	120
15	.48	180
20	.65	240
25	.81	300
30	.97	360
35	1.13	420
40	1.29	480
45	1.45	540
50	1.61	600
60	1.94	720
70	2.26	840
80	2.58	960
90	2.90	1080
100	3.23	1200
110	3.55	1320
120	3.87	1440
130	4.19	1560
140	4.52	1680
150	4.84	1800
160	5.16	1920
170	5.48	2400
180	5.81	2160
190	6.13	2280
200	6.45	2400
300	9.68	3600
400	12.90	4800
500	16.13	6000
600	19.35	7200
700	22.58	8400
800	25.81	9600
900	29.03	10800
1000	32.26	12000

Example

Current monthly payment is $150

Proposed monthly payment is $190

Monthly differential is $40—with daily difference only $1.29

Interest formulas

Simple interest $\quad I = P \times R \times T$

Compound interest $\quad S = P(I + R)^N$

I = Interest
P = Principal
R = Rate
T = Time
S = Compound Amount
N = # of Periods

Capitalization Table

Capitalization Rate	Factor	Capitalization Rate	Factor	Capitalization Rate	Factor
5%	20.00	8½%	11.76	12%	8.33
5½%	18.19	9%	11.11	12½%	8.00
6%	16.67	9½%	10.53	13%	7.69
6½%	15.38	10%	10.00	13½%	7.41
7%	14.29	10½%	9.52	14%	7.14
7½%	13.33	11%	9.09	14½%	6.90
8%	12.50	11½%	8.69	15%	6.67

Example: If a building is to be sold on the basis of its net income being capitalized at 8%, the net income multiplied by the factor for 8% would give the sale price as

Income $14,000 $ 14,000
Rate   8%   ×12.5
Factor   12.5 $175,000

Formula: SP = I × F
SP = Selling Price
  I = Income
  F = Capitalization Factor

Example: A building is to be sold on the basis of its net income being capitalized at 8%. The net income divided by 8% would give the sales price. Income is at $14,000.

Income $14,000 $\dfrac{\$14,000}{.08} = \$175,000$
Rate   8%
Value $175,000

Formula: $\dfrac{I}{R \times V}$

I = Income $I = R \times V$

R = Rate $R = \dfrac{I}{V}$

V = Value $V = \dfrac{I}{R}$

Amortization Tables

Following are amortization tables showing the amounts of monthly payments required to retire the principal and pay the interest on loans from $100 to $75,000, at interest rates from 8 percent through 14 percent in quarterly increments.

These charts are followed by a guide to monthly payments where the interest rates may be figured in quarters of a percent. This chart is based on a $1,000 loan. Multiples or fractions of $1,000 can be obtained by using the appropriate factor for multiplying the payment listed under the percent of the loan and the number of years it is to run.

Term in Years Amount	5	10	15	20	25	30
$ 25	.51	.31	.24	.21	.20	.19
50	1.02	.61	.48	.42	.39	.37
75	1.53	.91	.72	.63	.58	.56
100	2.03	1.22	.96	.84	.78	.74
200	4.06	2.43	1.92	1.68	1.55	1.47
300	6.09	3.64	2.87	2.51	2.32	2.21
400	8.12	4.86	3.83	3.35	3.09	2.94
500	10.14	6.07	4.78	4.19	3.86	3.67
600	12.17	7.28	5.74	5.02	4.64	4.41
700	14.20	8.50	6.69	5.86	5.41	5.14
800	16.23	9.71	7.65	6.70	6.18	5.88
900	18.25	10.92	8.61	7.53	6.95	6.61
1 000	20.28	12.14	9.56	8.37	7.72	7.34
2 000	40.56	24.27	19.12	16.73	15.44	14.68
3 000	60.83	36.40	28.67	25.10	23.16	22.02
4 000	81.11	48.54	38.23	33.46	30.88	29.36
5 000	101.39	60.67	47.79	41.83	38.60	36.69
6 000	121.66	72.80	57.34	50.19	46.31	44.03
7 000	141.94	84.93	66.90	58.56	54.03	51.37
8 000	162.22	97.07	76.46	66.92	61.75	58.71
9 000	182.49	109.20	86.01	75.28	69.47	66.04
10 000	202.77	121.33	95.57	83.65	77.19	73.38
11 000	223.05	133.47	105.13	92.01	84.90	80.72
12 000	243.32	145.60	114.68	100.38	92.62	88.06
13 000	263.60	157.73	124.24	108.74	100.34	95.39
14 000	283.87	169.86	133.80	117.11	108.06	102.73
15 000	304.15	182.00	143.35	125.47	115.78	110.07
16 000	324.43	194.13	152.91	133.84	123.50	117.41
17 000	344.70	206.26	162.47	142.20	131.21	124.74
18 000	364.98	218.39	172.02	150.56	138.93	132.08
19 000	385.26	230.53	181.58	158.93	146.65	139.42
20 000	405.53	242.66	191.14	167.29	154.37	146.76
21 000	425.81	254.79	200.69	175.66	162.09	154.10
22 000	446.09	266.93	210.25	184.02	169.80	161.43
23 000	466.36	279.06	219.80	192.39	177.52	168.77
24 000	486.64	291.19	229.36	200.75	185.24	176.11
25 000	506.91	303.32	238.92	209.12	192.96	183.45
26 000	527.19	315.46	248.47	217.48	200.68	190.78
27 000	547.47	327.59	258.03	225.84	208.40	198.12
28 000	567.74	339.72	267.59	234.21	216.11	205.46
29 000	588.02	351.86	277.14	242.57	223.83	212.80
30 000	608.30	363.99	286.70	250.94	231.55	220.13
31 000	628.57	376.12	296.26	259.30	239.27	227.47
32 000	648.85	388.25	305.81	267.67	246.99	234.81
33 000	669.13	400.39	315.37	276.03	254.70	242.15
34 000	689.40	412.52	324.93	284.39	262.42	249.48
35 000	709.68	424.65	334.48	292.76	270.14	256.82
40 000	811.06	485.32	382.27	334.58	308.73	293.51
45 000	912.44	545.98	430.05	376.40	347.32	330.20
50 000	1013.82	606.64	477.83	418.23	385.91	366.89
55 000	1115.21	667.31	525.61	460.05	424.50	403.58
60 000	1216.59	727.97	573.40	501.87	463.09	440.26
65 000	1317.97	788.63	621.18	543.69	501.69	476.95
70 000	1419.35	849.30	668.96	585.51	540.28	513.64
75 000	1520.73	909.96	716.74	627.34	578.87	550.33
80 000	1622.12	970.63	764.53	669.16	617.46	587.02
100 000	2027.64	1213.28	955.66	836.45	771.82	733.77

185

Term in Years Amount	5	10	15	20	25	30
$ 25	.51	.31	.25	.22	.20	.19
50	1.02	.62	.49	.43	.40	.38
75	1.53	.92	.73	.64	.60	.57
100	2.04	1.23	.98	.86	.79	.76
200	4.08	2.46	1.95	1.71	1.58	1.51
300	6.12	3.68	2.92	2.56	2.37	2.26
400	8.16	4.91	3.89	3.41	3.16	3.01
500	10.20	6.14	4.86	4.27	3.95	3.76
600	12.24	7.36	5.83	5.12	4.74	4.51
700	14.28	8.59	6.80	5.97	5.52	5.26
800	16.32	9.82	7.77	6.82	6.31	6.02
900	18.36	11.04	8.74	7.67	7.10	6.77
1 000	20.40	12.27	9.71	8.53	7.89	7.52
2 000	40.80	24.54	19.41	17.05	15.77	15.03
3 000	61.19	36.80	29.11	25.57	23.66	22.54
4 000	81.59	49.07	38.81	34.09	31.54	30.06
5 000	101.99	61.33	48.51	42.61	39.43	37.57
6 000	122.38	73.60	58.21	51.13	47.31	45.08
7 000	142.78	85.86	67.91	59.65	55.20	52.59
8 000	163.18	98.13	77.62	68.17	63.08	60.11
9 000	183.57	110.39	87.32	76.69	70.97	67.62
10 000	203.97	122.66	97.02	85.21	78.85	75.13
11 000	224.36	134.92	106.72	93.73	86.73	82.64
12 000	244.76	147.19	116.42	102.25	94.62	90.16
13 000	265.16	159.45	126.12	110.77	102.50	97.67
14 000	285.55	171.72	135.82	119.29	110.39	105.18
15 000	305.95	183.98	145.53	127.81	118.27	112.69
16 000	326.35	196.25	155.23	136.34	126.16	120.21
17 000	346.74	208.51	164.93	144.86	134.04	127.72
18 000	367.14	220.78	174.63	153.38	141.93	135.23
19 000	387.53	233.04	184.33	161.90	149.81	142.75
20 000	407.93	245.31	194.03	170.42	157.70	150.26
21 000	428.33	257.58	203.73	178.94	165.58	157.77
22 000	448.72	269.84	213.44	187.46	173.46	165.28
23 000	469.12	282.11	223.14	195.98	181.35	172.80
24 000	489.52	294.37	232.84	204.50	189.23	180.31
25 000	509.91	306.64	242.54	213.02	197.12	187.82
26 000	530.31	318.90	252.24	221.54	205.00	195.33
27 000	550.70	331.17	261.94	230.06	212.89	202.85
28 000	571.10	343.43	271.64	238.58	220.77	210.36
29 000	591.50	355.70	281.35	247.10	228.66	217.87
30 000	611.89	367.96	291.05	255.62	236.54	225.38
31 000	632.29	380.23	300.75	264.15	244.42	232.90
32 000	652.69	392.49	310.45	272.67	252.31	240.41
33 000	673.08	404.76	320.15	281.19	260.19	247.92
34 000	693.48	417.02	329.85	289.71	268.08	255.44
35 000	713.87	429.29	339.55	298.23	275.96	262.95
40 000	815.86	490.62	388.06	340.83	315.39	300.51
45 000	917.84	551.94	436.57	383.43	354.81	338.07
50 000	1019.82	613.27	485.08	426.04	394.23	375.64
55 000	1121.80	674.59	533.58	468.64	433.65	413.20
60 000	1223.78	735.92	582.09	511.24	473.08	450.76
65 000	1325.76	797.25	630.60	553.85	512.50	488.33
70 000	1427.74	858.57	679.10	596.45	551.92	525.89
75 000	1529.72	919.90	727.61	639.05	591.34	563.45
80 000	1631.71	981.23	776.12	681.66	630.77	601.02
100 000	2039.63	1226.53	970.15	852.07	788.46	751.27

186

Term in Years Amount	5	10	15	20	25	30
$ 25	.52	.31	.25	.22	.21	.20
50	1.03	.62	.50	.44	.41	.39
75	1.54	.93	.74	.66	.61	.58
100	2.06	1.24	.99	.87	.81	.77
200	4.11	2.48	1.97	1.74	1.62	1.54
300	6.16	3.72	2.96	2.61	2.42	2.31
400	8.21	4.96	3.94	3.48	3.23	3.08
500	10.26	6.20	4.93	4.34	4.03	3.85
600	12.31	7.44	5.91	5.21	4.84	4.62
700	14.37	8.68	6.90	6.08	5.64	5.39
800	16.42	9.92	7.88	6.95	6.45	6.16
900	18.47	11.16	8.87	7.82	7.25	6.93
1 000	20.52	12.40	9.85	8.68	8.06	7.69
2 000	41.04	24.80	19.70	17.36	16.11	15.38
3 000	61.55	37.20	29.55	26.04	24.16	23.07
4 000	82.07	49.60	39.39	34.72	32.21	30.76
5 000	102.59	62.00	49.24	43.40	40.27	38.45
6 000	123.10	74.40	59.09	52.07	48.32	46.14
7 000	143.62	86.79	68.94	60.75	56.37	53.83
8 000	164.14	99.19	78.78	69.43	64.42	61.52
9 000	184.65	111.59	88.63	78.11	72.48	69.21
10 000	205.17	123.99	98.48	86.79	80.53	76.90
11 000	225.69	136.39	108.33	95.47	88.58	84.59
12 000	246.20	148.79	118.17	104.14	96.63	92.27
13 000	266.72	161.19	128.02	112.82	104.68	99.96
14 000	287.24	173.58	137.87	121.50	112.74	107.65
15 000	307.75	185.98	147.72	130.18	120.79	115.34
16 000	328.27	198.38	157.56	138.86	128.84	123.03
17 000	348.79	210.78	167.41	147.53	136.89	130.72
18 000	369.30	223.18	177.26	156.21	144.95	138.41
19 000	389.82	235.58	187.11	164.89	153.00	146.10
20 000	410.34	247.98	196.95	173.57	161.05	153.79
21 000	430.85	260.37	206.80	182.25	169.10	161.48
22 000	451.37	272.77	216.65	190.93	177.15	169.17
23 000	471.89	285.17	226.50	199.60	185.21	176.86
24 000	492.40	297.57	236.34	208.28	193.26	184.54
25 000	512.92	309.97	246.19	216.96	201.31	192.23
26 000	533.43	322.37	256.04	225.64	209.36	199.92
27 000	553.95	334.77	265.88	234.32	217.42	207.61
28 000	574.47	347.16	275.73	243.00	225.47	215.30
29 000	594.98	359.56	285.58	251.67	233.52	222.99
30 000	615.50	371.96	295.43	260.35	241.57	230.68
31 000	636.02	384.36	305.27	269.03	249.63	238.37
32 000	656.53	396.76	315.12	277.71	257.68	246.06
33 000	677.05	409.16	324.97	286.39	265.73	253.75
34 000	697.57	421.56	334.82	295.06	273.78	261.44
35 000	718.08	433.95	344.66	303.74	281.83	269.12
40 000	820.67	495.95	393.90	347.13	322.10	307.57
45 000	923.25	557.94	443.14	390.53	362.36	346.02
50 000	1025.83	619.93	492.37	433.92	402.62	384.46
55 000	1128.41	681.93	541.61	477.31	442.88	422.91
60 000	1231.00	743.92	590.85	520.70	483.14	461.35
65 000	1333.58	805.91	640.09	564.09	523.40	499.80
70 000	1436.16	867.90	689.32	607.48	563.66	538.24
75 000	1538.74	929.90	738.56	650.87	603.93	576.69
80 000	1641.33	991.89	787.80	694.26	644.19	615.14
100 000	2051.66	1239.86	984.74	867.83	805.23	768.92

187

Term in Years / Amount	5	10	15	20	25	30
$ 25	.52	.32	.25	.23	.21	.20
50	1.04	.63	.50	.45	.42	.40
75	1.55	.94	.75	.67	.62	.60
100	2.07	1.26	1.00	.89	.83	.79
200	4.13	2.51	2.00	1.77	1.65	1.58
300	6.20	3.76	3.00	2.66	2.47	2.37
400	8.26	5.02	4.00	3.54	3.29	3.15
500	10.32	6.27	5.00	4.42	4.12	3.94
600	12.39	7.52	6.00	5.31	4.94	4.73
700	14.45	8.78	7.00	6.19	5.76	5.51
800	16.51	10.03	8.00	7.07	6.58	6.30
900	18.58	11.28	9.00	7.96	7.40	7.09
1 000	20.64	12.54	10.00	8.84	8.23	7.87
2 000	41.28	25.07	19.99	17.68	16.45	15.74
3 000	61.92	37.60	29.99	26.52	24.67	23.61
4 000	82.55	50.14	39.98	35.35	32.89	31.47
5 000	103.19	62.67	49.98	44.19	41.11	39.34
6 000	123.83	75.20	59.97	53.03	49.33	47.21
7 000	144.47	87.73	69.97	61.86	57.56	55.07
8 000	165.10	100.27	79.96	70.70	65.78	62.94
9 000	185.74	112.80	89.96	79.54	74.00	70.81
10 000	206.38	125.33	99.95	88.38	82.22	78.68
11 000	227.01	137.86	109.94	97.21	90.44	86.54
12 000	247.65	150.40	119.94	106.05	98.66	94.41
13 000	268.29	162.93	129.93	114.89	106.88	102.28
14 000	288.93	175.46	139.93	123.72	115.11	110.14
15 000	309.56	188.00	149.92	132.56	123.33	118.01
16 000	330.20	200.53	159.92	141.40	131.55	125.88
17 000	350.84	213.06	169.91	150.24	139.77	133.74
18 000	371.48	225.59	179.91	159.07	147.99	141.61
19 000	392.11	238.13	189.90	167.91	156.21	149.48
20 000	412.75	250.66	199.89	176.75	164.43	157.35
21 000	433.39	263.19	209.89	185.58	172.66	165.21
22 000	454.02	275.72	219.88	194.42	180.88	173.08
23 000	474.66	288.26	229.88	203.26	189.10	180.95
24 000	495.30	300.79	239.87	212.10	197.32	188.81
25 000	515.94	313.32	249.87	220.93	205.54	196.68
26 000	536.57	325.85	259.86	229.77	213.76	204.55
27 000	557.21	338.39	269.86	238.61	221.98	212.41
28 000	577.85	350.92	279.85	247.44	230.21	220.28
29 000	598.48	363.45	289.85	256.28	238.43	228.15
30 000	619.12	375.99	299.84	265.12	246.65	236.02
31 000	639.76	388.52	309.83	273.96	254.87	243.88
32 000	660.40	401.05	319.83	282.79	263.09	251.75
33 000	681.03	413.58	329.82	291.63	271.31	259.62
34 000	701.67	426.12	339.82	300.47	279.53	267.48
35 000	722.31	438.65	349.81	309.30	287.76	275.35
40 000	825.49	501.31	399.78	353.49	328.86	314.69
45 000	928.68	563.98	449.76	397.67	369.97	354.02
50 000	1031.87	626.64	499.73	441.86	411.08	393.36
55 000	1135.05	689.30	549.70	486.05	452.18	432.69
60 000	1238.24	751.97	599.67	530.23	493.29	472.03
65 000	1341.43	814.63	649.65	574.42	534.40	511.36
70 000	1444.61	877.29	699.62	618.60	575.51	550.70
75 000	1547.80	939.96	749.59	662.79	616.61	590.03
80 000	1650.98	1002.62	799.56	706.97	657.72	629.37
100 000	2063.73	1253.27	999.45	883.72	822.15	786.71

188

Term in Years Amount	5	10	15	20	25	30
$ 25	.52	.32	.26	.23	.21	.21
50	1.04	.64	.51	.45	.42	.41
75	1.56	.96	.77	.68	.63	.61
100	2.08	1.27	1.02	.90	.84	.81
200	4.16	2.54	2.03	1.80	1.68	1.61
300	6.23	3.81	3.05	2.70	2.52	2.42
400	8.31	5.07	4.06	3.60	3.36	3.22
500	10.38	6.34	5.08	4.50	4.20	4.03
600	12.46	7.61	6.09	5.40	5.04	4.83
700	14.54	8.87	7.10	6.30	5.88	5.64
800	16.61	10.14	8.12	7.20	6.72	6.44
900	18.69	11.41	9.13	8.10	7.56	7.25
1 000	20.76	12.67	10.15	9.00	8.40	8.05
2 000	41.52	25.34	20.29	18.00	16.79	16.10
3 000	62.28	38.01	30.43	27.00	25.18	24.14
4 000	83.04	50.68	40.58	35.99	33.57	32.19
5 000	103.80	63.34	50.72	44.99	41.96	40.24
6 000	124.56	76.01	60.86	53.99	50.36	48.28
7 000	145.31	88.68	71.00	62.99	58.75	56.33
8 000	166.07	101.35	81.15	71.98	67.14	64.37
9 000	186.83	114.01	91.29	80.98	75.53	72.42
10 000	207.59	126.68	101.43	89.98	83.92	80.47
11 000	228.35	139.35	111.57	98.97	92.32	88.51
12 000	249.11	152.02	121.72	107.97	100.71	96.56
13 000	269.86	164.68	131.86	116.97	109.10	104.61
14 000	290.62	177.35	142.00	125.97	117.49	112.65
15 000	311.38	190.02	152.14	134.96	125.88	120.70
16 000	332.14	202.69	162.29	143.96	134.28	128.74
17 000	352.90	215.35	172.43	152.96	142.67	136.79
18 000	373.66	228.02	182.57	161.96	151.06	144.84
19 000	394.41	240.69	192.72	170.95	159.45	152.88
20 000	415.17	253.36	202.86	179.95	167.84	160.93
21 000	435.93	266.02	213.00	188.95	176.24	168.98
22 000	456.69	278.69	223.14	197.94	184.63	177.02
23 000	477.45	291.36	233.29	206.94	193.02	185.07
24 000	498.21	304.03	243.43	215.94	201.41	193.11
25 000	518.96	316.69	253.57	224.94	209.80	201.16
26 000	539.72	329.36	263.71	233.93	218.20	209.21
27 000	560.48	342.03	273.86	242.93	226.59	217.25
28 000	581.24	354.70	284.00	251.93	234.98	225.30
29 000	602.00	367.36	294.14	260.93	243.37	233.35
30 000	622.76	380.03	304.28	269.92	251.76	241.39
31 000	643.51	392.70	314.43	278.92	260.16	249.44
32 000	664.27	405.37	324.57	287.92	268.55	257.48
33 000	685.03	418.04	334.71	296.91	276.94	265.53
34 000	705.79	430.70	344.86	305.91	285.33	273.58
35 000	726.55	443.37	355.00	314.91	293.72	281.62
40 000	830.34	506.71	405.71	359.90	335.68	321.85
45 000	934.13	570.05	456.42	404.88	377.64	362.09
50 000	1037.92	633.38	507.14	449.87	419.60	402.32
55 000	1141.71	696.72	557.85	494.85	461.56	442.55
60 000	1245.51	760.06	608.56	539.84	503.52	482.78
65 000	1349.30	823.40	659.28	584.83	545.48	523.01
70 000	1453.09	886.74	709.99	629.81	587.44	563.24
75 000	1556.88	950.07	760.70	674.80	629.40	603.47
80 000	1660.67	1013.41	811.42	719.79	671.36	643.70
100 000	2075.84	1266.76	1014.27	899.73	839.20	804.63

Monthly Loan Amortization Payments

Term in Years Amount	5	10	15	20	25	30
$ 25	.53	.33	.26	.23	.22	.21
50	1.05	.65	.52	.46	.43	.42
75	1.57	.97	.78	.69	.65	.62
100	2.09	1.29	1.03	.92	.86	.83
200	4.18	2.57	2.06	1.84	1.72	1.65
300	6.27	3.85	3.09	2.75	2.57	2.47
400	8.36	5.13	4.12	3.67	3.43	3.30
500	10.44	6.41	5.15	4.58	4.29	4.12
600	12.53	7.69	6.18	5.50	5.14	4.94
700	14.62	8.97	7.21	6.42	6.00	5.76
800	16.71	10.25	8.24	7.33	6.86	6.59
900	18.80	11.53	9.27	8.25	7.71	7.41
1 000	20.88	12.81	10.30	9.16	8.57	8.23
2 000	41.76	25.61	20.59	18.32	17.13	16.46
3 000	62.64	38.41	30.88	27.48	25.70	24.69
4 000	83.52	51.22	41.17	36.64	34.26	32.91
5 000	104.40	64.02	51.46	45.80	42.82	41.14
6 000	125.28	76.82	61.76	54.96	51.39	49.37
7 000	146.16	89.63	72.05	64.12	59.95	57.59
8 000	167.04	102.43	82.34	73.27	68.52	65.82
9 000	187.92	115.23	92.63	82.43	77.08	74.05
10 000	208.80	128.04	102.92	91.59	85.64	82.27
11 000	229.68	140.84	113.22	100.75	94.21	90.50
12 000	250.56	153.64	123.51	109.91	102.77	98.73
13 000	271.44	166.45	133.80	119.07	111.33	106.95
14 000	292.32	179.25	144.09	128.23	119.90	115.18
15 000	313.20	192.05	154.38	137.39	128.46	123.41
16 000	334.08	204.86	164.68	146.54	137.03	131.63
17 000	354.96	217.66	174.97	155.70	145.59	139.86
18 000	375.84	230.46	185.26	164.86	154.15	148.09
19 000	396.72	243.27	195.55	174.02	162.72	156.31
20 000	417.60	256.07	205.84	183.18	171.28	164.54
21 000	438.48	268.87	216.14	192.34	179.85	172.77
22 000	459.36	281.68	226.43	201.50	188.41	180.99
23 000	480.24	294.48	236.72	210.65	196.97	189.22
24 000	501.12	307.28	247.01	219.81	205.54	197.45
25 000	522.00	320.09	257.30	228.97	214.10	205.67
26 000	542.88	332.89	267.59	238.13	222.66	213.90
27 000	563.76	345.69	277.89	247.29	231.23	222.13
28 000	584.64	358.50	288.18	256.45	239.79	230.35
29 000	605.52	371.30	298.47	265.61	248.36	238.58
30 000	626.40	384.10	308.76	274.77	256.92	246.81
31 000	647.28	396.91	319.05	283.92	265.48	255.03
32 000	668.16	409.71	329.35	293.08	274.05	263.26
33 000	689.04	422.51	339.64	302.24	282.61	271.49
34 000	709.92	435.32	349.93	311.40	291.17	279.71
35 000	730.80	448.12	360.22	320.56	299.74	287.94
40 000	835.20	512.14	411.68	366.35	342.56	329.08
45 000	939.60	576.15	463.14	412.15	385.38	370.21
50 000	1044.00	640.17	514.60	457.94	428.20	411.34
55 000	1148.40	704.18	566.06	503.73	471.02	452.48
60 000	1252.80	768.20	617.52	549.53	513.83	493.61
65 000	1357.20	832.22	668.98	595.32	556.65	534.74
70 000	1461.60	896.23	720.44	641.11	599.47	575.88
75 000	1566.00	960.25	771.90	686.91	642.29	617.01
80 000	1670.40	1024.27	823.36	732.70	685.11	658.15
100 000	2087.99	1280.33	1029.20	915.87	856.39	822.68

190

9½%	Monthly Loan Amortization Payments					9½%
Term in Years Amount	5	10	15	20	25	30
$ 25	.53	.33	.27	.24	.22	.22
50	1.06	.65	.53	.47	.44	.43
75	1.58	.98	.79	.70	.66	.64
100	2.11	1.30	1.05	.94	.88	.85
200	4.21	2.59	2.09	1.87	1.75	1.69
300	6.31	3.89	3.14	2.80	2.63	2.53
400	8.41	5.18	4.18	3.73	3.50	3.37
500	10.51	6.47	5.23	4.67	4.37	4.21
600	12.61	7.77	6.27	5.60	5.25	5.05
700	14.71	9.06	7.31	6.53	6.12	5.89
800	16.81	10.36	8.36	7.46	6.99	6.73
900	18.91	11.65	9.40	8.39	7.87	7.57
1 000	21.01	12.94	10.45	9.33	8.74	8.41
2 000	42.01	25.88	20.89	18.65	17.48	16.82
3 000	63.01	38.82	31.33	27.97	26.22	25.23
4 000	84.01	51.76	41.77	37.29	34.95	33.64
5 000	105.01	64.70	52.22	46.61	43.69	42.05
6 000	126.02	77.64	62.66	55.93	52.43	50.46
7 000	147.02	90.58	73.10	65.25	61.16	58.86
8 000	168.02	103.52	83.54	74.58	69.90	67.27
9 000	189.02	116.46	93.99	83.90	78.64	75.68
10 000	210.02	129.40	104.43	93.22	87.37	84.09
11 000	231.03	142.34	114.87	102.54	96.11	92.50
12 000	252.03	155.28	125.31	111.86	104.85	100.91
13 000	273.03	168.22	135.75	121.18	113.59	109.32
14 000	294.03	181.16	146.20	130.50	122.32	117.72
15 000	315.03	194.10	156.64	139.82	131.06	126.13
16 000	336.03	207.04	167.08	149.15	139.80	134.54
17 000	357.04	219.98	177.52	158.47	148.53	142.95
18 000	378.04	232.92	187.97	167.79	157.27	151.36
19 000	399.04	245.86	198.41	177.11	166.01	159.77
20 000	420.04	258.80	208.85	186.43	174.74	168.18
21 000	441.04	271.74	219.29	195.75	183.48	176.58
22 000	462.05	284.68	229.73	205.07	192.22	184.99
23 000	483.05	297.62	240.18	214.40	200.96	193.40
24 000	504.05	310.56	250.62	223.72	209.69	201.81
25 000	525.05	323.50	261.06	233.04	218.43	210.22
26 000	546.05	336.44	271.50	242.36	227.17	218.63
27 000	567.06	349.38	281.95	251.68	235.90	227.04
28 000	588.06	362.32	292.39	261.00	244.64	235.44
29 000	609.06	375.26	302.83	270.32	253.38	243.85
30 000	630.06	388.20	313.27	279.64	262.11	252.26
31 000	651.06	401.14	323.71	288.97	270.85	260.67
32 000	672.06	414.08	334.16	298.29	279.59	269.08
33 000	693.07	427.02	344.60	307.61	288.32	277.49
34 000	714.07	439.96	355.04	316.93	297.06	285.90
35 000	735.07	452.90	365.48	326.25	305.80	294.30
40 000	840.08	517.60	417.69	372.86	349.48	336.35
45 000	945.09	582.29	469.91	419.46	393.17	378.39
50 000	1050.10	646.99	522.12	466.07	436.85	420.43
55 000	1155.11	711.69	574.33	512.68	480.54	462.47
60 000	1260.12	776.39	626.54	559.28	524.22	504.52
65 000	1365.13	841.09	678.75	605.89	567.91	546.56
70 000	1470.14	905.79	730.96	652.50	611.59	588.60
75 000	1575.14	970.49	783.17	699.10	655.28	630.65
80 000	1680.15	1035.19	835.38	745.71	698.96	672.69
100 000	2100.19	1293.98	1044.23	932.14	873.70	840.86

191

Term in Years Amount	5	10	15	20	25	30
$ 25	.53	.33	.27	.24	.23	.22
50	1.06	.66	.53	.48	.45	.43
75	1.59	.99	.80	.72	.67	.65
100	2.12	1.31	1.06	.95	.90	.86
200	4.23	2.62	2.12	1.90	1.79	1.72
300	6.34	3.93	3.18	2.85	2.68	2.58
400	8.45	5.24	4.24	3.80	3.57	3.44
500	10.57	6.54	5.30	4.75	4.46	4.30
600	12.68	7.85	6.36	5.70	5.35	5.16
700	14.79	9.16	7.42	6.64	6.24	6.02
800	16.90	10.47	8.48	7.59	7.13	6.88
900	19.02	11.77	9.54	8.54	8.03	7.74
1 000	21.13	13.08	10.60	9.49	8.92	8.60
2 000	42.25	26.16	21.19	18.98	17.83	17.19
3 000	63.38	39.24	31.79	28.46	26.74	25.78
4 000	84.50	52.31	42.38	37.95	35.65	34.37
5 000	105.63	65.39	52.97	47.43	44.56	42.96
6 000	126.75	78.47	63.57	56.92	53.47	51.55
7 000	147.87	91.54	74.16	66.40	62.38	60.15
8 000	169.00	104.62	84.75	75.89	71.30	68.74
9 000	190.12	117.70	95.35	85.37	80.21	77.33
10 000	211.25	130.78	105.94	94.86	89.12	85.92
11 000	232.37	143.85	116.53	104.34	98.03	94.51
12 000	253.50	156.93	127.13	113.83	106.94	103.10
13 000	274.62	170.01	137.72	123.31	115.85	111.70
14 000	295.74	183.08	148.32	132.80	124.76	120.29
15 000	316.87	196.16	158.91	142.28	133.68	128.88
16 000	337.99	209.24	169.50	151.77	142.59	137.47
17 000	359.12	222.31	180.10	161.25	151.50	146.06
18 000	380.24	235.39	190.69	170.74	160.41	154.65
19 000	401.37	248.47	201.28	180.22	169.32	163.24
20 000	422.49	261.55	211.88	189.71	178.23	171.84
21 000	443.61	274.62	222.47	199.19	167.14	180.43
22 000	464.74	287.70	233.06	208.68	196.06	189.02
23 000	485.86	300.78	243.66	218.16	204.97	197.61
24 000	506.99	313.85	254.25	227.65	213.88	206.20
25 000	528.11	326.93	264.85	237.13	222.79	214.79
26 000	549.24	340.01	275.44	246.62	231.70	223.39
27 000	570.36	353.08	286.03	256.10	240.61	231.98
28 000	591.48	366.16	296.63	265.59	249.52	240.57
29 000	612.61	379.24	307.22	275.07	258.43	249.16
30 000	633.73	392.32	317.81	284.56	267.35	257.75
31 000	654.86	405.39	328.41	294.05	276.26	266.34
32 000	675.98	418.47	339.00	303.53	285.17	274.93
33 000	697.11	431.55	349.59	313.02	294.08	283.53
34 000	718.23	444.62	360.19	322.50	302.99	292.12
35 000	739.35	457.70	370.78	331.99	311.90	300.71
40 000	844.97	523.09	423.75	379.41	356.46	343.67
45 000	950.60	588.47	476.72	426.84	401.02	386.62
50 000	1056.22	653.86	529.69	474.26	445.57	429.58
55 000	1161.84	719.24	582.65	521.69	490.13	472.54
60 000	1267.46	784.63	635.62	569.12	534.69	515.50
65 000	1373.08	850.01	688.59	616.54	579.24	558.46
70 000	1478.70	915.40	741.56	663.97	623.80	601.41
75 000	1584.32	980.78	794.53	711.39	668.36	644.37
80 000	1689.94	1046.17	847.50	758.82	712.91	687.33
100 000	2112.43	1307.71	1059.37	948.52	891.14	859.16

Term in Years Amount	5	10	15	20	25	30
$ 25	.54	.34	.27	.25	.23	.22
50	1.07	.67	.54	.49	.46	.44
75	1.60	1.00	.81	.73	.69	.66
100	2.13	1.33	1.08	.97	.91	.88
200	4.25	2.65	2.15	1.94	1.82	1.76
300	6.38	3.97	3.23	2.90	2.73	2.64
400	8.50	5.29	4.30	3.87	3.64	3.52
500	10.63	6.61	5.38	4.83	4.55	4.39
600	12.75	7.93	6.45	5.80	5.46	5.27
700	14.88	9.26	7.53	6.76	6.37	6.15
800	17.00	10.58	8.60	7.73	7.27	7.03
900	19.13	11.90	9.68	8.69	8.18	7.90
1 000	21.25	13.22	10.75	9.66	9.09	8.78
2 000	42.50	26.44	21.50	19.31	18.18	17.56
3 000	63.75	39.65	32.24	28.96	27.27	26.33
4 000	84.99	52.87	42.99	38.61	36.35	35.11
5 000	106.24	66.08	53.74	48.26	45.44	43.88
6 000	127.49	79.30	64.48	57.91	54.53	52.66
7 000	148.73	92.51	75.23	67.56	63.61	61.44
8 000	169.98	105.73	85.97	77.21	72.70	70.21
9 000	191.23	118.94	96.72	86.86	81.79	78.99
10 000	212.48	132.16	107.47	96.51	90.88	87.76
11 000	233.72	145.37	118.21	106.16	99.96	96.54
12 000	254.97	158.59	128.96	115.81	109.05	105.31
13 000	276.22	171.80	139.70	125.46	118.14	114.09
14 000	297.46	185.02	150.45	135.11	127.22	122.87
15 000	318.71	198.23	161.20	144.76	136.31	131.64
16 000	339.96	211.45	171.94	154.41	145.40	140.42
17 000	361.20	224.66	182.69	164.06	154.48	149.19
18 000	382.45	237.88	193.43	173.71	163.57	157.97
19 000	403.70	251.09	204.18	183.36	172.66	166.74
20 000	424.95	264.31	214.93	193.01	181.75	175.52
21 000	446.19	277.52	225.67	202.66	190.83	184.30
22 000	467.44	290.74	236.42	212.31	199.92	193.07
23 000	488.69	303.95	247.16	221.96	209.01	201.85
24 000	509.93	317.17	257.91	231.61	218.09	210.62
25 000	531.18	330.38	268.66	241.26	227.18	219.40
26 000	552.43	343.60	279.40	250.91	236.27	228.17
27 000	573.68	356.81	290.15	260.56	245.35	236.95
28 000	594.92	370.03	300.89	270.21	254.44	245.73
29 000	616.17	383.24	311.64	279.86	263.53	254.50
30 000	637.42	396.46	322.39	289.51	272.62	263.28
31 000	658.66	409.67	333.13	299.16	281.70	272.05
32 000	679.91	422.89	343.88	308.81	290.79	280.83
33 000	701.16	436.10	354.62	318.46	299.88	289.60
34 000	722.40	449.32	365.37	328.11	308.96	298.38
35 000	743.65	462.53	376.12	337.76	318.05	307.16
40 000	849.89	528.61	429.85	386.01	363.49	351.03
45 000	956.12	594.68	483.58	434.26	408.92	394.91
50 000	1062.36	660.76	537.31	482.52	454.36	438.79
55 000	1168.59	726.83	591.04	530.77	499.79	482.67
60 000	1274.83	792.91	644.77	579.02	545.23	526.55
65 000	1381.06	858.98	698.50	627.27	590.66	570.43
70 000	1487.30	925.06	752.23	675.52	636.10	614.31
75 000	1593.53	991.14	805.96	723.77	681.53	658.18
80 000	1699.77	1057.21	859.69	772.02	726.97	702.06
100 000	2124.71	1321.51	1074.61	965.03	908.71	877.58

193

Term in Years Amount	5	10	15	20	25	30
$ 25	.54	.34	.28	.25	.24	.23
50	1.07	.67	.55	.50	.47	.45
75	1.61	1.01	.82	.74	.70	.68
100	2.14	1.34	1.09	.99	.93	.90
200	4.28	2.68	2.18	1.97	1.86	1.80
300	6.42	4.01	3.27	2.95	2.78	2.69
400	8.55	5.35	4.36	3.93	3.71	3.59
500	10.69	6.68	5.45	4.91	4.64	4.49
600	12.83	8.02	6.54	5.89	5.56	5.38
700	14.96	9.35	7.63	6.88	6.49	6.28
800	17.10	10.69	8.72	7.86	7.42	7.17
900	19.24	12.02	9.81	8.84	8.34	8.07
1 000	21.38	13.36	10.90	9.82	9.27	8.97
2 000	42.75	26.71	21.80	19.64	18.53	17.93
3 000	64.12	40.07	32.70	29.45	27.80	26.89
4 000	85.49	53.42	43.60	39.27	37.06	35.85
5 000	106.86	66.77	54.50	49.09	46.32	44.81
6 000	128.23	80.13	65.40	58.90	55.59	53.77
7 000	149.60	93.48	76.30	68.72	64.85	62.73
8 000	170.97	106.84	87.20	78.54	74.12	71.69
9 000	192.34	120.19	98.10	88.35	83.38	80.65
10 000	213.71	133.54	109.00	98.17	92.64	89.62
11 000	235.08	146.90	119.90	107.99	101.91	98.58
12 000	256.45	160.25	130.80	117.80	111.17	107.54
13 000	277.82	173.61	141.70	127.62	120.43	116.50
14 000	299.19	186.96	152.60	137.44	129.70	125.46
15 000	320.56	200.31	163.50	147.25	138.96	134.42
16 000	341.93	213.67	174.40	157.07	148.23	143.38
17 000	363.30	227.02	185.30	166.88	157.49	152.34
18 000	384.67	240.38	196.20	176.70	166.75	161.30
19 000	406.04	253.73	207.10	186.52	176.02	170.26
20 000	427.41	267.08	218.00	196.33	185.28	179.23
21 000	448.78	280.44	228.89	206.15	194.55	188.19
22 000	470.15	293.79	239.79	215.97	203.81	197.15
23 000	491.52	307.14	250.69	225.78	213.07	206.11
24 000	512.89	320.50	261.59	235.60	222.34	215.07
25 000	534.26	333.85	272.49	245.42	231.60	224.03
26 000	555.63	347.21	283.39	255.23	240.86	232.99
27 000	577.00	360.56	294.29	265.05	250.13	241.95
28 000	598.37	373.91	305.19	274.87	259.39	250.91
29 000	619.74	387.27	316.09	284.68	268.66	259.87
30 000	641.11	400.62	326.99	294.50	277.92	268.84
31 000	662.48	413.98	337.89	304.31	287.18	277.80
32 000	683.85	427.33	348.79	314.13	296.45	286.76
33 000	705.22	440.68	359.69	323.95	305.71	295.72
34 000	726.59	454.04	370.59	333.76	314.98	304.68
35 000	747.96	467.39	381.49	343.58	324.24	313.64
40 000	854.82	534.16	435.99	392.66	370.56	358.45
45 000	961.67	600.93	490.48	441.74	416.88	403.25
50 000	1068.52	667.70	544.98	490.83	463.20	448.06
55 000	1175.37	734.47	599.48	539.91	509.52	492.86
60 000	1282.22	801.24	653.98	588.99	555.83	537.67
65 000	1389.07	868.01	708.47	638.07	602.15	582.47
70 000	1495.92	934.78	762.97	687.16	648.47	627.28
75 000	1602.77	1001.55	817.47	736.24	694.79	672.08
80 000	1709.63	1068.32	871.97	785.32	741.11	716.89
100 000	2137.03	1335.40	1089.96	981.65	926.39	896.11

194

10½ % Monthly Loan Amortization Payments 10½ %

Term in Years Amount	5	10	15	20	25	30
$ 25	.54	.34	.28	.25	.24	.23
50	1.08	.68	.56	.50	.48	.46
75	1.62	1.02	.83	.75	.71	.69
100	2.15	1.35	1.11	1.00	.95	.92
200	4.30	2.70	2.22	2.00	1.89	1.83
300	6.45	4.05	3.32	3.00	2.84	2.75
400	8.60	5.40	4.43	4.00	3.78	3.66
500	10.75	6.75	5.53	5.00	4.73	4.58
600	12.90	8.10	6.64	6.00	5.67	5.49
700	15.05	9.45	7.74	6.99	6.61	6.41
800	17.20	10.80	8.85	7.99	7.56	7.32
900	19.35	12.15	9.95	8.99	8.50	8.24
1 000	21.50	13.50	11.06	9.99	9.45	9.15
2 000	42.99	26.99	22.11	19.97	18.89	18.30
3 000	64.49	40.49	33.17	29.96	28.33	27.45
4 000	85.98	53.98	44.22	39.94	37.77	36.59
5 000	107.47	67.47	55.27	49.92	47.21	45.74
6 000	128.97	80.97	66.33	59.91	56.66	54.89
7 000	150.46	94.46	77.38	69.89	66.10	64.04
8 000	171.96	107.95	88.44	79.88	75.54	73.18
9 000	193.45	121.45	99.49	89.86	84.98	82.33
10 000	214.94	134.94	110.54	99.84	94.42	91.48
11 000	236.44	148.43	121.60	109.83	103.86	100.63
12 000	257.93	161.93	132.65	119.81	113.31	109.77
13 000	279.43	175.42	143.71	129.79	122.75	118.92
14 000	300.92	188.91	154.76	139.78	132.19	128.07
15 000	322.41	202.41	165.81	149.76	141.63	137.22
16 000	343.91	215.90	176.87	159.75	151.07	146.36
17 000	365.40	229.39	187.92	169.73	160.52	155.51
18 000	386.90	242.89	198.98	179.71	169.96	164.66
19 000	408.39	256.38	210.03	189.70	179.40	173.81
20 000	429.88	269.87	221.08	199.68	188.84	182.95
21 000	451.38	283.37	232.14	209.66	198.28	192.10
22 000	472.87	296.86	243.19	219.65	207.72	201.25
23 000	494.36	310.36	254.25	229.63	217.17	210.40
24 000	515.86	323.85	265.30	239.62	226.61	219.54
25 000	537.35	337.34	276.35	249.60	236.05	228.69
26 000	558.85	350.84	287.41	259.58	245.49	237.84
27 000	580.34	364.33	298.46	269.57	254.93	246.98
28 000	601.83	377.82	309.52	279.55	264.38	256.13
29 000	623.33	391.32	320.57	289.54	273.82	265.28
30 000	644.82	404.81	331.62	299.52	283.26	274.43
31 000	666.32	418.30	342.68	309.50	292.70	283.57
32 000	687.81	431.80	353.73	319.49	302.14	292.72
33 000	709.30	445.29	364.79	329.47	311.58	301.87
34 000	730.80	458.78	375.84	339.45	321.03	311.02
35 000	752.29	472.28	386.89	349.44	330.47	320.16
40 000	859.76	539.74	442.16	399.36	377.68	365.90
45 000	967.23	607.21	497.43	449.28	424.89	411.64
50 000	1074.70	674.68	552.70	499.19	472.10	457.37
55 000	1182.17	742.15	607.97	549.11	519.30	503.11
60 000	1289.64	809.61	663.24	599.03	566.51	548.85
65 000	1397.11	877.08	718.51	648.95	613.72	594.59
70 000	1504.58	944.55	773.78	698.87	660.93	640.32
75 000	1612.05	1012.02	829.05	748.79	708.14	686.06
80 000	1719.52	1079.48	884.32	798.71	755.35	731.80
100 000	2149.40	1349.35	1105.40	998.38	944.19	914.74

195

Monthly Loan Amortization Payments

Term in Years Amount	5	10	15	20	25	30
$ 25	.55	.35	.29	.26	.25	.24
50	1.09	.69	.57	.51	.49	.47
75	1.63	1.03	.85	.77	.73	.71
100	2.17	1.37	1.13	1.02	.97	.94
200	4.33	2.73	2.25	2.04	1.93	1.87
300	6.49	4.10	3.37	3.05	2.89	2.81
400	8.65	5.46	4.49	4.07	3.85	3.74
500	10.81	6.82	5.61	5.08	4.82	4.67
600	12.98	8.19	6.73	6.10	5.78	5.61
700	15.14	9.55	7.85	7.11	6.74	6.54
800	17.30	10.91	8.97	8.13	7.70	7.47
900	19.46	12.28	10.09	9.14	8.66	8.41
1 000	21.62	13.64	11.21	10.16	9.63	9.34
2 000	43.24	27.27	22.42	20.31	19.25	18.67
3 000	64.86	40.91	33.63	30.46	28.87	28.01
4 000	86.48	54.54	44.84	40.61	38.49	37.34
5 000	108.09	68.17	56.05	50.77	48.11	46.68
6 000	129.71	81.81	67.26	60.92	57.73	56.01
7 000	151.33	95.44	78.47	71.07	67.35	65.35
8 000	172.95	109.08	89.68	81.22	76.97	74.68
9 000	194.57	122.71	100.89	91.38	86.59	84.02
10 000	216.18	136.34	112.10	101.53	96.21	93.35
11 000	237.80	149.98	123.31	111.68	105.84	102.69
12 000	259.42	163.61	134.52	121.83	115.46	112.02
13 000	281.04	177.25	145.73	131.98	125.08	121.36
14 000	302.66	190.88	156.94	142.14	134.70	130.69
15 000	324.27	204.51	168.15	152.29	144.32	140.03
16 000	345.89	218.15	179.36	162.44	153.94	149.36
17 000	367.51	231.78	190.57	172.59	163.56	158.70
18 000	389.13	245.41	201.78	182.75	173.18	168.03
19 000	410.75	259.05	212.99	192.90	182.80	177.37
20 000	432.36	272.68	224.19	203.05	192.42	186.70
21 000	453.98	286.32	235.40	213.20	202.04	196.04
22 000	475.60	299.95	246.61	223.36	211.67	205.37
23 000	497.22	313.58	257.82	233.51	221.29	214.71
24 000	518.84	327.22	269.03	243.66	230.91	224.04
25 000	540.45	340.85	280.24	253.81	240.53	233.38
26 000	562.07	354.49	291.45	263.96	250.15	242.71
27 000	583.69	368.12	302.66	274.12	259.77	252.04
28 000	605.31	381.75	313.87	284.27	269.39	261.38
29 000	626.93	395.39	325.08	294.42	279.01	270.71
30 000	648.54	409.02	336.29	304.57	288.63	280.05
31 000	670.16	422.65	347.50	314.73	298.25	289.38
32 000	691.78	436.29	358.71	324.88	307.87	298.72
33 000	713.40	449.92	369.92	335.03	317.50	308.05
34 000	735.02	463.56	381.13	345.18	327.12	317.39
35 000	756.63	477.19	392.34	355.34	336.74	326.72
40 000	864.72	545.36	448.38	406.10	384.84	373.40
45 000	972.81	613.53	504.43	456.86	432.95	420.07
50 000	1080.90	681.70	560.48	507.62	481.05	466.75
55 000	1188.99	749.87	616.53	558.38	529.16	513.42
60 000	1297.08	818.04	672.57	609.14	577.26	560.09
65 000	1405.17	886.21	728.62	659.90	625.37	606.77
70 000	1513.26	954.38	784.67	710.67	673.47	653.44
75 000	1621.35	1022.55	840.72	761.43	721.57	700.12
80 000	1729.44	1090.71	896.76	812.19	769.68	746.79
100 000	2161.80	1363.39	1120.95	1015.23	962.10	933.49

Term in Years Amount	5	10	15	20	25	30
$ 25	.55	.35	.29	.26	.25	.24
50	1.09	.69	.57	.52	.50	.48
75	1.64	1.04	.86	.78	.74	.72
100	2.18	1.38	1.14	1.04	.99	.96
200	4.35	2.76	2.28	2.07	1.97	1.91
300	6.53	4.14	3.41	3.10	2.95	2.86
400	8.70	5.52	4.55	4.13	3.93	3.81
500	10.88	6.89	5.69	5.17	4.91	4.77
600	13.05	8.27	6.82	6.20	5.89	5.72
700	15.22	9.65	7.96	7.23	6.87	6.67
800	17.40	11.03	9.10	8.26	7.85	7.62
900	19.57	12.40	10.23	9.29	8.83	8.58
1 000	21.75	13.78	11.37	10.33	9.81	9.53
2 000	43.49	27.56	22.74	20.65	19.61	19.05
3 000	65.23	41.33	34.10	30.97	29.41	28.57
4 000	86.97	55.11	45.47	41.29	39.21	38.10
5 000	108.72	68.88	56.83	51.61	49.01	47.62
6 000	130.46	82.66	68.20	61.94	58.81	57.14
7 000	152.20	96.43	79.57	72.26	68.61	66.67
8 000	173.94	110.21	90.93	82.58	78.41	76.19
9 000	195.69	123.98	102.30	92.90	88.22	85.71
10 000	217.43	137.76	113.66	103.22	98.02	95.24
11 000	239.17	151.53	125.03	113.55	107.82	104.76
12 000	260.91	165.31	136.40	123.87	117.62	114.28
13 000	282.66	179.08	147.76	134.19	127.42	123.81
14 000	304.40	192.86	159.13	144.51	137.22	133.33
15 000	326.14	206.63	170.49	154.83	147.02	142.85
16 000	347.88	220.41	181.86	165.16	156.82	152.38
17 000	369.63	234.18	193.23	175.48	166.62	161.90
18 000	391.37	247.96	204.59	185.80	176.43	171.42
19 000	413.11	261.73	215.96	196.12	186.23	180.95
20 000	434.85	275.51	227.32	206.44	196.03	190.47
21 000	456.60	289.28	238.69	216.76	205.83	199.99
22 000	478.34	303.06	250.06	227.09	215.63	209.52
23 000	500.08	316.83	261.42	237.41	225.43	219.04
24 000	521.82	330.61	272.79	247.73	235.23	228.56
25 000	543.57	344.38	284.15	258.05	245.03	238.09
26 000	565.31	358.16	295.52	268.37	254.83	247.61
27 000	587.05	371.93	306.89	278.70	264.64	257.13
28 000	608.79	385.71	318.25	289.02	274.44	266.66
29 000	630.54	399.48	329.62	299.34	284.24	276.18
30 000	652.28	413.26	340.98	309.66	294.04	285.70
31 000	674.02	427.03	352.35	319.98	303.84	295.23
32 000	695.76	440.81	363.72	330.31	313.64	304.75
33 000	717.50	454.58	375.08	340.63	323.44	314.27
34 000	739.25	468.36	386.45	350.95	333.24	323 79
35 000	760.99	482.13	397.81	361.27	343.04	333.32
40 000	869.70	551.01	454.64	412.88	392.05	380.93
45 000	978.41	619.88	511.47	464.49	441.06	428.55
50 000	1087.13	688.76	568.30	516.10	490.06	476.17
55 000	1195.84	757.63	625.13	567.71	539.07	523.78
60 000	1304.55	826.51	681.96	619.32	588.07	571.40
65 000	1413.26	895.38	738.79	670.93	637.08	619.02
70 000	1521.97	964.26	795.62	722.54	686.08	666.63
75 000	1630.69	1033.13	852.45	774.15	735.09	714.25
80 000	1739.40	1102.01	909.28	825.76	784.10	761.86
100 000	2174.25	1377.51	1136.60	1032.19	980.12	952.33

197

Term in Years Amount	5	10	15	20	25	30
$ 25	.55	.35	.29	.27	.25	.25
50	1.10	.70	.58	.53	.50	.49
75	1.65	1.05	.87	.79	.75	.73
100	2.19	1.40	1.16	1.05	1.00	.98
200	4.38	2.79	2.31	2.10	2.00	1.95
300	6.57	4.18	3.46	3.15	3.00	2.92
400	8.75	5.57	4.61	4.20	4.00	3.89
500	10.94	6.96	5.77	5.25	5.00	4.86
600	13.13	8.36	6.92	6.30	5.99	5.83
700	15.31	9.75	8.07	7.35	6.99	6.80
800	17.50	11.14	9.22	8.40	7.99	7.78
900	19.69	12.53	10.38	9.45	8.99	8.75
1 000	21.87	13.92	11.53	10.50	9.99	9.72
2 000	43.74	27.84	23.05	20.99	19.97	19.43
3 000	65.61	41.76	34.58	31.48	29.95	29.14
4 000	87.47	55.67	46.10	41.98	39.93	38.86
5 000	109.34	69.59	57.62	52.47	49.92	48.57
6 000	131.21	83.51	69.15	62.96	59.90	58.28
7 000	153.08	97.42	80.67	73.45	69.88	67.99
8 000	174.94	111.34	92.19	83.95	79.86	77.71
9 000	196.81	125.26	103.72	94.44	89.85	87.42
10 000	218.68	139.17	115.24	104.93	99.83	97.13
11 000	240.55	153.09	126.76	115.42	109.81	106.84
12 000	262.41	167.01	138.29	125.92	119.79	116.56
13 000	284.28	180.92	149.81	136.41	129.78	126.27
14 000	306.15	194.84	161.33	146.90	139.76	135.98
15 000	328.01	208.76	172.86	157.39	149.74	145.69
16 000	349.88	222.68	184.38	167.89	159.72	155.41
17 000	371.75	236.59	195.90	178.38	169.71	165.12
18 000	393.62	250.51	207.43	188.87	179.69	174.83
19 000	415.48	264.43	218.95	199.36	189.67	184.54
20 000	437.35	278.34	230.47	209.86	199.65	194.26
21 000	459.22	292.26	242.00	220.35	209.64	203.97
22 000	481.09	306.18	253.52	230.84	219.62	213.68
23 000	502.95	320.09	265.04	241.33	229.60	223.40
24 000	524.82	334.01	276.57	251.83	239.58	233.11
25 000	546.69	347.93	288.09	262.32	249.56	242.82
26 000	568.56	361.84	299.61	272.81	259.55	252.53
27 000	590.42	375.76	311.14	283.30	269.53	262.25
28 000	612.29	389.68	322.66	293.80	279.51	271.96
29 000	634.16	403.59	334.18	304.29	289.49	281.67
30 000	656.02	417.51	345.71	314.78	299.48	291.38
31 000	677.89	431.43	357.23	325.27	309.46	301.10
32 000	699.76	445.35	368.76	335.77	319.44	310.81
33 000	721.63	459.26	380.28	346.26	329.42	320.52
34 000	743.49	473.18	391.80	356.75	339.41	330.23
35 000	765.36	487.10	403.33	367.24	349.39	339.95
40 000	874.70	556.68	460.94	419.71	399.30	388.51
45 000	984.03	626.27	518.56	472.17	449.21	437.07
50 000	1093.37	695.85	576.18	524.63	499.12	485.64
55 000	1202.71	765.43	633.79	577.10	549.04	534.20
60 000	1312.04	835.02	691.41	629.56	598.95	582.76
65 000	1421.38	904.60	749.03	682.02	648.86	631.32
70 000	1530.72	974.19	806.65	734.48	698.77	679.89
75 000	1640.05	1043.77	864.26	786.95	748.68	728.45
80 000	1749.39	1113.36	921.88	839.41	798.60	777.01
100 000	2186.74	1391.69	1152.35	1049.26	998.24	971.27

198

Term in Years Amount	5	10	15	20	25	30
$ 25	.55	.36	.30	.27	.26	.25
50	1.10	.71	.59	.54	.51	.50
75	1.65	1.06	.88	.80	.77	.75
100	2.20	1.41	1.17	1.07	1.02	1.00
200	4.40	2.82	2.34	2.14	2.04	1.99
300	6.60	4.22	3.51	3.20	3.05	2.98
400	8.80	5.63	4.68	4.27	4.07	3.97
500	11.00	7.03	5.85	5.34	5.09	4.96
600	13.20	8.44	7.01	6.40	6.10	5.95
700	15.40	9.85	8.18	7.47	7.12	6.94
800	17.60	11.25	9.35	8.54	8.14	7.93
900	19.80	12.66	10.52	9.60	9.15	8.92
1 000	22.00	14.06	11.69	10.67	10.17	9.91
2 000	43.99	28.12	23.37	21.33	20.33	19.81
3 000	65.98	42.18	35.05	32.00	30.50	29.71
4 000	87.98	56.24	46.73	42.66	40.66	39.62
5 000	109.97	70.30	58.41	53.33	50.83	49.52
6 000	131.96	84.36	70.10	63.99	60.99	59.42
7 000	153.95	98.42	81.78	74.66	71.16	69.33
8 000	175.95	112.48	93.46	85.32	81.32	79.23
9 000	197.94	126.54	105.14	95.98	91.49	89.13
10 000	219.93	140.60	116.82	106.65	101.65	99.03
11 000	241.92	154.66	128.51	117.31	111.82	108.94
12 000	263.92	168.72	140.19	127.98	121.98	118.84
13 000	285.91	182.78	151.87	138.64	132.15	128.74
14 000	307.90	196.84	163.55	149.31	142.31	138.65
15 000	329.89	210.90	175.23	159.97	152.48	148.55
16 000	351.89	224.96	186.92	170.63	162.64	158.45
17 000	373.88	239.02	198.60	181.30	172.80	168.35
18 000	395.87	253.08	210.28	191.96	182.97	178.26
19 000	417.86	267.14	221.96	202.63	193.13	188.16
20 000	439.86	281.20	233.64	213.29	203.30	198.06
21 000	461.85	295.26	245.32	223.96	213.46	207.97
22 000	483.84	309.31	257.01	234.62	223.63	217.87
23 000	505.83	323.37	268.69	245.28	233.79	227.77
24 000	527.83	337.43	280.37	255.95	243.96	237.67
25 000	549.82	351.49	292.05	266.61	254.12	247.58
26 000	571.81	365.55	303.73	277.28	264.29	257.48
27 000	593.81	379.61	315.42	287.94	274.45	267.38
28 000	615.80	393.67	327.10	298.61	284.62	277.29
29 000	637.79	407.73	338.78	309.27	294.78	287.19
30 000	659.78	421.79	350.46	319.93	304.95	297.09
31 000	681.78	435.85	362.14	330.60	315.11	307.00
32 000	703.77	449.91	373.83	341.26	325.28	316.90
33 000	725.76	463.97	385.51	351.93	335.44	326.80
34 000	747.75	478.03	397.19	362.59	345.60	336.70
35 000	769.75	492.09	408.87	373.26	355.77	346.61
40 000	879.71	562.39	467.28	426.58	406.59	396.12
45 000	989.67	632.68	525.69	479.90	457.42	445.64
50 000	1099.64	702.98	584.10	533.22	508.24	495.15
55 000	1209.60	773.28	642.51	586.54	559.06	544.67
60 000	1319.56	843.58	700.92	639.86	609.89	594.18
65 000	1429.52	913.88	759.33	693.18	660.71	643.69
70 000	1539.49	984.17	817.74	746.51	711.53	693.21
75 000	1649.45	1054.47	876.15	799.83	762.36	742.72
80 000	1759.41	1124.77	934.56	853.15	813.18	792.24
100 000	2199.27	1405.96	1168.19	1066.43	1016.47	990.30

199

Term in Years Amount	5	10	15	20	25	30
$ 25	.56	.36	.30	.28	.26	.26
50	1.11	.72	.60	.55	.52	.51
75	1.66	1.07	.89	.82	.78	.76
100	2.22	1.43	1.19	1.09	1.04	1.01
200	4.43	2.85	2.37	2.17	2.07	2.02
300	6.64	4.27	3.56	3.26	3.11	3.03
400	8.85	5.69	4.74	4.34	4.14	4.04
500	11.06	7.11	5.93	5.42	5.18	5.05
600	13.28	8.53	7.11	6.51	6.21	6.06
700	15.49	9.95	8.29	7.59	7.25	7.07
800	17.70	11.37	9.48	8.67	8.28	8.08
900	19.91	12.79	10.66	9.76	9.32	9.09
1 000	22.12	14.21	11.85	10.84	10.35	10.10
2 000	44.24	28.41	23.69	21.68	20.70	20.19
3 000	66.36	42.61	35.53	32.52	31.05	30.29
4 000	88.48	56.82	47.37	43.35	41.40	40.38
5 000	110.60	71.02	59.21	54.19	51.74	50.48
6 000	132.71	85.22	71.05	65.03	62.09	60.57
7 000	154.83	99.43	82.89	75.86	72.44	70.66
8 000	176.95	113.63	94.74	86.70	82.79	80.76
9 000	199.07	127.83	106.58	97.54	93.14	90.85
10 000	221.19	142.03	118.42	108.38	103.48	100.95
11 000	243.31	156.24	130.26	119.21	113.83	111.04
12 000	265.42	170.44	142.10	130.05	124.18	121.13
13 000	287.54	184.64	153.94	140.89	134.53	131.23
14 000	309.66	198.85	165.78	151.72	144.88	141.32
15 000	331.78	213.05	177.62	162.56	155.22	151.42
16 000	353.90	227.25	189.47	173.40	165.57	161.51
17 000	376.02	241.46	201.31	184.24	175.92	171.60
18 000	398.13	255.66	213.15	195.07	186.27	181.70
19 000	420.25	269.86	224.99	205.91	196.62	191.79
20 000	442.37	284.06	236.83	216.75	206.96	201.89
21 000	464.49	298.27	248.67	227.58	217.31	211.98
22 000	486.61	312.47	260.51	238.42	227.66	222.08
23 000	508.73	326.67	272.36	249.26	238.01	232.17
24 000	530.84	340.88	284.20	260.09	248.36	242.26
25 000	552.96	355.08	296.04	270.93	258.70	252.36
26 000	575.08	369.28	307.88	281.77	269.05	262.45
27 000	597.20	383.48	319.72	292.61	279.40	272.55
28 000	619.32	397.69	331.56	303.44	289.75	282.64
29 000	641.44	411.89	343.40	314.28	300.10	292.73
30 000	663.55	426.09	355.24	325.12	310.44	302.83
31 000	685.67	440.30	367.09	335.95	320.79	312.92
32 000	707.79	454.50	378.93	346.79	331.14	323.02
33 000	729.91	468.70	390.77	357.63	341.49	333.11
34 000	752.03	482.91	402.61	368.47	351.84	343.20
35 000	774.15	497.11	414.45	379.30	362.18	353.30
40 000	884.74	568.12	473.66	433.49	413.92	403.77
45 000	995.33	639.14	532.86	487.67	465.66	454.24
50 000	1105.92	710.15	592.07	541.86	517.40	504.71
55 000	1216.51	781.17	651.28	596.04	569.14	555.18
60 000	1327.10	852.18	710.48	650.23	620.88	605.65
65 000	1437.70	923.20	769.69	704.41	672.62	656.12
70 000	1548.29	994.21	828.90	758.60	724.36	706.59
75 000	1658.88	1065.23	888.10	812.79	776.10	757.06
80 000	1769.47	1136.24	947.31	866.97	827.84	807.53
100 000	2211.84	1420.30	1184.14	1083.71	1034.80	1009.41

200

Term in Years Amount	5	10	15	20	25	30
$ 25	.56	.36	.31	.28	.27	.26
50	1.12	.72	.61	.56	.53	.52
75	1.67	1.08	.91	.83	.79	.78
100	2.23	1.44	1.21	1.11	1.06	1.03
200	4.45	2.87	2.41	2.21	2.11	2.06
300	6.68	4.31	3.61	3.31	3.16	3.09
400	8.90	5.74	4.81	4.41	4.22	4.12
500	11.13	7.18	6.01	5.51	5.27	5.15
600	13.35	8.61	7.21	6.61	6.32	6.18
700	15.58	10.05	8.41	7.71	7.38	7.21
800	17.80	11.48	9.61	8.81	8.43	8.23
900	20.03	12.92	10.81	9.91	9.48	9.26
1 000	22.25	14.35	12.01	11.02	10.54	10.29
2 000	44.49	28.70	24.01	22.03	21.07	20.58
3 000	66.74	43.05	36.01	33.04	31.60	30.86
4 000	88.98	57.39	48.01	44.05	42.13	41.15
5 000	111.23	71.74	60.01	55.06	52.67	51.44
6 000	133.47	86.09	72.02	66.07	63.20	61.72
7 000	155.72	100.43	84.02	77.08	73.73	72.01
8 000	177.96	114.78	96.02	88.09	84.26	82.29
9 000	200.21	129.13	108.02	99.10	94.80	92.58
10 000	222.45	143.48	120.02	110.11	105.33	102.87
11 000	244.69	157.82	132.02	121.12	115.86	113.15
12 000	266.94	172.17	144.03	132.14	126.39	123.44
13 000	289.18	186.52	156.03	143.15	136.92	133.72
14 000	311.43	200.86	168.03	154.16	147.46	144.01
15 000	333.67	215.21	180.03	165.17	157.99	154.30
16 000	355.92	229.56	192.03	176.18	168.52	164.58
17 000	378.16	243.91	204.03	187.19	179.05	174.87
18 000	400.41	258.25	216.04	198.20	189.59	185.16
19 000	422.65	272.60	228.04	209.21	200.12	195.44
20 000	444.89	286.95	240.04	220.22	210.65	205.73
21 000	467.14	301.29	252.04	231.23	221.18	216.01
22 000	489.38	315.64	264.04	242.24	231.71	226.30
23 000	511.63	329.99	276.04	253.25	242.25	236.59
24 000	533.87	344.34	288.05	264.27	252.78	246.87
25 000	556.12	358.68	300.05	275.28	263.31	257.16
26 000	578.36	373.03	312.05	286.29	273.84	267.44
27 000	600.61	387.38	324.05	297.30	284.38	277.73
28 000	622.85	401.72	336.05	308.31	294.91	288.02
29 000	645.09	416.07	348.05	319.32	305.44	298.30
30 000	667.34	430.42	360.06	330.33	315.97	308.59
31 000	689.58	444.76	372.06	341.34	326.50	318.87
32 000	711.83	459.11	384.06	352.35	337.04	329.16
33 000	734.07	473.46	396.06	363.36	347.57	339.45
34 000	756.32	487.81	408.06	374.37	358.10	349.73
35 000	778.56	502.15	420.06	385.39	368.63	360.02
40 000	889.78	573.89	480.07	440.44	421.29	411.45
45 000	1001.01	645.62	540.08	495.49	473.96	462.88
50 000	1112.23	717.36	600.09	550.55	526.62	514.31
55 000	1223.45	789.10	660.10	605.60	579.28	565.74
60 000	1334.67	860.83	720.11	660.66	631.94	617.17
65 000	1445.89	932.57	780.11	715.71	684.60	668.60
70 000	1557.12	1004.30	840.12	770.77	737.26	720.03
75 000	1668.34	1076.04	900.13	825.82	789.92	771.46
80 000	1779.56	1147.77	960.14	880.87	842.58	822.90
100 000	2224.45	1434.71	1200.17	1101.09	1053.23	1028.62

201

Term in Years Amount	5	10	15	20	25	30
$ 25	.56	.37	.31	.28	.27	.27
.50	1.12	.73	.61	.56	.54	.53
75	1.68	1.09	.92	.84	.81	.79
100	2.24	1.45	1.22	1.12	1.08	1.05
200	4.48	2.90	2.44	2.24	2.15	2.10
300	6.72	4.35	3.65	3.36	3.22	3.15
400	8.95	5.80	4.87	4.48	4.29	4.20
500	11.19	7.25	6.09	5.60	5.36	5.24
600	13.43	8.70	7.30	6.72	6.44	6.29
700	15.66	10.15	8.52	7.83	7.51	7.34
800	17.90	11.60	9.74	8.95	8.58	8.39
900	20.14	13.05	10.95	10.07	9.65	9.44
1 000	22.38	14.50	12.17	11.19	10.72	10.48
2 000	44.75	28.99	24.33	22.38	21.44	20.96
3 000	67.12	43.48	36.49	33.56	32.16	31.44
4 000	89.49	57.97	48.66	44.75	42.87	41.92
5 000	111.86	72.46	60.82	55.93	53.59	52.40
6 000	134.23	86.96	72.98	67.12	64.31	62.88
7 000	156.60	101.45	85.15	78.30	75.03	73.36
8 000	178.97	115.94	97.31	89.49	85.74	83.84
9 000	201.34	130.43	109.47	100.68	96.46	94.32
10 000	223.71	144.92	121.63	111.86	107.18	104.79
11 000	246.09	159.42	133.80	123.05	117.90	115.27
12 000	268.46	173.91	145.96	134.23	128.61	125.75
13 000	290.83	188.40	158.12	145.42	139.33	136.23
14 000	313.20	202.89	170.29	156.60	150.05	146.71
15 000	335.57	217.38	182.45	167.79	160.77	157.19
16 000	357.94	231.88	194.61	178.98	171.48	167.67
17 000	380.31	246.37	206.78	190.16	182.20	178.15
18 000	402.68	260.86	218.94	201.35	192.92	188.63
19 000	425.05	275.35	231.10	212.53	203.64	199.11
20 000	447.42	289.84	243.26	223.72	214.35	209.58
21 000	469.80	304.34	255.43	234.90	225.07	220.06
22 000	492.17	318.83	267.59	246.09	235.79	230.54
23 000	514.54	333.32	279.75	257.27	246.51	241.02
24 000	536.91	347.81	291.92	268.46	257.22	251.50
25 000	559.28	362.30	304.08	279.65	267.94	261.98
26 000	581.65	376.80	316.24	290.83	278.66	272.46
27 000	604.02	391.29	328.41	302.02	289.38	282.94
28 000	626.39	405.78	340.57	313.20	300.09	293.42
29 000	648.76	420.27	352.73	324.39	310.81	303.89
30 000	671.13	434.76	364.89	335.57	321.53	314.37
31 000	693.51	449.26	377.06	346.76	332.25	324.85
32 000	715.88	463.75	389.22	357.95	342.96	335.33
33 000	738.25	478.24	401.38	369.13	353.68	345.81
34 000	760.62	492.73	413.55	380.32	364.40	356.29
35 000	782.99	507.22	425.71	391.50	375.12	366.77
40 000	894.84	579.68	486.52	447.43	428.70	419.16
45 000	1006.70	652.14	547.34	503.36	482.29	471.56
50 000	1118.55	724.60	608.15	559.29	535.88	523.95
55 000	1230.41	797.06	668.97	615.22	589.46	576.35
60 000	1342.26	869.52	729.78	671.14	643.05	628.74
65 000	1454.12	941.98	790.60	727.07	696.64	681.14
70 000	1565.97	1014.44	851.41	783.00	750.23	733.53
75 000	1677.83	1086.90	912.23	838.93	803.81	785.93
80 000	1789.68	1159.36	973.04	894.86	857.40	838.32
100 000	2237.10	1449.20	1216.30	1118.57	1071.75	1047.90

202

Term in Years Amount	5	10	15	20	25	30
$ 25	.57	.37	.31	.29	.28	.27
50	1.13	.74	.62	.57	.55	.54
75	1.69	1.10	.93	.86	.82	.81
100	2.25	1.47	1.24	1.14	1.10	1.07
200	4.50	2.93	2.47	2.28	2.19	2.14
300	6.75	4.40	3.70	3.41	3.28	3.21
400	9.00	5.86	4.94	4.55	4.37	4.27
500	11.25	7.32	6.17	5.69	5.46	5.34
600	13.50	8.79	7.40	6.82	6.55	6.41
700	15.75	10.25	8.63	7.96	7.64	7.48
800	18.00	11.72	9.87	9.09	8.73	8.54
900	20.25	13.18	11.10	10.23	9.82	9.61
1 000	22.50	14.64	12.33	11.37	10.91	10.68
2 000	45.00	29.28	24.66	22.73	21.81	21.35
3 000	67.50	43.92	36.98	34.09	32.72	32.02
4 000	90.00	58.56	49.31	45.45	43.62	42.70
5 000	112.49	73.19	61.63	56.81	54.52	53.37
6 000	134.99	87.83	73.96	68.17	65.43	64.04
7 000	157.49	102.47	86.28	79.53	76.33	74.71
8 000	179.99	117.11	98.61	90.90	87.23	85.39
9 000	202.49	131.74	110.93	102.26	98.14	96.06
10 000	224.98	146.38	123.26	113.62	109.04	106.73
11 000	247.48	161.02	135.58	124.98	119.94	117.40
12 000	269.98	175.66	147.91	136.34	130.85	128.08
13 000	292.48	190.29	160.23	147.70	141.75	138.75
14 000	314.98	204.93	172.56	159.06	152.65	149.42
15 000	337.47	219.57	184.88	170.43	163.56	160.09
16 000	359.97	234.21	197.21	181.79	174.46	170.77
17 000	382.47	248.84	209.53	193.15	185.37	181.44
18 000	404.97	263.48	221.86	204.51	196.27	192.11
19 000	427.47	278.12	234.18	215.87	207.17	202.78
20 000	449.96	292.76	246.51	227.23	218.08	213.46
21 000	472.46	307.39	258.83	238.59	228.98	224.13
22 000	494.96	322.03	271.16	249.96	239.88	234.80
23 000	517.46	336.67	283.49	261.32	250.79	245.47
24 000	539.96	351.31	295.81	272.68	261.69	256.15
25 000	562.45	365.95	308.14	284.04	272.59	266.82
26 000	584.95	380.58	320.46	295.40	283.50	277.49
27 000	607.45	395.22	332.79	306.76	294.40	288.16
28 000	629.95	409.86	345.11	318.12	305.30	298.84
29 000	652.45	424.50	357.44	329.49	316.21	309.51
30 000	674.94	439.13	369.76	340.85	327.11	320.18
31 000	697.44	453.77	382.09	352.21	338.01	330.85
32 000	719.94	468.41	394.41	363.57	348.92	341.53
33 000	742.44	483.05	406.74	374.93	359.82	352.20
34 000	764.93	497.68	419.06	386.29	370.73	362.87
35 000	787.43	512.32	431.39	397.65	381.63	373.55
40 000	899.92	585.51	493.01	454.46	436.15	426.91
45 000	1012.41	658.70	554.64	511.27	490.66	480.27
50 000	1124.90	731.89	616.27	568.08	545.18	533.63
55 000	1237.39	805.07	677.89	624.88	599.70	587.00
60 000	1349.88	878.26	739.52	681.69	654.22	640.36
65 000	1462.37	951.45	801.14	738.50	708.74	693.72
70 000	1574.86	1024.64	862.77	795.30	763.25	747.09
75 000	1687.35	1097.83	924.40	852.11	817.77	800.45
80 000	1799.84	1171.01	986.02	908.92	872.29	853.81
100 000	2249.80	1463.77	1232.53	1136.15	1090.36	1067.26

203

Term in Years Amount	5	10	15	20	25	30
$ 25	.57	.37	.32	.29	.28	.28
50	1.14	.74	.63	.58	.56	.55
75	1.70	1.11	.94	.87	.84	.82
100	2.27	1.48	1.25	1.16	1.11	1.09
200	4.53	2.96	2.50	2.31	2.22	2.18
300	6.79	4.44	3.75	3.47	3.33	3.27
400	9.06	5.92	5.00	4.62	4.44	4.35
500	11.32	7.40	6.25	5.77	5.55	5.44
600	13.58	8.88	7.50	6.93	6.66	6.53
700	15.84	10.35	8.75	8.08	7.77	7.61
800	18.11	11.83	10.00	9.24	8.88	8.70
900	20.37	13.31	11.24	10.39	9.99	9.79
1 000	22.63	14.79	12.49	11.54	11.10	10.87
2 000	45.26	29.57	24.98	23.08	22.19	21.74
3 000	67.88	44.36	37.47	34.62	33.28	32.61
4 000	90.51	59.14	49.96	46.16	44.37	43.47
5 000	113.13	73.92	62.45	57.70	55.46	54.34
6 000	135.76	88.71	74.94	69.23	66.55	65.21
7 000	158.38	103.49	87.42	80.77	77.64	76.07
8 000	181.01	118.28	99.91	92.31	88.73	86.94
9 000	203.63	133.06	112.40	103.85	99.82	97.81
10 000	226.26	147.84	124.89	115.39	110.91	108.67
11 000	248.88	162.63	137.38	126.92	122.00	119.54
12 000	271.51	177.41	149.87	138.46	133.09	130.41
13 000	294.13	192.20	162.35	150.00	144.18	141.28
14 000	316.76	206.98	174.84	161.54	155.27	152.14
15 000	339.38	221.76	187.33	173.08	166.36	163.01
16 000	362.01	236.55	199.82	184.61	177.45	173.88
17 000	384.64	251.33	212.31	196.15	188.54	184.74
18 000	407.26	266.12	224.80	207.69	199.63	195.61
19 000	429.89	280.90	237.28	219.23	210.72	206.48
20 000	452.51	295.68	249.77	230.77	221.82	217.34
21 000	475.14	310.47	262.26	242.31	232.91	228.21
22 000	497.76	325.25	274.75	253.84	244.00	239.08
23 000	520.39	340.04	287.24	265.38	255.09	249.94
24 000	543.01	354.82	299.73	276.92	266.18	260.81
25 000	565.64	369.60	312.21	288.46	277.27	271.68
26 000	588.26	384.39	324.70	300.00	288.36	282.55
27 000	610.89	399.17	337.19	311.53	299.45	293.41
28 000	633.51	413.96	349.68	323.07	310.54	304.28
29 000	656.14	428.74	362.17	334.61	321.63	315.15
30 000	678.76	443.52	374.66	346.15	332.72	326.01
31 000	701.39	458.31	387.14	357.69	343.81	336.88
32 000	724.01	473.09	399.63	369.22	354.90	347.75
33 000	746.64	487.88	412.12	380.76	365.99	358.61
34 000	769.27	502.66	424.61	392.30	377.08	369.48
35 000	791.89	517.44	437.10	403.84	388.17	380.35
40 000	905.02	591.36	499.54	461.53	443.63	434.68
45 000	1018.14	665.28	561.98	519.22	499.08	489.02
50 000	1131.27	739.20	624.42	576.91	554.53	543.35
55 000	1244.40	813.12	686.87	634.60	609.98	597.69
60 000	1357.52	887.04	749.31	692.29	665.44	652.02
65 000	1470.65	960.96	811.75	749.98	720.89	706.36
70 000	1583.78	1034.88	874.19	807.67	776.34	760.69
75 000	1696.90	1108.80	936.63	865.36	831.79	815.02
80 000	1810.03	1182.72	999.07	923.05	887.25	869.36
100 000	2262.54	1478.40	1248.84	1153.82	1109.06	1086.70

Term in Years Amount	5	10	15	20	25	30
$ 25	.57	.38	.32	.30	.29	.28
50	1.14	.75	.64	.59	.57	.56
75	1.71	1.12	.95	.88	.85	.83
100	2.28	1.50	1.27	1.18	1.13	1.11
200	4.56	2.99	2.54	2.35	2.26	2.22
300	6.83	4.48	3.80	3.52	3.39	3.32
400	9.11	5.98	5.07	4.69	4.52	4.43
500	11.38	7.47	6.33	5.86	5.64	5.54
600	13.66	8.96	7.60	7.03	6.77	6.64
700	15.93	10.46	8.86	8.21	7.90	7.75
800	18.21	11.95	10.13	9.38	9.03	8.85
900	20.48	13.44	11.39	10.55	10.16	9.96
1 000	22.76	14.94	12.66	11.72	11.28	11.07
2 000	45.51	29.87	25.31	23.44	22.56	22.13
3 000	68.26	44.80	37.96	35.15	33.84	33.19
4 000	91.02	59.73	50.61	46.87	45.12	44.25
5 000	113.77	74.66	63.27	58.58	56.40	55.31
6 000	136.52	89.59	75.92	70.30	67.68	66.38
7 000	159.28	104.52	88.57	82.02	78.95	77.44
8 000	182.03	119.45	101.22	93.73	90.23	88.50
9 000	204.78	134.38	113.88	105.45	101.51	99.56
10 000	227.54	149.32	126.53	117.16	112.79	110.62
11 000	250.29	164.25	139.18	128.88	124.07	121.69
12 000	273.04	179.18	151.83	140.59	135.35	132.75
13 000	295.79	194.11	164.49	152.31	146.62	143.81
14 000	318.55	209.04	177.14	164.03	157.90	154.87
15 000	341.30	223.97	189.79	175.74	169.18	165.93
16 000	364.05	238.90	202.44	187.46	180.46	177.00
17 000	386.81	253.83	215.10	199.17	191.74	188.06
18 000	409.56	268.76	227.75	210.89	203.02	199.12
19 000	432.31	283.70	240.40	222.60	214.29	210.18
20 000	455.07	298.63	253.05	234.32	225.57	221.24
21 000	477.82	313.56	265.71	246.04	236.85	232.31
22 000	500.57	328.49	278.36	257.75	248.13	243.37
23 000	523.33	343.42	291.01	269.47	259.41·	254.43
24 000	546.08	358.35	303.66	281.18	270.69	265.49
25 000	568.83	373.28	316.32	292.90	281.96	276.55
26 000	591.58	388.21	328.97	304.61	293.24	287.62
27 000	614.34	403.14	341.62	316.33	304.52	298.68
28 000	637.09	418.08	354.27	328.05	315.80	309.74
29 000	659.84	433.01	366.93	339.76	327.08	320.80
30 000	682.60	447.94	379.58	351.48	338.36	331.86
31 000	705.35	462.87	392.23	363.19	349.63	342.93
32 000	728.10	477.80	404.88	374.91	360.91	353.99
33 000	750.86	492.73	417.53	386.62	372.19	365.05
34 000	773.61	507.66	430.19	398.34	383.47	376.11
35 000	796.36	522.59	442.84	410.06	394.75	387.17
40 000	910.13	597.25	506.10	468.64	451.14	442.48
45 000	1023.89	671.90	569.36	527.21	507.53	497.79
50 000	1137.66	746.56	632.63	585.79	563.92	553.10
55 000	1251.42	821.21	695.89	644.37	620.31	608.41
60 000	1365.19	895.87	759.15	702.95	676.71	663.72
65 000	1478.95	970.52	822.41	761.53	733.10	719.03
70 000	1592.72	1045.18	885.67	820.11	789.49	774.34
75 000	1706.49	1119.84	948.94	878.69	845.88	829.65
80 000	1820.25	1194.49	1012.20	937.27	902.27	884.96
100 000	2275.31	1493.11	1265.25	1171.58	1127.84	1106.20

205

Term in Years Amount	5	10	15	20	25	30
$ 25	.58	.38	.33	.30	.29	.29
50	1.15	.76	.65	.60	.58	.57
75	1.72	1.14	.97	.90	.87	.85
100	2.29	1.51	1.29	1.19	1.15	1.13
200	4.58	3.02	2.57	2.38	2.30	2.26
300	6.87	4.53	3.85	3.57	3.45	3.38
400	9.16	6.04	5.13	4.76	4.59	4.51
500	11.45	7.54	6.41	5.95	5.74	5.63
600	13.73	9.05	7.70	7.14	6.89	6.76
700	16.02	10.56	8.98	8.33	8.03	7.89
800	18.31	12.07	10.26	9.52	9.18	9.01
900	20.60	13.58	11.54	10.71	10.33	10.14
1 000	22.89	15.08	12.82	11.90	11.47	11.26
2 000	45.77	30.16	25.64	23.79	22.94	22.52
3 000	68.65	45.24	38.46	35.69	34.41	33.78
4 000	91.53	60.32	51.27	47.58	45.87	45.04
5 000	114.41	75.40	64.09	59.48	57.34	56.29
6 000	137.29	90.48	76.91	71.37	68.81	67.55
7 000	160.17	105.56	89.73	83.27	80.27	78.81
8 000	183.06	120.64	102.54	95.16	91.74	90.07
9 000	205.94	135.72	115.36	107.05	103.21	101.32
10 000	228.82	150.79	128.18	118.95	114.68	112.58
11 000	251.70	165.87	141.00	130.84	126.14	123.84
12 000	274.58	180.95	153.81	142.74	137.61	135.10
13 000	297.46	196.03	166.63	154.63	149.08	146.36
14 000	320.34	211.11	179.45	166.53	160.54	157.61
15 000	343.22	226.19	192.27	178.42	172.01	168.87
16 000	366.11	241.27	205.08	190.31	183.48	180.13
17 000	388.99	256.35	217.90	202.21	194.94	191.39
18 000	411.87	271.43	230.72	214.10	206.41	202.64
19 000	434.75	286.50	243.53	226.00	217.88	213.90
20 000	457.63	301.58	256.35	237.89	229.35	225.16
21 000	480.51	316.66	269.17	249.79	240.81	236.42
22 000	503.39	331.74	281.99	261.68	252.28	247.68
23 000	526.27	346.82	294.80	273.57	263.75	258.93
24 000	549.16	361.90	307.62	285.47	275.21	270.19
25 000	572.04	376.98	320.44	297.36	286.68	281.45
26 000	594.92	392.06	333.26	309.26	298.15	292.71
27 000	617.80	407.14	346.07	321.15	309.61	303.96
28 000	640.68	422.21	358.89	333.05	321.08	315.22
29 000	663.56	437.29	371.71	344.94	332.55	326.48
30 000	686.44	452.37	384.53	356.83	344.02	337.74
31 000	709.32	467.45	397.34	368.73	355.48	348.99
32 000	732.21	482.53	410.16	380.62	366.95	360.25
33 000	755.09	497.61	422.98	392.52	378.42	371.51
34 000	777.97	512.69	435.80	404.41	389.88	382.77
35 000	800.85	527.77	448.61	416.31	401.35	394.03
40 000	915.26	603.16	512.70	475.78	458.69	450.31
45 000	1029.66	678.56	576.79	535.25	516.02	506.60
50 000	1144.07	753.95	640.87	594.72	573.36	562.89
55 000	1258.47	829.34	704.96	654.19	630.69	619.18
60 000	1372.88	904.74	769.05	713.66	688.03	675.47
65 000	1487.29	980.13	833.13	773.13	745.36	731.76
70 000	1601.69	1055.53	897.22	832.61	802.70	788.05
75 000	1716.10	1130.92	961.31	892.08	860.03	844.34
80 000	1830.51	1206.32	1025.39	951.55	917.37	900.62
100 000	2288.13	1507.89	1281.74	1189.44	1146.71	1125.78

Term in Years Amount	5	10	15	20	25	30
$ 25	.58	.39	.33	.31	.30	.29
50	1.16	.77	.65	.61	.59	.58
75	1.73	1.15	.98	.91	.88	.86
100	2.31	1.53	1.30	1.21	1.17	1.15
200	4.61	3.05	2.60	2.42	2.34	2.30
300	6.91	4.57	3.90	3.63	3.50	3.44
400	9.21	6.10	5.20	4.83	4.67	4.59
500	11.51	7.62	6.50	6.04	5.83	5.73
600	13.81	9.14	7.79	7.25	7.00	6.88
700	16.11	10.66	9.09	8.46	8.16	8.02
800	18.41	12.19	10.39	9.66	9.33	9.17
900	20.71	13.71	11.69	10.87	10.50	10.31
1 000	23.01	15.23	12.99	12.08	11.66	11.46
2 000	46.02	30.46	25.97	24.15	23.32	22.91
3 000	69.03	45.69	38.95	36.23	34.97	34.37
4 000	92.04	60.91	51.94	48.30	46.63	45.82
5 000	115.05	76.14	64.92	60.37	58.29	57.28
6 000	138.06	91.37	77.90	72.45	69.94	68.73
7 000	161.07	106.60	90.89	84.52	81.60	80.18
8 000	184.08	121.82	103.87	96.59	93.26	91.64
9 000	207.09	137.05	116.85	108.67	104.91	103.09
10 000	230.10	152.28	129.84	120.74	116.57	114.55
11 000	253.11	167.51	142.82	132.82	128.23	126.00
12 000	276.12	182.73	155.80	144.89	139.88	137.45
13 000	299.13	197.96	168.79	156.96	151.54	148.91
14 000	322.14	213.19	181.77	169.04	163.20	160.36
15 000	345.15	228.42	194.75	181.11	174.85	171.82
16 000	368.16	243.64	207.74	193.18	186.51	183.27
17 000	391.17	258.87	220.72	205.26	198.16	194.73
18 000	414.18	274.10	233.70	217.33	209.82	206.18
19 000	437.19	289.33	246.69	229.41	221.48	217.63
20 000	460.20	304.55	259.67	241.48	233.13	229.09
21 000	483.21	319.78	272.65	253.55	244.79	240.54
22 000	506.22	335.01	285.64	265.63	256.45	252.00
23 000	529.23	350.24	298.62	277.70	268.10	263.45
24 000	552.24	365.46	311.60	289.77	279.76	274.90
25 000	575.25	380.69	324.58	301.85	291.42	286.36
26 000	598.26	395.92	337.57	313.92	303.07	297.81
27 000	621.27	411.15	350.55	326.00	314.73	309.27
28 000	644.28	426.37	363.53	338.07	326.39	320.72
29 000	667.29	441.60	376.52	350.14	338.04	332.17
30 000	690.30	456.83	389.50	362.22	349.70	343.63
31 000	713.31	472.06	402.48	374.29	361.35	355.08
32 000	736.32	487.28	415.47	386.36	373.01	366.54
33 000	759.33	502.51	428.45	398.44	384.67	377.99
34 000	782.34	517.74	441.43	410.51	396.32	389.45
35 000	805.35	532.97	454.42	422.59	407.98	400.90
40 000	920.40	609.10	519.33	482.95	466.26	458.17
45 000	1035.45	685.24	584.25	543.32	524.55	515.44
50 000	1150.50	761.38	649.16	603.69	582.83	572.71
55 000	1265.55	837.51	714.08	664.06	641.11	629.98
60 000	1380.60	913.65	779.00	724.43	699.39	687.25
65 000	1495.64	989.79	843.91	784.80	757.67	744.52
70 000	1610.69	1065.93	908.83	845.17	815.96	801.79
75 000	1725.74	1142.06	973.74	905.54	874.24	859.06
80 000	1840.79	1218.20	1038.66	965.90	932.52	916.33
100 000	2300.99	1522.75	1298.32	1207.38	1165.65	1145.42

207

Term in Years Amount	5	10	15	20	25	30
$ 25	.58	.39	.33	.31	.30	.30
50	1.16	.77	.66	.62	.60	.59
75	1.74	1.16	.99	.92	.89	.88
100	2.32	1.54	1.32	1.23	1.19	1.17
200	4.63	3.08	2.63	2.46	2.37	2.34
300	6.95	4.62	3.95	3.68	3.56	3.50
400	9.26	6.16	5.26	4.91	4.74	4.67
500	11.57	7.69	6.58	6.13	5.93	5.83
600	13.89	9.23	7.89	7.36	7.11	7.00
700	16.20	10.77	9.21	8.58	8.30	8.16
800	18.52	12.31	10.52	9.81	9.48	9.33
900	20.83	13.84	11.84	11.03	10.67	10.49
1 000	23.14	15.38	13.15	12.26	11.85	11.66
2 000	46.28	30.76	26.30	24.51	23.70	23.31
3 000	69.42	46.14	39.45	36.77	35.54	34.96
4 000	92.56	61.51	52.60	49.02	47.39	46.61
5 000	115.70	76.89	65.75	61.28	59.24	58.26
6 000	138.84	92.27	78.90	73.53	71.08	69.91
7 000	161.98	107.64	92.05	85.78	82.93	81.56
8 000	185.12	123.02	105.20	98.04	94.78	93.21
9 000	208.25	138.40	118.35	110.29	106.62	104.87
10 000	231.39	153.77	131.50	122.55	118.47	116.52
11 000	254.53	169.15	144.65	134.80	130.32	128.17
12 000	277.67	184.53	157.80	147.05	142.16	139.82
13 000	300.81	199.90	170.95	159.31	154.01	151.47
14 000	323.95	215.28	184.10	171.56	165.86	163.12
15 000	347.09	230.66	197.25	183.82	177.70	174.77
16 000	370.23	246.03	210.40	196.07	189.55	186.42
17 000	393.37	261.41	223.55	208.32	201.40	198.07
18 000	416.50	276.79	236.70	220.58	213.24	209.73
19 000	439.64	292.16	249.85	232.83	225.09	221.38
20 000	462.78	307.54	263.00	245.09	236.94	233.03
21 000	485.92	322.92	276.15	257.34	248.78	244.68
22 000	509.06	338.29	289.30	269.59	260.63	256.33
23 000	532.20	353.67	302.45	281.85	272.48	267.98
24 000	555.34	369.05	315.60	294.10	284.32	279.63
25 000	578.48	384.42	328.75	306.36	296.17	291.28
26 000	601.61	399.80	341.90	318.61	308.02	302.93
27 000	624.75	415.18	355.05	330.86	319.86	314.59
28 000	647.89	430.55	368.20	343.12	331.71	326.24
29 000	671.03	445.93	381.35	355.37	343.56	337.89
30 000	694.17	461.31	394.50	367.63	355.40	349.54
31 000	717.31	476.68	407.65	379.88	367.25	361.19
32 000	740.45	492.06	420.80	392.13	379.10	372.84
33 000	763.59	507.44	433.95	404.39	390.94	384.49
34 000	786.73	522.81	447.10	416.64	402.79	396.14
35 000	809.86	538.19	460.25	428.90	414.64	407.79
40 000	925.56	615.07	526.00	490.17	473.87	466.05
45 000	1041.25	691.96	591.75	551.44	533.10	524.31
50 000	1156.95	768.84	657.50	612.71	592.34	582.56
55 000	1272.64	845.72	723.25	673.98	651.57	640.82
60 000	1388.34	922.61	789.00	735.25	710.80	699.07
65 000	1504.03	999.49	854.75	796.52	770.04	757.33
70 000	1619.72	1076.37	920.50	857.79	829.27	815.58
75 000	1735.42	1153.26	986.25	919.06	888.50	873.84
80 000	1851.11	1230.14	1051.99	980.33	947.74	932.10
100 000	2313.89	1537.67	1314.99	1225.41	1184.67	1165.12

Term in Years Amount	5	10	15	20	25	30
$ 25	.59	.39	.34	.32	.31	.30
50	1.17	.78	.67	.63	.61	.60
75	1.75	1.17	1.00	.94	.91	.89
100	2.33	1.56	1.34	1.25	1.21	1.19
200	4.66	3.11	2.67	2.49	2.41	2.37
300	6.99	4.66	4.00	3.74	3.62	3.56
400	9.31	6.22	5.33	4.98	4.82	4.74
500	11.64	7.77	6.66	6.22	6.02	5.93
600	13.97	9.32	8.00	7.47	7.23	7.11
700	16.29	10.87	9.33	8.71	8.43	8.30
800	18.62	12.43	10.66	9.95	9.64	9.48
900	20.95	13.98	11.99	11.20	10.84	10.67
1 000	23.27	15.53	13.32	12.44	12.04	11.85
2 000	46.54	31.06	26.64	24.88	24.08	23.70
3 000	69.81	46.58	39.96	37.31	36.12	35.55
4 000	93.08	62.11	53.27	49.75	48.16	47.40
5 000	116.35	77.64	66.59	62.18	60.19	59.25
6 000	139.61	93.16	79.91	74.62	72.23	71.10
7 000	162.88	108.69	93.23	87.05	84.27	82.95
8 000	186.15	124.22	106.54	99.49	96.31	94.79
9 000	209.42	139.74	119.86	111.92	108.34	106.64
10 000	232.69	155.27	133.18	124.36	120.38	118.49
11 000	255.96	170.80	146.50	136.79	132.42	130.34
12 000	279.22	186.32	159.81	149.23	144.46	142.19
13 000	302.49	201.85	173.13	161.66	156.49	154.04
14 000	325.76	217.38	186.45	174.10	168.53	165.89
15 000	349.03	232.90	199.77	186.53	180.57	177.74
16 000	372.30	248.43	213.08	198.97	192.61	189.58
17 000	395.57	263.96	226.40	211.40	204.64	201.43
18 000	418.83	279.48	239.72	223.84	216.68	213.28
19 000	442.10	295.01	253.04	236.27	228.72	225.13
20 000	465.37	310.54	266.35	248.71	240.76	236.98
21 000	488.64	326.06	279.67	261.14	252.79	248.83
22 000	511.91	341.59	292.99	273.58	264.83	260.68
23 000	535.17	357.12	306.31	286.01	276.87	272.53
24 000	558.44	372.64	319.62	298.45	288.91	284.37
25 000	581.71	388.17	332.94	310.89	300.95	296.22
26 000	604.98	403.70	346.26	323.32	312.98	308.07
27 000	628.25	419.22	359.58	335.76	325.02	319.92
28 000	651.52	434.75	372.89	348.19	337.06	331.77
29 000	674.78	450.28	386.21	360.63	349.10	343.62
30 000	698.05	465.80	399.53	373.06	361.13	355.47
31 000	721.32	481.33	412.84	385.50	373.17	367.32
32 000	744.59	496.86	426.16	397.93	385.21	379.16
33 000	767.86	512.38	439.48	410.37	397.25	391.01
34 000	791.13	527.91	452.80	422.80	409.28	402.86
35 000	814.39	543.44	466.11	435.24	421.32	414.71
40 000	930.74	621.07	532.70	497.41	481.51	473.95
45 000	1047.08	698.70	599.29	559.59	541.70	533.20
50 000	1163.42	776.34	665.88	621.77	601.89	592.44
55 000	1279.76	853.97	732.46	683.94	662.07	651.68
60 000	1396.10	931.60	799.05	746.12	722.26	710.93
65 000	1512.44	1009.24	865.64	808.29	782.45	770.17
70 000	1628.78	1086.87	932.22	870.47	842.64	829.42
75 000	1745.12	1164.50	998.81	932.65	902.83	888.66
80 000	1861.47	1242.14	1065.40	994.82	963.01	947.90
100 000	2326.83	1552.67	1331.75	1243.53	1203.77	1184.88

209

Monthly Payments Necessary to Amortize a Loan of $1,000

No. of Years	Annual Interest Rate				
	8%	8¼%	8½%	8¾%	9%
5	$20.28	$20.40	$20.52	$20.64	$20.76
6	17.54	17.66	17.78	17.91	18.03
7	15.59	15.72	15.84	15.97	16.09
8	14.14	14.27	14.40	14.53	14.66
9	13.02	13.15	13.28	13.42	13.55
10	12.14	12.27	12.40	12.54	12.67
11	11.42	11.56	11.69	11.83	11.97
12	10.83	10.97	11.11	11.24	11.39
13	10.34	10.48	10.62	10.76	10.90
14	9.92	10.06	10.20	10.35	10.49
15	9.56	9.71	9.85	10.00	10.15
16	9.25	9.40	9.55	9.70	9.85
17	8.99	9.14	9.29	9.44	9.59
18	8.75	8.91	9.06	9.21	9.37
19	8.55	8.70	8.86	9.02	9.17
20	8.37	8.53	8.68	8.84	9.00
25	7.72	7.89	8.06	8.23	8.40
30	7.34	7.52	7.69	7.87	8.05
35	7.11	7.29	7.47	7.66	7.84

Monthly Payments Necessary to Amortize a Loan of $1,000

No. of Years	Annual Interest Rate				
	10½%	10¾%	11%	11¼%	11½%
5	$21.50	$21.62	$21.75	$21.87	$22.00
6	18.78	18.91	19.04	19.17	19.30
7	16.87	17.00	17.13	17.26	17.39
8	15.45	15.58	15.71	15.85	15.98
9	14.36	14.49	14.63	14.77	14.91
10	13.50	13.64	13.78	13.92	14.06
11	12.81	12.95	13.10	13.24	13.39
12	12.25	12.39	12.54	12.69	12.84
13	11.78	11.93	12.08	12.23	12.38
14	11.39	11.54	11.70	11.85	12.01
15	11.06	11.21	11.37	11.53	11.69
16	10.78	10.94	11.10	11.26	11.42
17	10.54	10.70	10.86	11.02	11.19
18	10.33	10.49	10.66	10.82	10.99
19	10.15	10.31	10.48	10.65	10.82
20	9.99	10.16	10.33	10.50	10.67
25	9.45	9.63	9.81	9.99	10.17
30	9.15	9.34	9.53	9.72	9.91
35	8.99	9.18	9.37	9.57	9.77

Annual Interest Rate				
9¼%	9½%	9¾	10%	10¼%
$20.88	$21.01	$21.13	$21.25	$21.38
18.15	18.28	18.41	18.53	18.66
16.22	16.35	16.48	16.61	16.74
14.79	14.92	15.05	15.18	15.31
13.68	13.81	13.95	14.08	14.22
12.81	12.94	13.08	13.22	13.36
12.10	12.24	12.38	12.52	12.67
11.53	11.67	11.81	11.96	12.10
11.05	11.19	11.34	11.48	11.63
10.64	10.79	10.94	11.09	11.24
10.30	10.45	10.60	10.75	10.90
10.00	10.15	10.31	10.46	10.62
9.75	9.90	10.06	10.22	10.38
9.53	9.68	9.84	10.00	10.16
9.33	9.49	9.65	9.82	9.98
9.16	9.33	9.49	9.66	9.82
8.57	8.74	8.92	9.09	9.27
8.23	8.41	8.60	8.78	8.97
8.03	8.22	8.41	8.60	8.79

Annual Interest Rate				
11¾%	12%	12¼%	12½%	12¾%
$22.12	$22.25	$22.38	$22.50	$22.63
19.43	19.56	19.69	19.82	19.95
17.52	17.66	17.79	17.93	18.06
16.12	16.26	16.40	16.53	16.67
15.05	15.19	15.33	15.47	15.62
14.21	14.35	14.50	14.64	14.79
13.54	13.68	13.83	13.98	14.13
12.99	13.14	13.29	13.44	13.60
12.54	12.69	12.85	13.00	13.16
12.16	12.32	12.48	12.64	12.80
11.85	12.01	12.17	12.33	12.49
11.58	11.74	11.91	12.07	12.24
11.35	11.52	11.68	11.85	12.02
11.16	11.32	11.49	11.67	11.84
10.99	11.16	11.33	11.50	11.68
10.84	11.02	11.19	11.37	11.54
10.35	10.54	10.72	10.91	11.10
10.10	10.29	10.48	10.68	10.87
9.96	10.16	10.36	10.56	10.76

Monthly Payments Necessary to Amortize a Loan of $1,000

No. of Years	Annual Interest Rate				
	13%	13¼ %	13½ %	13¾ %	14%
5	$22.76	$22.89	$23.01	$23.14	$23.27
6	20.08	20.21	20.34	20.48	20.61
7	18.20	18.33	18.47	18.61	18.75
8	16.81	16.95	17.09	17.23	17.38
9	15.76	15.90	16.05	16.19	16.34
10	14.94	15.08	15.23	15.38	15.53
11	14.28	14.43	14.58	14.74	14.89
12	13.75	13.91	14.06	14.22	14.38
13	13.32	13.48	13.63	13.80	13.96
14	12.96	13.12	13.28	13.45	13.61
15	12.66	12.82	12.99	13.15	13.32
16	12.40	12.57	12.74	12.91	13.08
17	12.19	12.36	12.23	12.71	12.88
18	12.01	12.18	12.36	12.53	12.71
19	11.85	12.03	12.21	12.39	12.56
20	11.72	11.90	12.08	12.26	12.44
25	11.28	11.47	11.66	11.85	12.04
30	11.07	11.26	11.46	11.66	11.85
35	10.96	11.16	11.36	11.56	11.76

Index

217

Notes